ENDORSEMENT

CW01594230

This fictional mystery sto[illegible] age of the earth and the very relevant eruption of Mount Saint Helens in 1980 in Washington state, America. Once started, you won't want to put it down! It's a story of intrigue, adventure and danger, with surprising twists and turns. The characters are well-developed, and it has an engaging plot. The geological evidence (both for and against the earth being millions of years old), which the book's characters discuss, is referenced at the end of the book for those who want to dig deeper. The characters (both believers and sceptics) discuss the gospel and other important issues in a way that is accurate and true to life. The book will entertain and inform Christians and non-Christians alike. I highly recommend it!

Dr. Terry Mortenson
Speaker, writer and researcher
Answers in Genesis

Copyright © 2025 by Day One Publications

Unless otherwise indicated, Scripture quotations are from the New King James Version (NKJV)®. Copyright © 1982 by Thomas Nelson, Inc. Used by permission. All rights reserved.

Published in Great Britain by
Day One, Ryelands Road, Leominster, HR6 8NZ
Email: sales@dayone.co.uk
Website: www.dayone.co.uk

All rights reserved. No part of this publication may be reproduced, stored in a retrieval system or transmitted in any form or by any means, electronic, mechanical, photocopying, recording or otherwise, without the prior permission of the publisher or the Copyright Licensing Agency.

British Library Cataloguing in Publication Data available

ISBN: 978-1-84625-808-4

Cover design by Kathryn Chedgzoy

Printed by 4edge

Dedication

This book is dedicated to the biologist, Professor Gary Parker—a man I have never met. To a large degree, it is as a result of Gary's testimony (*Evolution to Creation*[1]) that *Set in Stone* has been written. I am extremely grateful to Gary for the massive influence he has had on my life.

CONTENTS

ACKNOWLEDGEMENTS

I would very much like to thank the following people:

Firstly, my heartfelt thanks go to Mark Roberts and all at Day One Publications for taking a chance on this book. Thanks for all your help and advice.

Grateful thanks to Steve Austin whose brilliant DVD on Mount St. Helens was the primary inspiration for this book.

Thanks to Dr Andrew Snelling who provided me with technical and detailed information on radioactive decay in rocks. He also provided most of the photographs in the book.

Thanks also to Dr Terry Mortenson and his wife Margie who reviewed the book, making many helpful revisions and giving other vital assistance.

Thanks to all at Answers in Genesis whose DVDs and literature have been invaluable.

Thanks to Francesca Spencer who gave me some great suggestions about the book as well as doing a detailed edit.

Thanks to Tim Ollier for help with research and all his encouragement during the writing of the book.

Thanks to Oly Naedefam for her helpful suggestions about the book.

Thanks to Brett Hagger for providing additional specialist information.

Thanks to the owners of Jenner's Café and the Blue Mugge pub for allowing me to use the names of their businesses in the book.

Thanks to my brother, Chris, for the photo on the back cover of this book.

Special and particular thanks to my wife, Sue, who, as ever, has been very supportive.

Last but definitely not least, thank you to my Creator, Lord and Saviour whose guidance and inspiration has made the writing of this book possible.

Thank you all.

Tony Green

PREFACE

There are certain subjects within the world of science which, it seems, are not open to scrutiny. Darwinian Evolution is one of these, and my first book, *Deception*, was a novel which dealt with that issue. However, Darwinian Evolution is not the only subject where this kind of bias occurs.

Another seemingly indisputable issue involves the age of the earth. As with Darwinism, arguments which question the great age of our planet are virtually never heard in our mainstream media. This is curious, as many of the geological clocks which have been used to provide an age for the earth give ages far younger than that required by evolution. Sadly, most people are completely unaware of this.

Set in Stone is a fictional novel that has been written as a sequel to the book, *Deception*. In *Set in Stone*, geological processes which are usually assumed to take a huge period of time are discussed in a more critical way. These include rock strata being deposited in a matter of hours, the rapid formation of fossils, canyons being carved out in a single day, as well as others. Rather than just accepting the beliefs of the old-earth proponents, in this book, their beliefs are put under the spotlight.

As with *Deception*, I have included statements from the conventional scientific community to add weight to those arguments. Also, a note section is included at the back of the book so people can check the sources of any details given.

My hope is the same for *Set in Stone* as it was for *Deception*. I am trying to reach people who are open-minded enough to listen to new information. If you are prepared to honestly consider these details and have your worldview challenged, please read on.

Obviously, no one has to change their position having read this book. However, if you check the details it contains, and find that they are accurate, hopefully, you will seriously think about the potential implications.

I realize, of course, that some will read this book from a position of deep scepticism and I completely understand. I, myself, when first coming across this subject, was absolutely certain that claims of a young earth were ridiculous. Thankfully, I was open-minded enough to listen to and check up on the information being presented to me. The question is, 'Are you?'

Chapter 1
A Second Adventure

A sudden movement out of the corner of my eye caused me to glance out of the window at the grey, miserable weather. My eye was drawn to a small, male blackbird in my front garden who was industriously pecking away at the ground.

It was a Saturday morning in early April and I was sitting in my lounge with my brother, Sam, discussing the events from an adventure we had shared just over a year ago. Sam is three years younger than me and had been a keen sportsman. That was until his situation had been permanently changed due to the events surrounding that ill-fated trip. We had both been invited to act as independent observers on an expedition to the Congo in Central Africa. The main purpose of the excursion was to investigate rumours of the existence of a dinosaur-like creature, known in those parts as Mokele-mbembe. Our expenses had been covered, and the only expectation from us was to provide unbiased feedback on any events we might witness while on the trip.

None of the events of that lifechanging adventure had faded from our minds and, as we had done so often over the last year, we sat that morning again discussing the massive footprints that our team had discovered.

I had just mildly mocked Sam by reminding him of his rush to view the footprints when we were interrupted by a sharp wrap at the front door. As I entered the hall and swung the door open, to my amazement, there, standing on the step, was Kevin Robinson. I was delighted to see him.

'Kevin, come in,' I said.

Kevin had been the microbiologist who had led our expedition to the African continent. He was knowledgeable, friendly, and an all-round great guy. However, unfortunately, the expedition had left us all with a number of scars. My own scars had been emotional and mental, but some members of the team had received physical scars as permanent and painful reminders of the trip.

After making some drinks, I returned to the lounge to join Sam and Kevin.

'What are you doing with yourself at the moment, Kevin?' I asked, handing him a mug.

'I'm manically busy. What with my speaking engagements on top of my main job, I could do with forty-eight hours in a day. And if that weren't enough, we're putting together another trip.' He took a quick sip of coffee and looked at me over the top of his mug. 'Actually, that's the main reason for me calling in on you today.'

I raised my eyebrows in anticipation. 'Are you going back to the Congo?'

He shook his head. 'No, I'm afraid that's not going to be possible for a while. The political situation there isn't stable enough for a second expedition.'

This was disappointing, as the discoveries we had made on the trip certainly deserved further investigation.

'I was wondering if either of you two gents would be interested in joining me on another trip,' he said. 'This one would be to the United States.'

Kevin's offer inevitably reminded me of the problems we had encountered on our last trip. I glanced at Sam and wondered what was going through his mind. He returned my gaze but was giving nothing away in his expression.

'You'll obviously want to know what it's all about,' Kevin said.

Although no one could possibly say that our first adventure had not been exciting, I certainly did not want to repeat some of the experiences. I needed to ask a few questions.

'Kevin? There are people in this country who are obviously desperate to discredit your work. There's no chance that we'd bump into any of them on this trip, is there?'

Kevin gave an apologetic smile. 'You're right, Rob. Some of those people appear to be very concerned about the influence we've already had on certain members of the scientific community, as well as some prominent individuals within academia. I think it's probably true to say that concern may even be growing. But it's very difficult to say how far they'd go to interfere with our work.'

I considered his comments. Kevin and his colleagues were biblical creationists. They believed the Bible to be the divinely inspired, inerrant Word of God and, as such, they believed that an Intelligent Designer was responsible for the creation of our universe. They had no time for Darwin's theory of evolution, believing that God had created different kinds of plants and animals, and had created man distinct from the animal kingdom.

My own background is in computer programming which is heavily based on logical problem-solving. When I had been introduced to the whole creation/evolution controversy before the previous expedition, I had been highly sceptical about their beliefs. However, having listened to their scientific arguments as well as doing all I could to find problems with their statements, my honest investigations had not been able to refute their stance. In fact, the checking I had done subsequent to the African trip had strengthened their case rather than weakened it. While I'd still not completely signed up to their position, their reasoning did appear sound.

One thing was for certain: there were obviously people in the world who did not appreciate their attempts to highlight potential issues with the origin and evolution of life on our planet. From what Kevin had just said, it sounded as if this opposition might even be increasing.

'What makes you think the opposition's getting worse?' I asked.

There was a short pause. Kevin shifted uncomfortably in his seat, a look of concern on his face.

'Well, I can't really say too much because the information has come from a source who is in a fairly delicate situation. That source is close to some of those who are upset by our work, and before you ask, yes, we're confident that this person's information is trustworthy.'

This was unwelcome news. I knew the debate over creation and evolution was a highly controversial one, but it sounded as if there might be a significant element of danger. With the offer of a new trip looming in the air, my thoughts ran back to last year as the scenes played through my mind like the reel of a film: the excitement of discovery mingled with the moments of terror. Then, my thoughts went back even further. I recalled a mysterious conversation with my grandfather, which had been responsible for our later introduction to Kevin and his friends.

My eyes had returned to the blackbird who was now pulling a worm from the soil in the garden. The sound of Kevin placing his coffee cup on the table brought my mind back to the present.

If I was to get involved in this latest trip, might I be leaving myself open to more grief?

'So, Kevin, what's the main purpose of this trip?'

'This one's more to do with geological time than biological evolution,' he said. 'We're carrying out some potentially valuable geological research, but we also have the opportunity to take a few laymen on the trip with us. Once again, we're keen for people to hear the truth about the evidence often used to support the views of the conventional scientific community. The arguments we'll be countering on this trip will involve the earth's supposed great age.'

That piqued my interest and I saw a glint in Sam's eye as I looked over at my brother, who, so far, had been unusually quiet. The information I had gained from the last adventure had significantly changed my view of science and the natural world, particularly with regard to the theory of evolution. However, I did still have doubts over their beliefs about the age of the earth. Once more, my mind returned to the more tragic consequences of that previous trip.

'Presumably you're not expecting to face the same kind of disruption we faced in the Congo?'

Kevin's smile contained more than a little sadness. 'I certainly hope not,' he said. 'Unfortunately, as you've already discovered, we have the habit of ruffling feathers. It's ironic, because most of the time, all we're doing is pointing out verifiable facts. It would appear that that's unacceptable for many who follow the religion of naturalism.'

I probed further. 'Is there a lot of secrecy surrounding this trip?'

He shook his head. 'No. We're taking a different approach to that of our last expedition. Instead of trying to keep everything under wraps, we're letting people know about the trip. In fact, we outlined our intentions in February's edition of *Creation Monthly*.'

Creation Monthly was a magazine promoting arguments supporting a straightforward reading of the first book of the Bible. Many of the articles within its pages dealt with scientific issues, and I had found it to be very informative on the occasions when I had scanned through it.

Kevin continued: 'We announced that we'd be carrying out some exciting new research and that there could be scientific and even financial benefits to the work.'

‘Was that wise?’ I asked doubtfully.

‘That’s a question we discussed for hours,’ he said. ‘As you know, we tried to keep the Congo trip quiet, but people found out about it anyway.’

This had been a source of great personal embarrassment for Kevin, as he felt a degree of responsibility for the leak of information in that instance.

‘Anyway,’ he went on, ‘although we’d like people to leave us alone to carry out our work, we feel that’s unrealistic. We came to the conclusion that if we were more open about our plans and publicised the trip, people might consider it to be less interesting and therefore, not worth interfering with. Also, we figured that the publicity would make it much more difficult for anyone wishing to bother us to carry out any illegal acts. I guess time will tell whether or not we were right.’

He laughed humourlessly. ‘Guys, let me be completely candid. There’s no way I can give you any assurance that no one will try to interfere with our work. In fact, we’ve even discussed the possibility that any such interference could potentially work in our favour. As you know, part of the motivation in our work is to encourage our opponents out into the open; to cause them to actively and openly engage with us in debate.’

Kevin looked at Sam and then back at me again. ‘Because of your involvement in our last expedition, we wanted to give you two guys the first opportunity to be involved. Bearing in mind the information I’ve just given you as well as your experiences on the last trip, I suspect I know the answer, but are either of you interested?'

Sam briefly glanced down at the coffee table before staring out of the window. Our African expedition had cost him a lot: specifically, his left leg. Although he was now able to discuss his disability without the feelings of bitterness which had initially consumed him, I was not sure he would want to repeat the experience.

There was an extended silence as Sam considered the prospect. Then came the answer I was expecting:

'No thanks, Kevin. I'm afraid I won't be joining you on this one.'

Kevin nodded. 'I completely understand, Sam.'

He shifted his attention to me: 'How do you feel about it, Rob?'

Again, my gaze turned to the gloomy morning outside. The drizzle had turned to rain, and the blackbird had flown away. I had also been tremendously affected by Sam's injury and, while I certainly did not blame anyone, I still felt a stab of resentment.

I looked back at Kevin. 'You'll have to tell me much more about it before I make a decision.'

'That's fine, Rob,' he said. 'It's actually pretty encouraging. I expected you to turn it down flat.'

'Can you tell me where you're going?' I asked.

'It's an excursion to Mount Saint Helens in the States.'

I'd heard of Mount Saint Helens. 'Isn't that an active volcano?'

Kevin gave a slight chuckle. 'It is, but it hasn't erupted since January 2008. As far as I know, there have been no indications that she's about to go up again.'

Once again, images from our previous trip flooded my mind. Kevin had taken Sam and me on an expedition to the Congo to search for surviving pre-historic creatures. On that trip, we had been approached by a deadly snake, our party was attacked by a hostile group, we had been shot at, Sam was badly injured, and two people had even lost their lives. Apart from that, everything had gone fine, I thought wryly. Now, this same man wanted to take me on a jaunt to visit an active volcano.

I gave a mildly ironic laugh and asked, 'OK. And what exactly will you be doing?'

After another sip of coffee, Kevin explained the plan:

'There are two main purposes of this trip. The first, and actually the main purpose, is the research aspect.

My colleagues are very excited about this work. However, the part of the work you'd be involved in is basically an information-sharing exercise.

'Over recent decades there has been a tremendous amount of thorough, high-quality, geological investigatory work performed at Mount Saint Helens by some of our American colleagues. Unfortunately, however, very few people have ever been exposed to the results of this work.

'As you know, it's our desire that the general public are allowed to hear both sides of the argument. You know yourselves that many of the details we put to you on the first expedition were completely new to you. The reason for this is so that the general public doesn't get to hear about the very real issues that exist for Darwinian theory. By the same token, this subject of the age of the earth is equally one-sided when it comes to what the public gets to hear. We want to put that right. By asking people like yourselves to come on a trip like this, we hope to make it possible for this subject to be dealt with a little more fairly.'

I could not help feeling a degree of excitement. As I have already mentioned, my own investigations over the details given by Kevin and his colleagues relating to evolution had been surprising. I had been pretty thorough in my checking of the quotes and other facts presented by Kevin. If their details relating to the age of the earth were as trustworthy as their evolutionary facts had proved to be, this was going to be a fascinating journey.

Then I remembered that there were two purposes of the trip. 'What's the research that you mentioned?'

Kevin looked thoughtful. 'It's a bit difficult,' he said. 'I can give you a rough outline, but I don't think there would be much chance of you understanding it without me giving you a bit of background as to why we're doing that work.' Then he added, hurriedly, 'Please don't take that as a slight on your intelligence. That isn't how it's meant at all. It's just that the research is technical and, without certain information, it almost certainly wouldn't mean much to you. However, if you really grasp the information we're going to give you on the trip, you might be excited by the research as well.'

I laughed. 'Hey, hold on, Kevin, I haven't said I'm going yet.'

He grinned. 'No, but you sound as if you're seriously considering it.'

My own smile was at least partly an acknowledgement of this assessment.

'Anyway,' he continued, 'we at the Genesis Foundation have been doing some geological research on predicting where certain minerals can be found in rocks. However, just as importantly, we want to show people like you a different way of interpreting the hard geological evidence.

'As you know from our previous expedition, one of our biggest concerns is over the way in which science is taught in the schools, colleges and universities of our western nations. The millions or billions of years of earth's history is just accepted as hard fact. Our young people are never given any information about the real problems that exist for this interpretation of the rocks. As a result, and as creationists are dismissed as scientifically ignorant crackpots, the earth's great age is just accepted as fact.'

'If I go,' I said, 'what will you expect of me?'

'You'll be going on a number of excursions to view some incredible evidence,' Kevin said. 'We just want you to think about that evidence and the details we give you about it. I tell you what, let me take you lads out for a spot of lunch. I'll explain more about what we'll be doing then.'

The rain had eased to a gentle drizzle and the air smelled fresh as we headed into town. With a welcoming smile, the barman handed us a menu as we sat down in the corner of Sam's favourite pub, 'The Boar's Head'.

When we had chosen our meals, our conversation turned again to the age of the earth. Kevin began to run through some of the arguments which had been used to convince everyone that the earth is very old.

‘Most geologists would say that our planet is about 4.5 billion years old. To support this belief, they point to thick sequences of sedimentary rock, fossils of creatures presumed to be extinct, canyon systems, stalactites, petrified trees, coal, oil and many others. A number of those pieces of evidence have been called into question and even totally overturned as a result of the work that has been carried out at Mount Saint Helens. On our trip, evidence will be presented that suggests these “old earth” claims are not to be trusted.’

As our food arrived, we continued to asked questions as Kevin ran through many of these ‘old earth’ arguments. He then spent a short time giving an overview of the other research to which he had alluded.

‘The other work we’ll be doing is related to one of the most convincing scientific arguments against an old earth.’

I was often amused when Kevin began talking about research that he felt to be significant. His enthusiasm was infectious. He would lean forward and become incredibly intense. He had not changed at all, as this is what happened now.

He said, ‘As I mentioned earlier, some of our discoveries suggest that it’s possible to predict where certain ore deposits might be found.’

‘That does sound exciting,’ I said.

‘Yes,’ he said, laughing. ‘Don’t let anyone tell you that creation science has no practical benefits.’

‘So, what’s all that about, Kevin?’ I asked.

He looked thoughtful:

'Well, as I say, it's difficult to explain without giving you a fair bit of background information. Also, I'm not an expert myself. But let's just say that there is physical damage that occurs in rocks as a result of radioactive decay. There are phenomena called radiohalos which are formed as a result of alpha decay of certain radioactive elements. As a result of the work of some of my colleagues on these radiohalos, we believe we can show that radioactive decay has occurred much faster in the past. However, another consequence of this work suggests that ore deposits may be found in locations which contain high numbers of these radiohalos.'

I laughed. 'You're right,' I said. 'Most of that went right over my head.'

In spite of having very little knowledge of the relevant subjects, superficially, it did sound intriguing. Having said that, our previous experiences had left me with a significant amount of caution when it came to getting involved in future creationist expeditions. And the expedition to the Congo had supposedly been planned in secret. This latest jaunt had apparently been freely disclosed and even advertised to the world. If, as was obviously the case, people were so violently opposed to the work of Kevin and his friends, then perhaps the safety of those taking part in this current work might once more be questionable.

I thought back to the events surrounding the Congo expedition. There had been a number of people who had shown antagonism towards the work of Kevin and his team. Our own expedition had been shadowed by a group of evolutionists. They had disrupted our work and had caused a good deal of hurt and upset. Some of these people had been academics, but there had also been a particularly nefarious individual involved who appeared to have been hired specifically to threaten and even use violence against us if that proved necessary.

Rather unconvincingly, this man had claimed his name was John Smith, but no one believed him. Unfortunately, although the authorities knew the true identity of the individual concerned, he had never been traced by the police and was therefore still at large. This was especially concerning, as he was the type of person who was likely to bear a grudge. I now brought him up.

'Kevin, how do we know John Smith isn't going to turn up and wreak havoc on our mission?'

Kevin gazed across the pub. 'We don't. As I said before, I'm afraid there are no guarantees.' He looked back at me. 'Having said that, you have to admit, it's one thing indulging in criminal activity in the middle of the Congo rainforest where there's no police presence. It's something else again to do that in America. In our judgement, Smith wouldn't dare try it.'

Sam and I swapped glances. I could not read Sam's face, and I wanted to know what was going through my brother's mind, but his presence was a reminder of the violence of which John Smith was capable. After all, it had been his bullet that was responsible for shattering Sam's knee. Smith had seemed to me to be a complete psychopath, and I was not as sure as Kevin appeared to be over the matter.

As a result of the Congo trip, Smith was a hunted man.

Additionally, he had been badly outmanoeuvred and made to look rather foolish. I suspected he might not be exactly thrilled by that.

Another character involved in the drama had been Charles Thompson, the head of biology at Denbridge University and the organizer of the evolutionist expedition. My first introduction to this man had been when I had seen him take on Kevin in a debate on evolution. My own assessment of that encounter was that Charles Thompson had taken a bit of a battering. This was even more significant as, at the start of the debate, I had expected to come down on his side of the argument.

During this debate, Thompson had displayed what I judged to be something approaching hatred for Kevin. I had discovered later that Thompson bore a significant grudge against Kevin and had been highly motivated to do all he could to undermine Kevin's research. Although there had been serious criminal activity involved from members of the evolutionists' team in the Congo, Thompson had never been charged with any offence. He had been arrested but, in spite of the fact that he undoubtedly had a clear motive, he had somehow managed to convince the authorities that the criminal action had been entirely the work of John Smith. In addition, although it had been Thompson who had hired the crook, he claimed to know nothing at all about the man's subsequent movements.

'What about Charles Thompson?' I asked. 'Where is he now? And has he made any further attempts to interfere with your work?'

'No,' he said. 'It's all gone very quiet on that front. I don't think we'll hear from him again. He lost his job at Denbridge University over that whole matter. The last I heard about Charles was that he had almost completely withdrawn from society and was living in the Derby area as a virtual recluse.'

Another man with a grudge, I thought to myself. Thinking about the results of the expedition he had put together, I could not muster too much sympathy for Dr Charles Thompson.

Then there was Jim Redfern. He had also been a lecturer at Denbridge University and part of the evolutionist expedition. Initially, he too, had come across as a nasty individual, but as events had turned out, he had shown signs of genuine remorse for his part in the proceedings. To his credit, he had turned up to see my brother in hospital and had also given the police useful information as they had investigated the events.

'Have you heard any more about Jim Redfern?' I asked.

'Actually, yes. I've been in touch with Jim on a number of occasions. He's a good man and, believe it or not, he's very interested to know more, particularly with regard to the arguments against Darwinian theory.'

I remembered my meeting with Redfern in a pub in Reading, and getting the impression that he was genuinely sorry for his part in our problems in the Congo. Although the news about Sam losing his leg was particularly raw to me at that time, when I had left Redfern at the end of that meeting, I had actually begun to like the man. There were even aspects of his story which had caused me to feel a degree of sympathy for him.

But there had also been another mysterious individual. This

was not anyone directly involved with the expedition, but a shadowy character in the background who may have had some influence on the subsequent police investigation.

I had been told that the 'creation evolution' debate upset people in a number of areas including the government, the education system and scientific research. This mysterious character was a lady who appeared to be connected with both the government and education. It suggested that there were people in fairly high places who did not appreciate the work Kevin and his colleagues were doing. That being the case, and given our experiences on the previous expedition, I wondered again how sensible it was to get involved in another trip designed to promote Kevin's position. Were these the people Kevin was alluding to about a group of people who appeared determined to disrupt their work? My grandfather had warned me that the subject I was getting involved with was controversial and that I might run into significant opposition. My heart ached as I thought of him; that wise man who never got ruffled about anything.

'I suppose you didn't hear any more about that woman from the Ministry of Education?'

Kevin looked confused.

I realized that he may know nothing at all about her. Although he had briefly seen the woman in question, we had never really discussed her. I had had most of my conversations about this woman with a policeman called Andy Phillips.

'Sorry Kevin, you've probably forgotten her.'

I reminded him about an incident immediately following his

debate with Charles Thompson. We had been discussing the debate in a corridor backstage when Charles Thompson had come barging past us and had nearly knocked Kevin to the ground.

'Yes, I remember,' he said.

'Well, it was the woman from the Ministry of Education who Charles had been speaking to just before that incident.'

Kevin gave a nod of understanding. Then, suddenly, he froze and stared sightlessly across the bar.

'You OK, Kevin?' I asked.

His eyes briefly flicked in my direction before becoming fixed on his glass of Coke. 'I'd forgotten about that.'

'Is it significant?' I enquired.

'Not sure,' he said. 'Rob, if I could get a photo of this woman, do you think you'd recognize her?'

I considered. 'I don't know, Kevin. It's a good while ago, and I wasn't really paying much attention to her physical appearance. I was more interested in the comments she was making.'

'That's a shame,' he said to his Coke. 'Never mind. I might try to get a picture of her anyway. If you don't recognize her, we haven't lost anything.'

As I looked at Sam, I thought about another member of that first expedition. Sam had struck up what appeared to be a very close friendship with a young lady called Jane Walker. Jane was a nurse and had been introduced to us as our 'medical insurance' for the trip. She and Sam had got on extremely well and, at least from Sam's side, there had been strong indications that he would have liked that friendship to develop into something more serious.

It had been right at the end of our time in the Congo that Sam had been wounded. Ordinarily, he would have loved to have Jane giving him her undivided attention, but his injury was so serious that I do not think he was even aware of her presence for most of that time.

When Sam had eventually been flown back to Britain, the medical staff had been very pleased with Sam's physical progress, but his mental condition was another thing altogether. Having been a very active sportsman and fairly gifted footballer, the fact that his playing days were over, threw him into a state of depression which was impossible to shift. This was bad enough, but it was not his biggest concern. He had an overwhelming fear that his disability would mean that he would no longer be seen as attractive by the opposite sex.

Partly because of this concern, I had been greatly heartened to hear that Jane had visited him in hospital a number of times. On one of these occasions, I had turned up to see Sam while Jane was still visiting. After a brief, joyful reunion, I told them I would go for a coffee until they had said their goodbyes.

I had still been in the restaurant when Jane came over to see me. After exchanging a few pleasantries, Jane had asked how I felt Sam was doing. In a way it had put me in a slightly tricky spot. I wanted to be honest and tell her the issues Sam was struggling with, but I did not want to make her feel uncomfortable in any way.

In the end, I did decide to tell her Sam's fears about feeling less attractive to women. She had smiled sadly and said that he should not have any fears on that front. She had said something along the lines that if young ladies were put off because he had a disability, then he was probably better off without them anyway. In some ways that was comforting, because it clearly showed Jane's own attitude to Sam's position. However, I thought that it might not necessarily allay all Sam's fears.

When Sam had recovered to the point where he was out of hospital and starting to get out and about, he had taken Jane out for a meal on a couple of occasions. After their first date, I had spoken to Sam, who was as up-beat as I had seen him since that fateful day when he had been shot on the Likouala Aux Herbes River. He was full of life and much more like his old self. It all looked promising.

During their second date, however, a problem became apparent. Sam had asked Jane if she would be interested in a more serious relationship, and that was when things went downhill. Jane, who took her Christian faith very seriously, told Sam that she could not start a relationship with someone who had not given their life to Christ. Unfortunately, Sam took that badly. He became frustrated and irritable. Although Jane had tried to explain to Sam why she felt the way she did, her attempts to reason with him fell on stony ground.

Unfortunately, that had been the end of it. Sam had been in a foul mood for weeks. At least a fortnight went by before he could refer to the incident at all. When he did, all he would say was that her fairytale God was too important to her. Nothing I did or said made any difference. Ironically, this incident had the effect of pushing Sam further away from Christianity.

Jane and I had spoken to each other about three weeks after the fateful meal. She informed me that the Bible said Christians should not be unequally yoked. Apparently, this meant that Christians ought to be in relationships with people who shared their faith in Jesus. In truth, I was somewhere between Sam's and Jane's position. I understood why Sam would be upset when he had very little trust in the Bible, but I could also see it from Jane's point of view. If she believed that the Bible was the Word of God, I could see why she would not want to go against its teaching. Anyway, she was adamant that she would not be starting a relationship with anyone who was not a Christian. She was very sad about the situation because she genuinely liked Sam, but there was no way she would compromise on this.

After a few weeks, I tried to talk to Sam about Jane, but he was not having any of it. I could tell he was upset, but his hurt was most likely mingled with pride. He was not used to being turned down by women.

I dragged my thoughts back to the matter in hand. After another round of drinks, we spent the next forty-five minutes discussing the pros and cons of me joining the team. I asked a number of questions and, for the most part, Kevin's responses satisfied me. Yet still, an uncomfortable sense of foreboding crept up on me each time I thought of committing myself to the project.

The feeling of discomfort and apprehension seemed totally irrational. Generally speaking, I am not someone who regularly claims to have premonitions of doom. Having said that, I remembered the sense I had had on a number of occasions in the Congo of being watched. At the time, I had told myself that I was being foolish and had rejected the idea. Later, however, that sense had proved to be accurate.

As I sat in the pub and recalled these events, I told myself that I was letting the negative situations we had experienced on that last trip affect my judgement of a completely different set of circumstances. On that last expedition, we had been miles from anywhere and it would have been impossible to call the authorities for help. However, on this latest proposed trip, we would be in the State of Washington in the U.S. Surely, we would be safer there? I was to be reminded of this reasoning later.

Time passed as I continued to reflect on the offer; Kevin patiently waited for my decision.

Eventually, I said, 'OK, what do you want from me?'

Kevin positively beamed. 'That's brilliant,' he said. 'I was sure you'd say "no".' He leant forward, resting his crossed forearms on the table. 'Well, if you're happy to take it on, I'd like you to see if you can find someone who teaches geology, who is open-minded enough to honestly consider our position, and who might like to join us on the trip.'

I frowned. 'And how do I go about locating someone like that?'

'I'll leave that up to you,' he said. 'Use your imagination. But it's vitally important that we find some people involved in the teaching of the sciences in this country to be exposed to some of the great evidence which goes against the idea of millions or billions of years of earth's history.'

I studied him for a few seconds before transferring my gaze to my coffee cup. 'OK,' I said. 'I'll give it some thought.'

He nodded briefly. 'I'll give you a couple of weeks, and then I'll call you to see how you're getting on.'

Another thought popped into my head. 'Kevin, you'd better tell me when we're going. That might be a piece of information that a potential recruit will be interested to know.'

'Good point,' he said. 'The plan is that we go in early August. I mentioned to the other members that if we wanted a teacher to come on board it would obviously have to be in the school summer holidays.'

So that's how we left it. We expressed our grateful thanks to Kevin for lunch, said our goodbyes with hearty handshakes, and Kevin left to make the journey back up to Manchester.

Sam and I returned to my house and we spent some time discussing the proposed new adventure. Although Sam was adamant over his decision not to go on the trip, he was very keen to receive daily updates from me as my journey of exploration progressed. In some respects, he almost seemed more excited about it than I was. This may have had something to do with the fact that I was still considering the opposition shown by many to the work of Kevin and his mates.

Chapter 2
A New Addition

The following morning, having no important tasks planned for the day, I decided to head to my study. The small box room, currently brilliantly lit by the morning sunshine, lifted my spirits and gave me hope for the task ahead. That task was to locate a geology teacher who would accept an invitation to a scientific trip to the USA, and who was also happy to embrace controversial subjects.

While clearing away some papers on my desk and switching on the computer, I suddenly found the task quite daunting. Starting my search, as I came across each individual I recorded their name along with any additional relevant information.

On looking at the list of possible candidates two hours later, I was rather disappointed at only having half a dozen names scribbled down. Determined to be successful in my quest, I picked up the list, hoping one of them would be suitable. I decided to attempt to make contact straight away. The first potential candidate was a gentleman who was forty-seven years old from Ealing in West London. Locating his email address, I wrote:

> My name is Robert Granger and I live in Maidenhead in Berkshire. I have been tasked with finding an individual who would be interested in learning more about the ages of geological features and the way in which they may have been formed. Part of this learning would involve a trip to the USA.
>
> I was drawn to your name as you appear to have attended the debate on evolution approximately eighteen months ago between Dr Charles Thompson and Professor Kevin Robinson in Harrow. In addition, some of your online comments lead me to believe that you might possibly have something to do with the teaching profession. Is this true? I am specifically looking for someone who has taught or is teaching geology.
>
> Should you be interested in knowing more about this, please respond to this mail. However, if you would rather discuss it over the phone, my number can be found below.
>
> Regards, Robert Granger

Similar messages were sent to each of the other five people on my list. The gurgling noises from my stomach reminded me it was time for lunch. Having spent all morning researching geologists, hopefully at least one would reply. Taking a steaming mug of coffee and sandwich back to my study, I decided to attempt to identify more potential participants. I had not even finished my sandwich when, to my amazement, a notification popped up—a response from my first email:

> Hi Robert,
>
> Yes, I did attend that debate. Fascinating! I am interested in geology and would love a trip to the States, but I'm afraid I've never had anything to do with teaching.

Responding immediately, I thanked him for his reply and told him that I may well be back in touch. Best to keep my options open, I thought.

Later in the afternoon as I was still researching, my spirits lifted as more responses came in. The second respondent was involved in teaching. However, sadly, while one of his comments which I had seen about the debate had sounded promising, it turned out that he was very much opposed to the creation position. After sharing another couple of emails, it was clear that he had no desire to be involved in Kevin's trip.

The third response was a different case altogether. Susan King was a thirty-two-year-old geography teacher. Her location was an additional bonus. It turned out that she lived in the Slough area, just a few miles from Maidenhead. After exchanging a few brief emails, it became obvious that Susan was going to be a far more promising prospect than my previous two contacts.

As a geography teacher, her work included elements of geology, and she had stated in her emails that, while she was certainly no creationist, her overall attitude appeared to be one of open-mindedness. Like me, when she had attended the evolution debate, she had assumed that all she had been taught about evolution was true. But again, like me, she had found Kevin Robinson's arguments to be surprisingly persuasive.

Susan certainly sounded promising. Kevin had not been that specific about the attributes of the candidate he wanted but, from what I did know, Susan seemed ideal.

As we exchanged messages by email, I found that explaining the reason for our trip to Mount Saint Helens was not the easiest to put in writing. It would be much easier in person. However, suggesting a meeting with a young woman you have just contacted out of the blue by email was not that straightforward either. Hoping she would not think me some online predator, I invited her to suggest a suitable time and place for a meeting and hit the send button. I was amazed when, a few moments later, she agreed a suitable rendezvous the following Saturday lunchtime at Jenner's Café, close to Boulter's Lock on the River Thames in Maidenhead. It was all coming together; hopefully she would be what Kevin had in mind.

It was 12:25pm on Saturday when I pulled into the car park at Jenner's Café feeling a tinge of nervousness. A smell of coffee and bacon greeted me as I opened the door and found a table just inside and waited.

Ten minutes later, Susan arrived. She was about 5 feet, 4 inches tall, with shoulder-length, slightly wavy, light brown hair and a friendly and cheerful face.

'Susan?' I asked, rising to my feet.

She turned towards me and smiled. 'Rob? Hi, nice to meet you.'

I took the few steps towards her and held out my hand. 'Nice to meet you too, Susan,' I said, returning the smile. 'By the way, are you a "Susan" or a "Sue"?'

She laughed. 'Most people call me "Sue", but I answer to either.'

'Great,' I said. 'What can I get you to drink, Sue?'

'I'll have a cappuccino, thanks.'

We walked up to the counter together.

'I take it you've been here before?' I said.

She nodded. 'I've been coming here for years. My sister and I used to come here with my parents when we were kids. I've always had a thing about the river.'

'What can I get you, folks?' The softly spoken words came from a broad smile behind the counter.

I ordered our coffees.

'Can I get you anything else?' the woman asked.

'I'm going to have a cheese and tomato roll,' I said to Sue. 'What would you like?'

She studied the sandwiches in the glass display case. 'I think I'll have a tuna and cucumber sandwich, if that's OK?' She opened her handbag. 'Hold on; let me give you the money.'

'No chance,' I said. 'I've asked you to come over here. I'm getting these. By the way, would you like a cake to go with your sandwich?'

'No thanks, Rob,' she said with a smile. 'I've got to watch my figure.'

I ordered the additional items from the woman behind the counter and handed over the requisite amount of money.

A minute later, we were sitting at a table in the corner of the café, with two cups of coffee between us.

Sue leant forward, rested her forearms on the table and said, 'OK, Rob, tell me what all this is about.'

As we munched our way through our sandwiches, I explained to Sue what Kevin had told me about the proposed trip to Mount Saint Helens. Susan listened intently and seemed genuinely interested in the details. As we talked, I noticed she had vibrant green eyes that sparkled when she smiled. She wore a light blue blouse and a cream jacket, and she had a gentle and friendly demeanour.

It turned out that Sue was head of her geography department at the school and had a degree in Geology. This was getting better and better, I thought as she began telling me about herself and her job. I was curious about what was taught in schools, having heard Kevin comment frequently about the education system. The question came up easily as we talked.

'When you discuss geological features visible around the world with your students, what explanation is given for them in the classroom?'

Sue was informative, explaining the core teaching elements. We briefly discussed the teaching of geology in schools, and I learned that it was all done from a position of millions of years. This did not surprise me one bit. If what people like Kevin believed was anything like accurate, none of the young-earth arguments that we would be hearing about at Mount Saint Helens would ever be heard by people in the schools, colleges and universities of our nation. Although I was still unsure about the arguments for a young earth, I was adamant that if there were two ways of interpreting the data, then our students should at least be made aware of that. I mentioned this to Sue.

Sue was doubtful about the Bible, but certainly open-minded enough to discuss the subject. The conversation was easy, and we quickly built up a rapport. I thought it might be helpful to enlighten her about the journey of discovery I had undertaken, and in which I was actually still involved.

'Would you mind if I explained to you a bit about my own exposure to the creation subject?' I asked. 'I've already been on one expedition with these people and it had a profound effect on my opinion of the Bible.'

'Not at all,' she said. 'I'd love to hear about it.'

So, I started right at the beginning. I told her about my grandfather's conversion to Christianity and the affect that had had on me as an agnostic, bordering on atheism. I explained about his background in teaching the sciences and the confusion into which his profession of faith had thrown me. The fact that it had been my grandfather's desire that I get involved in the creation/evolution debate really interested Sue.

'Was it your granddad who introduced you to these creationists?' she asked.

'In a way, it was,' I said. 'Unfortunately, he died only two weeks after telling us about his faith.'

'Oh, I'm sorry, Rob,' she said with feeling, stretching out her hand and resting it lightly on my forearm.

'Don't worry. He was ninety-two and he'd had a great life. Anyway, he left me a book in his will and I believe it was designed, in part, to provoke an interest in this subject. It worked.'

She smiled. 'What was the book?'

'*The Lost World* by Sir Arthur Conan Doyle,' I said.

I told her about my initial meeting with one of the creationists and his suggestion that I attend the evolution debate in Harrow. As Sue had attended this event, there was no need to elaborate, but I did explain that, later on, Sam and I had had a fascinating discussion with Kevin Robinson about dinosaurs.

Throughout this account, Sue seemed curious, but her body language told me that she was not particularly convinced about Kevin's position. However, when I told her about going to Carlisle to view engravings of dinosaurs on Bishop Richard Bell's tomb, she was amazed.

'You mean these dinosaurs were engraved in the 1400s?' she said with bewilderment.

I nodded. 'That's right. Amazing, isn't it?'

She shook her head in wonder. 'Go on,' she said, looking intently at me.

Naturally, I told her about the expedition to the Congo to look for Mokele-mbembe; I recounted the journey, picking up our guides and trackers and our long search for the creature, as well as all the problems we had to deal with at the end of our time in the rainforest. I finished the account by telling her that we had to hurriedly leave the area, and that this had ultimately led to Sam's injury.

Sue had listened earnestly and seemed genuinely interested as I relayed the details of the account of our epic adventure. At times, the look in her eyes suggested that she was finding it hard to digest some of the details I was relaying.

As she sat taking it all in, there was a look of wonder on her face as she said, 'Rob, that's incredible.' Then, after a short pause, she asked, 'How is your brother?'

'He lost his left leg just above the knee,' I said.

Once again, Sue looked horrified as she repeated the words she had said before. 'Oh no, I'm sorry, Rob.'

I shrugged slightly. 'I know. At the time it was terrible. Sam took it badly at first, but he's much more positive about things now.'

I looked up and smiled at her. 'Anyway, that's a rough outline of what has happened to me. I started out from a position of almost complete atheism, but that has changed. I haven't become a Christian myself, but I'm much less certain about this whole universe having been the product of 14 billion years of unguided natural processes.'

Sue looked thoughtful. 'Well, Rob, it's all very interesting, but I'm afraid I'm going to take a lot of convincing.'

'That's fair enough,' I said. 'All I would say is that I believe it's important to keep an open mind about these things.'

She nodded vigorously. 'Oh, I agree. I'll certainly be doing that.' As if suddenly remembering something, she asked, 'Have you done any further research since you got back from the Congo?'

I was hoping she would ask. Subsequent to the expedition, I had been digging and researching myself and was astonished at the evidence against evolution. I was keen to share what I had found.

Sue listened attentively and appeared to be honestly considering all the information I was throwing at her. Eventually she glanced down at her watch.

'Good grief,' she said. 'Is that the time? I'm supposed to be meeting a friend at 2:30pm.'

As we got up to leave, I had an idea. 'Sue,' I said, 'how about I send you a list of quotes that Kevin used in his arguments. You could Google them as I did and check they are accurate.'

She nodded. 'OK; good idea.'

We walked around to the car park and over to where she had parked her car.

'Give me a ring when you've had a chance to look at some of those quotes. Let me know what you think.' She opened her car door, about to get in. A waft of pine air freshener drifted through the air.

'I will,' she said. 'Thanks, Rob. I've enjoyed it. It's been fascinating.' And with that, she got in the car and pulled off.

I smiled and waved as she pulled out of the car park. It was some time before I stopped looking at the point where I had last seen her car. When I did eventually move, I turned and strolled over to my own jalopy. I sat there for some minutes thinking how enjoyable our meeting had been, and realized I had a big dopey grin on my face. I thought about how her green eyes sparkled and her voice rose with enthusiasm when she was talking about her work, and how her whole face seemed to shine when she smiled.

Out of the blue, I was hit by a memory from three and a half years ago when Karen and I broke up. We had been together for five years and the relationship had been going well; or at least, I had thought it had been going well. That was until I caught her in a drunken embrace with one of her colleagues at a work's Christmas party. I subsequently discovered that they had been carrying on behind my back for a couple of months.

That little episode had hit me hard. My own attitude towards that relationship had been pretty serious. I had never plucked up the courage to propose to Karen, but it was the plan at some point. As a result of the trauma that the break-up of that relationship had caused me, in the years since, I had found it almost impossible to trust women.

However, this situation felt different. Although I had only spent a couple of hours with Sue, I could not ever remember having this kind of reaction to meeting a young woman before. I actually felt like pulling out of the car park and racing after her to try to find out where she lived. This was ridiculous! Laughing at myself, I shook myself out of my soppy contemplations, put the car into gear and headed for home.

On the following Monday evening, I got a call from Sue. I had sent her a list of quotes along with their sources on the Saturday afternoon and, since then, she had spent some time checking them.

'Rob, if you've got some time to spare during the week, I'd like to meet up with you again.'

My heart skipped and I grinned to myself. I would quite like us to meet up as well, I thought. 'Sure. When would be best for you?' I replied, trying not to sound too eager.

'I've got a lot of work to do over the next couple of evenings,' she said, 'but I could meet you on Wednesday? It would probably have to be after 7:30pm.'

'That'll be fine,' I said. 'Do you want me to come over to you this time?'

There was a slight hesitation on the line. 'Err ... yes, OK. Do you know where 'The Swan' is?'

'I don't, but I'm sure I'll be able to find it. Is there something specific you want to go through?'

'Yes. The quotes you sent are very interesting. I'd like to ask you a bit about your subsequent investigations into some of these issues. I'd also like to know more about our proposed trip, if that's all right?'

Those two days felt like a week but finally, on Wednesday evening, after a quick search for the location of 'The Swan', I drove the 5 miles to Slough.

Pulling into the pub car park ten minutes early, I glanced at the other vehicles already parked there. I could not see Sue's car, so I parked up and headed into the pub.

The pub was not busy, but I chose a table as far away from others as I could manage and sat down to wait. I received one or two curious glances from a couple of the locals but avoided eye-contact to reduce the need for conversation. I looked around briefly, wondering if this was Sue's local, and if we would be interrupted by acquaintances wanting a catch up with Sue.

I had been sitting there in a state of increasing nervous anticipation for about fifteen minutes when Sue arrived. She was wearing a very attractive white short-sleeved blouse, along with a two-tone, blue skirt which came down to just below the knee.

I jumped up and crossed to intercept her. 'Hi, Sue, how are you?'

A couple of minutes later, we were sitting back at the table I had first occupied, accompanied by a pint of bitter shandy and a medium-sized glass of merlot.

As Sue took a sip of her wine, she said, 'By the way, don't worry, I'm not driving. I only live about half a mile from here.'

I smiled and nodded. I also mentally filed the information about her home away just in case.

We began by talking about the teaching of evolution in schools. However, after a while, the subject of religion came up. Suddenly, Sue stared sightlessly across the room as if recalling something from her past.

'When I was a child, I used to go to church with my grandma,' she said. 'I'm sure some of it went in, but I can't remember much of it now. I do remember her telling me that God was a good God. I know about the main claims of Christianity; that Jesus is supposed to have died for our sins and so on, but I haven't given it any thought for about twenty years. I have a vague recollection of Christmas nativities and harvest festivals, but not really much more than that. From about the age of twelve, I stopped going to church and, with the exception of weddings and funerals, I haven't really been since.'

'Well, to be honest, I've never been at all,' I said. 'Until my grandfather's conversion, none of our family had ever been churchgoers. I have never been exposed to what I think of as real Bible teaching. I can't tell you how weird I found it when I was introduced to Kevin and he spoke of the Bible as a reliable source of historical events. I thought it was totally nuts.'

'It sounds very much as if you've changed your mind,' she said.

I hesitated, wondering what exactly I did think. 'I'm not sure I'd put it exactly like that, but it's certainly changed my overall outlook. Having been through many of the arguments, I do think there are significant issues for the secular world to resolve. I'm not saying that evolution is definitely wrong, I'm just saying that there seem to be plenty of unanswered questions. What I would say is that, in many respects, I can see why Kevin and his friends assert that the Bible's account of creation is a better fit with the physical evidence than the naturalistic evolutionary one.'

Sue looked surprised. 'Really? You'd go that far?'

'Yes,' I said. 'I understand your surprise, but I do think that's so.'

Again, Sue looked thoughtful. 'Having checked on some of the quotes you sent me, I can see how someone might reach that conclusion. The trouble is, Rob, that it's all so new to me. This has the potential to turn everything I thought I knew completely on its head. Although I'm determined to deal with this honestly, I have a sense that I could end up feeling quite uncomfortable about all this.'

'You said you wanted to hear more about my investigations,' I interjected, remembering her stated purpose of this meeting. 'Was there anything specific that you had in mind?'

Sue nodded enthusiastically. 'Yes. I was fascinated about the creationists' argument over information always originating from an intelligent source. As I thought about it, I certainly couldn't come up with any immediate exceptions to that rule. But you've had much longer to consider their claims. So, one of my questions is, during your investigations, have you come across any languages, codes or information which you can prove do not come from an intelligent source?'

I thought back to when I had been looking into this issue. 'The short answer is "no",' I said. 'As far as I'm aware, there is no example of any of these things coming from a non-intelligent source. Now, I would qualify that by saying there are forms of communication in the animal kingdom and we don't know where they come from. However, that certainly doesn't refute their point. Firstly, most people would agree that animals which use some form of communication are themselves intelligent. But secondly, even in those cases, we can't prove where those languages came from. We certainly can't prove the source of those languages was not an intelligent creator.'

Sue nodded; the very slight frown on her features clearly betrayed the serious contemplation she was giving the subject.

I went on. 'The other thing which I found completely fascinating was SETI.'

Sue had been thoughtfully gazing at her wine glass.

She now looked up. 'SETI? What's that?'

'The Search for Extra-Terrestrial Intelligence,' I said.

'How's that relevant?' she asked.

I gave a little smile. 'Well, I'd never thought of it before it was pointed out to me, but how do they try to detect extra-terrestrial life?'

Sue thought for a moment. 'Don't they listen for radio signals coming from some distant galaxy?'

I nodded. 'Exactly, but what in particular are they listening for? What is it that would convince them that they had found an intelligent race?'

'I assume because they had received some kind of intelligent message.'

'That's right. But how will they determine whether the message is intelligent or not?'

A smile appeared on Sue's face. 'Because it contains a language, some type of verifiable code system, or recognizable information of some kind.'

'Precisely. But do you know what's really crazy?' I continued without waiting for a response. 'In the 1970s, some astronomers were listening for such a message from outer space and they heard this series of blips, one and one third seconds apart. They were delighted. They thought, this is it; we've found extra-terrestrial life. We're not alone after all. They actually nicknamed this phenomenon LGM1. It stood for Little Green Men 1.[2] In fact, what they had found was the first pulsar. This is a highly magnetized, rotating neutron star that emits a beam of electromagnetic radiation. This pulsar was rotating very quickly. As it did this, each revolution resulted in a radio signal being fired into space.

That's what had been picked up by our excited astronomers. It had absolutely zero to do with any intelligent alien life.

'So, think about it. In human DNA, we have 3.5 billion letters of detailed, functional, encoded information. That information holds all the genetic instructions that go to make a human being. It contains the information to build the structure of all the cells in our bodies. It holds the information to build tiny molecular machines within those cells. It has the information to create organs like eyes, ears, lungs, livers and kidneys; to create bone, hair and skin; to create systems like the central nervous system, the respiratory system, the circulatory system and the reproductive system. We have all that functional information within our cells and yet these geniuses say that it all happened through natural processes. The sad thing is that those same geniuses hear blip, blip, blip and believe they've just found intelligent life on another planet. It's idiotic!'

While I had been speaking, Sue had been staring at me with an expression of wonder on her face. All of a sudden, she collapsed into a fit of giggles. When she was eventually able to speak again, she said, 'You're right, Rob. It is idiotic. What do these people say in response?'

I shrugged. 'Don't know. I'm not convinced that they have any rational comeback.'

As we continued talking, the conversation was frequently interrupted as the ridiculousness of the issue would once more hit Sue. Every now and again she would break into what she was saying and say 'blip, blip, blip,' and begin another fit of giggles.

Each time this happened, our fits of laughter grew longer. This seemed to be a cause of irritation for three men who were sitting at the bar and they were giving us some very disdainful looks. I could not care less. I felt so relaxed in Sue's company. Her light-hearted, easy-going nature was refreshing, and while her giggles might be a cause of irritation for some, I found them strangely endearing.

As our fits of laughter died down and the conversation began to lapse, I asked Sue if there were any other issues she wanted to discuss.

'There is one thing,' she said. 'You remember the quote you sent me about genetic mutations? It was from a guy called Lee Spetner.'[3]

I did remember. 'Yep. It was about the fact that genetic mutations lose information.'

'That's right. Well, can you remember what the evolutionist said at the debate? I know he came back and said something about bacteria acquiring antibiotic resistance. Isn't that right?'

I was delighted that Sue had brought this up. My investigations into this subject had unearthed some fascinating details about a British expedition undertaken over 170 years ago. I decided to tell her about it.

'Have you ever heard of the Franklin Expedition?'[4] I asked.

Sue briefly shook her head.

'No, and nor had I, until I began gathering information on bacteria becoming resistant to antibiotics.' I had a quick sip of my shandy before continuing. 'I heard about this expedition to the Arctic in 1845 to explore the last unnavigated section of the North-west passage. It was led by Sir John Franklin, a Royal Navy officer and experienced explorer. The members of the expedition did not return and were presumed dead.'

Again, Sue looked rather puzzled. 'What's that got to do with antibiotic resistance in bacteria?'

I did not immediately answer her question. 'Do you remember what Kevin Robinson said at the debate? He said that creationists have no problem with the idea that organisms can adapt to changes in environment.'

'Yes,' Sue said. 'I grasped that.'

'Well, the Franklin Expedition provided another fascinating piece of the puzzle. You see, we're often told that bacteria become resistant to antibiotics by coming into contact with these drugs. One of the most popular theories is that when a patient fails to finish a course of antibiotics, if that course hasn't completely killed off the target bacteria, some of those surviving bacteria will be likely to develop resistance to that particular antibiotic.'

'Yes, I realize that too.'

'Well, the Franklin Expedition called that line of reasoning into question.'

'How?'

'In the 1980s, some of those men were found. They had been frozen in the ice for over 130 years. A number of scientists thought it would be a great idea to have a look at the bacteria in the stomachs of these men and compare them with those around today. So, that's what they did. Now, if you think about it, if those men were frozen solid for over 130 years, that would also be true of the contents of their stomachs. Therefore, the bacteria would be as they had been in the 1840s.' Sue nodded her understanding

'As antibiotics are a relatively recent weapon in our fight against infection, those men would never have come into contact with those antibiotics. Therefore, if the scientists' belief about how bacteria acquire their resistance is true, then none of the bacteria in the stomachs of those expedition members should have developed resistance.'

I could tell from Sue's face that she had already anticipated my next piece of information. This was confirmed when she said, 'And you're obviously about to tell me that those bacteria did have resistance.'

'Not all of them,' I said, 'but a few had.'

Sue sat there just staring at me for a few moments. Eventually she asked, 'So, do the creation scientists believe contact with antibiotics has nothing to do with resistance in bacteria?'

'No, I don't think so,' I said. 'You'd have to ask them to be sure, but I don't think they have any particular problem with bacteria adapting to an antibiotic-flooded environment. However, what the Franklin Expedition does show is that bacteria can develop a mutation which results in them being resistant, without there being any contact with the antibiotic concerned.'

Sue appeared to be staring at her wine; a slight frown was etched on her brow. After a moment she looked up at me. 'How come we don't hear about any of this, Rob?'

I laughed with genuine amusement. 'If you knew how many

times I'd asked myself exactly the same question, you'd be amazed.'

She smiled. 'I'm not surprised, if this is the kind of information you've unearthed.'

We continued to kick these matters around for some time before drifting onto other issues. We spent some time talking about our respective families, some about our past, and some about our interests.

At 10:15pm, Sue glanced down at her watch. 'I must be going,' she said. She looked up at me and smiled. 'Rob, I've had a lovely evening. Thank you.'

I felt exactly the same. It had been a wonderful evening spent with a wonderful girl.

I smiled back at her. 'Well, I've certainly enjoyed myself, Sue. Maybe we can do it again at some point?' Hoping for an immediate acceptance of that invitation, there was no response, and I could not read her face. I was certain that she had felt relaxed in my company, as I had in her's. We both stood and, with Sue picking up her handbag, we headed for the door.

'Can I give you a lift home?' I asked.

She smiled. 'No thanks, Rob, I'll walk. I don't get enough exercise as it is.'

As Sue held out her hand, I felt my stomach drop. I had no idea how the evening would end, but I had secretly been hoping for at least a peck on the cheek. Never mind, it was refreshing to find a young lady who had a well-developed sense of morals, I thought, as I took her delicate hand in a short, formal shake.

'Good night, Rob,' she said. 'I'll give you a ring in a day or two. I'm sure I'll have some more questions for you.'

'I hope so,' I thought. 'I'll look forward to it,' I said, smiling. 'Good night, Sue.'

I walked over to my car and got in. As I started the car, I glanced in Sue's direction to see which way she had gone. She had turned left out of the car park and was walking in the direction of the town.

I pulled out of the car park and headed in the same direction. Approaching her, I slowed and dropped the passenger-side window. As I slowly drove past her, I shouted, 'Blip, blip, blip.' Giving a quick toot on the horn, I drove off, but I could see her in the wing mirror and could tell that she was laughing.

Chapter 3
America: Here We Come

It was a bright, humid Saturday morning about two months later, and Sue and I were travelling to attend a meeting with Kevin Robinson at his offices in Manchester. We were both excited about our upcoming adventure, and Sue was very much looking forward to meeting Kevin. As we rode up on the train from London Euston, there was one thing I was highly curious about. When I had spoken to Kevin about this meeting, he had made a comment suggesting that I might be in for a 'slight surprise'. He had said that he hoped it would not affect my decision to go on the trip, which, to be honest, had caused me some concern. What might affect my decision?

Despite the fact that he had been quite upbeat himself, my curiosity had taken me on a trip already, wondering what awaited me. I mentioned the mystery to Sue.

'What do you think it might be?' she asked.

I frowned. 'I've got no idea. It was said in a fairly light-hearted way, but I did feel that it wasn't entirely frivolous.'

The speculation continued for a while, but to take my mind off it, I asked Sue to tell me a bit more about her geology degree. After all, it was her education in this area which was the main reason for me considering her to be such a good candidate for part of the team.

As we entered Kevin's place of work at 10:15am, I was greeted warmly by the receptionist, Sally. 'Hello! Nice to see you again.' I had come up to Manchester on a number of occasions with Sam prior to our last adventure in the Congo. It had usually been Sally who had accompanied us to the meeting room where we had had our sessions with Kevin. She must see dozens of people a week, and I thought it was lovely that she remembered me.

'Hi Sally,' I said cheerfully. 'I'd like to introduce you to Sue.'

After the greetings, Sally took us along to the meeting room. I explained who Sue was and why we were there.

Sally put her hand on my arm. 'Well, I hope this adventure isn't as eventful as the last one was. I heard about your brother. How is he?'

'He's doing well, thanks, Sally. I'll tell him you were asking about him.'

I sat in the seat I had occupied on previous visits, with Sue taking the seat to my left which had been Sam's old seat. When Kevin turned up a couple of minutes later, we stood and I went through the introductions again.

'OK, Kevin, what's this great mystery?'

He looked at me with an enigmatic smile on his face. 'Patience, Rob. All will be revealed.'

Kevin and Sue had been discussing the teaching of geology for about a quarter of an hour when Kevin's mobile phone sprang into life. He answered it and listened.

'OK, Sally. Thanks. I'll be out immediately.'

He got to his feet and smiled at me. 'Your curiosity is about to be satisfied, Rob.' And with that, he left the room. I glanced at Sue. 'Well, here we go,' I said. 'I have no idea what to expect.'

If I had expected anything, it certainly was not the answer that was revealed when Kevin returned with a new arrival.

My mouth fell open. I remembered a similar unexpected meeting with this man; I had been visiting my brother in a hospital in Reading following the amputation of his left leg.

'Dr Redfern,' I fumbled for words. 'How are you?'

Jim Redfern was from the States and had been a member of the team of evolutionists that had caused us so many problems on our previous expedition. Although he had opposed our work, he had subsequently had an attack of guilt over how our party had been treated. He had actually been very helpful to the police during their investigation into the circumstances surrounding the events of that trip. Although I was grateful to him for his participation in attempting to bring the real crooks to justice, rightly or wrongly, I still connected him with those who had caused Sam so much suffering.

'Mr Granger,' Redfern said. 'It's great to see you again. I'm fine, thanks. How are you? And more importantly, how is your brother?'

I rose from my seat and went to shake hands with the American. 'Sam's doing much better, thanks,' I said. 'He still has the odd bout of self-pity, but he's getting on with his life pretty well.'

I thought I detected a fleeting glimpse of pain in the doctor's eyes before he turned to look at Sue. After a few more pleasantries and introducing Sue to Dr Redfern, we all sat down to discuss the upcoming trip.

Kevin started to explain to us some of the scientific evidence we would be viewing on our visit to Mount Saint Helens. This included finely laminated rock strata, recently cut canyon systems, steam explosion pits and potential coal deposits.

'Sam's really keen to know what we'll be doing and when we'll be doing it,' I said. 'Although he's not coming with us, he very much wants to keep up to date with everything we're doing. Have you got a set itinerary for the trip?'

'We have a provisional list,' Kevin said, 'but it's very likely to change. I'll go and get a copy.'

As Kevin left the room, I turned to Jim Redfern. I had a burning desire to learn something of his news since our last meeting.

'Did you hear any more from John Smith?' I asked as casually as I could.

Jim looked uncomfortable. 'He tried to contact me on a few different occasions,' he said. 'Recognizing his number, I ignored the call. However, one day he called from a different phone. I answered and was cross-examined about my contact with the police. I told him that I'd said nothing that would incriminate him, but he didn't believe me and was quite abusive. I then had to endure a fifteen-minute lecture on what would happen to me if he ever found out that I'd grassed him up.'

'Have you heard anything from him since that call?'

Jim hesitated for a split second, then he said, 'Just once—probably four or five months ago. He was after some kind of specialist information. Anyway, it was something I couldn't help him with. Thankfully, I haven't heard from him since.'

At that moment, Kevin came back into the room holding a few sheets of A4 paper. 'OK,' he said. 'We've got a rough idea of the order we want to do things, but we're going to have to be a bit flexible about it. We'll need assistance for some of the trips we're going to make, and it will depend on when those people are available as to when we go. Also, the weather might have a bearing on some of the trips. So, at present, very little is set in stone.'

A little giggle came from my left and I glanced at Sue. 'Isn't that exactly what it is?' she said.

The others looked as confused as I felt.

'Set in stone,' she explained. 'From what you were saying earlier, almost all the evidence we'll be studying is exactly that.'

'Oh, ha ha ha,' I said.

The others laughed.

For once, Kevin was not having to rush off to another meeting, and suggested we went for a spot of lunch together. Unfortunately, Jim Redfern could not spare the time and had to return to his university, but Kevin, Sue and I took a five-minute stroll from his offices to a gastro pub to grab a bite to eat.

Sue was curious to know whether Kevin was intending to go back to the Congo. I was just as keen to hear this myself.

Kevin looked a little frustrated. 'A couple of months after

returning from the last trip, Ruth and I began to discuss the possibility of going back.'

'Ruth?' Sue enquired.

I realized I had never given Sue a complete list of those on the expedition. She had heard of many of them because they featured in the accounts I had related to her, but Ruth's name had never come up.

'Ruth was my right-hand man,' Kevin told her. 'Perhaps I should say, "woman". She was helping me with the scientific data. Anyway, having discovered the evidence we had, we naturally wanted to get back to the Congo. Unfortunately, there were a number of difficulties. One of these inevitably was funding. These trips are not cheap. We have a very generous supporter who funded a significant part of that last trip. He was delighted with the work we had done and excited about our discoveries. Unfortunately, our enforced departure prevented us from obtaining the evidence which could have really made a difference.'

'Do you still have his support?' I asked.

'Oh, yes. He's incredibly enthusiastic. However, as with everyone else, his resources are not limitless. We're hoping to be able to reimburse him for some of his outlay sometime in the future, but we're certainly not at that point yet. Anyway, funding isn't the only issue. The situation in the Congo is rather unstable politically at the moment.'

For the next half an hour, the discussion turned to his plans to follow up on our discoveries when things in the Congo had improved. Kevin then moved on to tell us some of the other things he had been doing in the previous year or so.

My mind went back to our discussion in Maidenhead when Kevin had first proposed this trip. He had mentioned having a friend in a fairly delicate situation who was informing him of a group that were opposed to his work.

'Have you heard any more from your source?' I enquired. For a moment, he looked confused, but then the penny dropped.

'No, not much. It's all gone a bit quiet on that front.'

Understandably, Sue was curious to know what we were talking about, so Kevin briefly filled her in. Suddenly remembering something, he said, 'I'm glad you brought that up. I said I'd try to get a photo of that woman at the Ministry for Education.' He produced his phone and spent a few moments studying it.

'Is this her?' he asked, turning his phone so I could see the screen.

Although it had been some time since I had seen the woman, there was no doubt in my mind that this was the same person. 'That's her,' I said.

'Sure?'

'Certain.'

He nodded. 'I thought so,' he said. 'She's not said a great deal in public, but privately, she's one of our fiercest critics.'

'Who is she?' asked Sue.

'Her name is Jennifer Davies. She's worked at the Ministry for Education for the last six years.'

'Is she an MP?' I asked.

Kevin shook his head. 'No. Initially, I thought she was, but it turns out that she's a high-ranking civil servant. However, my friend has the impression that she's very highly thought of by the Education Secretary. It would seem that she's trying to influence people to strengthen legislation against even discussing creation science in the classroom. Worryingly, this includes teaching in Christian schools and Christians who are home-schooling their children.'

'I thought civil servants were supposed to remain neutral,' Sue observed.

Kevin nodded. 'They are—except, it would seem, when it comes to biblical issues.'

On Saturday, 3rd August, Kevin, Jim, Sue and I flew out from Heathrow to Portland, Oregon. It was a flight of nearly ten hours which would carry us the best part of 5000 miles. Taking off from Heathrow at 9:15 in the morning, we were due to arrive in Portland at about 11:10am. Not having done a huge amount of travelling myself, I pondered on how we would get to our destination nearly two hours after leaving Heathrow, but I would actually be ten hours older than I'd been when we took off.

On arriving at Portland International Airport, we were met by an amazingly cheerful lady called Dr Jenny White. As we introduced ourselves, Jenny explained that she would be one of the geologists who would be part of our team for the duration of our stay. Her job would be to impart information to us about geology in general, and Mount Saint Helens, in particular.

I immediately took to Jenny. She was incredibly enthusiastic and had a wonderfully sunny disposition, with a positivity that oozed out of her. I guessed she might be in her early forties, and of African American descent.

As we left the terminal, the temperature was a very pleasant 20 degrees Celsius—much more comfortable than the humid August day we had left behind in London. We followed Jenny to a sleek black car. Kevin sat next to Jenny in the front, while Jim, Sue and I got in the back.

'It's great to meet all you folks,' Jenny said, in her American drawl. 'I'm really looking forward to working with you. I can't wait for you to see the evidence from Mount Saint Helens.'

'Well, Jenny,' Sue said, 'I can't speak for the others, but I'm very excited to see all you've got to show us.'

'I think we all feel the same, Sue,' Kevin agreed.

'Was it a good flight?' Jenny asked.

The next few minutes were taken up with small talk relaying our journey. I glanced through the side window to study the local environment. The roads were very busy, but Jenny appeared to be a highly competent driver. I wondered how far we had to go.

'Where are we staying, Jenny?' I asked.

'We're booked in to a hotel in a small town called Kelso,' she said. 'It's pretty convenient as far as access to Mount Saint Helens is concerned.'

We discovered that Kelso was in the southwest corner of Washington State, while Portland was in the far north of the State of Oregon. We would be heading north for about 50 miles on Interstate 5 to get to Kelso. The road to Mount Saint Helens left the I-5 at Exit 49 which was another 7 or 8 miles beyond Kelso. The actual volcano was another 45 miles east on Highway 504, Spirit Lake Memorial Highway.

Although our journey took about an hour, it seemed to pass in no time. We had many questions for Jenny and she was very happy to satisfy our curiosity.

Before we knew it, we were coming off the I-5 at Exit 39.

As the car slowed down, Jenny said, 'Here we are,' and pulled into the drive of a very smart looking hotel. As I got out of the car, I looked around, checking out the grounds. It was a very attractive place.

Retrieving our luggage from the vehicle, I had a bit of a chuckle to myself. Whatever this trip threw at us, I was fairly confident that the food and sleeping conditions would be a vast improvement on those I had experienced in the Congo, eighteen months earlier.

On entering the reception area, we were greeted heartily by a man who introduced himself as Steve Collins. Steve was white, just shy of 6 feet tall and looked as if he were in his late fifties.

'It's great to see you guys,' he said, shaking us all warmly by the hand. 'Let's get the keys to your rooms and we'll get you settled in.' He turned to Jenny and asked, 'Jen, can you get everything set up in the meeting room, please?'

'Sure,' she said, and disappeared down a corridor towards the back of the building.

Turning back to us, Steve continued, 'Two of our colleagues will be arriving shortly. I'll introduce you to them later. We also have another couple joining us but, unfortunately, they can't get here till Wednesday. When you're settled in and we've had a bite to eat, we're going to get together and I'll give you some information about the history of Mount Saint Helens.'

A thrill of anticipation went through me. I suspected that the afternoon's presentation was not going to be the highlight of our trip, but I was certainly looking forward to our first session on the volcano.

After booking in with one of the receptionists and receiving our cardkeys, Steve led us to our rooms. I made a mental note of everyone's room number. We were on the first floor. The first room we came to was my own. As I pushed open the door, I immediately saw that it was spacious and airy. I heaved my case on to the bed and looked round.

When I had finished unpacking and checking the facilities, I sent a quick message to Sam and another to my parents to inform them of my safe arrival. Then, I left the room and went to see if I could locate the others. While I had no idea where Steve's and Jenny's rooms were, Sue, Kevin and Jim were all in rooms very close to my own. I tapped lightly on Kevin's door. Getting no response, I moved on to the next room which was Sue's and tapped again. I could hear movement from within and heard a distant, 'Hold on.' After a little rustling there was the sound of footsteps approaching the door.

'Hi, Rob,' she said, pulling the door open. 'Is everyone ready to go down?'

'There's no response from Kevin's room,' I said, 'and I haven't spoken to Jim yet.'

'OK,' she said. 'Give me a couple of minutes and I should be with you. Do you want to give Jim a knock and see if he's ready?'

Jim's room was right opposite Sue's. I turned and once more gave a tap.

The door opened almost immediately. 'Hi, Rob,' Jim said. 'Are we going down?'

I told him that Sue was still going to be a couple of minutes.

'OK,' he said. 'Come in and have a seat. Prop the door open and we'll be able to see when Sue comes out.'

Jim's room was a mirror image of my own. I went in and sat on the edge of the bed.

'They're nice, clean and spacious rooms,' I said. 'It beats a bug-infested tent in the middle of Africa.' As soon as the words were out of my mouth, I realized I'd said something wrong.

Jim hung his head and there was a short silence. Eventually, he said, 'I hate thinking about it, Rob. Since I met you again in Kevin's office, I haven't been able to get your brother out of my head. I'm so ashamed of the way we treated you in the Congo.'

'I'm sorry, Jim,' I said. 'Please don't think I was having a dig.'

He looked at me and gave a sad smile. 'I know you weren't, Rob. You're not like that. If you were, it might not be so difficult. Both you and your brother are decent guys. You didn't deserve to have that happen to you.'

I did not know what to say to him. The reminder of that previous expedition and the terrible events that had taken place appeared to have sent Jim into a state of dejection.

In the end, I said, 'Look Jim, Sam and I both know who was

behind the violence out there. Neither of us blame you, and you shouldn't either. You can't go through the rest of your life beating yourself up over it.'

He just stood there slowly shaking his head. Then, he glanced over at me. 'Rob, you're a good man. I appreciate your words. I'm not sure I deserve them but thank you.'

'Jim, forget it. I've forgiven you; now, you need to forgive yourself. What's done is done. No amount of self-condemnation can change anything. Please let it go.'

He smiled at me again—this time with a tiny bit more conviction. 'I'll try,' he said.

At that moment, we heard the door to Sue's room open. She spotted us and stuck her head in the door.

'Sorry to keep you waiting, folks. Shall we go?'

We had arranged to meet up with Steve and Jenny in the bar area. As we walked in, they were talking to Kevin, as well as two others who I had not seen before. They saw us approaching and paused their conversation as they waited for us to join them.

We discovered that the two new individuals were Stephanie Manning and Benjamin O'Conner. They were both employees of the American branch of the Genesis Foundation and would be accompanying us on each of our Mount Saint Helens' trips. Benjamin was actually a medical doctor, while Stephanie had a degree in the history of geology. After all the introductions had been completed, we were asked to enter the restaurant area where a buffet-style late lunch had been ordered for our party.

My lunchtime was spent with Sue, Steve and Jenny. Most of

the conversation involved questions about each other's lives in an attempt to get to know one another. Sue and I did ask a few questions about Mount Saint Helens, but Steve suggested that these details would be coming out when the whole group was together.

When we had all finished eating, Steve stood. 'OK, folks, if everyone's ready, we'll go down to the meeting room which has been made available to us for the duration of our stay here.'

We all got to our feet and followed Steve out of the bar area.

The room was bigger than I had expected. At the left-hand end was a large screen which I guessed Steve would be using to assist with any presentations. In the body of the room, there were five round tables each surrounded by half a dozen chairs. Our team occupied some of the chairs around the two tables which were closest to the screen.

Over lunch, Sue and Jenny had really hit it off, and both Jenny and Steph came over to our table and sat the other side of Sue. To my left, Kevin, Jim and Ben occupied the next table. Steve had already gone to sit behind a small console situated just to the right of the screen and on which was a laptop. From his position, Steve could see anything displayed on the screen but could also look at his audience. I placed a small notebook and a pen on the table in front of me. Over the next couple of weeks, I suspected I would be hearing a lot of information that was new to me. I felt it might be an idea to make some notes.

My phone gave a ping, indicating the arrival of a message. I glanced over at Steve but he was still setting up, so I quickly looked down to read the message. It was from Sam. He told me that everything was OK at his end. Mum and Dad were also well and had suggested that Sam and I correspond and Sam would fill them in with my news. That was fine with me.

As I looked up, I noticed that Steve was preparing to address us.

'Right, folks, welcome to what I believe will be an exciting educational course on Mount Saint Helens. This first session is a presentation designed to give background information on the volcano. I'll briefly explain where the volcano is situated and its type, but then I'll give a bit more information about its eruptive history. Please feel free to jump in at any time if you have any questions.'

After a brief pause, he continued. 'OK, folks, this presentation will take about an hour, plus any time taken as you ask any questions. At the end of that time, we'll stop and have a coffee break. After the break, it's up to you what we do.'

He looked up at the screen and displayed a high-level map of the region. 'Right, Mount Saint Helens is one of a number of volcanos situated within the Cascade Range of the Pacific Northwest.[5] This range runs from British Columbia in Canada all the way down to northern California. From your journey here, you'll already be aware that Mount Saint Helens is located in Southwestern Washington, approximately 50 miles north of Portland, Oregon.'

The map disappeared and was replaced by an amazing photograph of the subject of our study [see image 1]. Steve told us that volcanoes like Mount Saint Helens are described as composite or stratovolcanoes. He said that they tend to be

Image 1: Mount Saint Helens before the 1980 eruption
Public domain.

steep-sided, symmetrical, cone-shaped volcanoes formed by alternating sequences of lava, ash, and other volcanic material. Apparently, this type of volcano can often erupt explosively, posing considerable danger to nearby life and property. Steve spent some time giving real-world examples of some destructive volcanic eruptions but then moved on to the history of Mount Saint Helens itself:

'When speaking about the history of this area, most geologists will tell you that Mount Saint Helens has experienced nine eruptive periods in the last 50,000 years. As I'm sure you're all aware, we entirely reject the timescale given by the conventional scientific community with regard to many of these dates.

'You'll appreciate that there is no human eyewitness testimony for many of these events. Furthermore, the dating methods used to provide these timelines have been shown to be highly unreliable. As a result, I only intend to give you dates of eruptions for which we have eyewitness testimony. Any dates you hear attributed to some of these periods that are over 500 years old, I suggest you take with a large pinch of salt.'

One eruptive period, Steve said, that they did have a fair degree of confidence in, started in 1800. This was probably the best known pre-1980 eruptive period, and it began with a major explosive eruption. He told us that this event was followed by intermittent and much smaller eruptions and lava flows. Steve looked from the screen towards us. 'If we assume that Mount Saint Helens behaves in the future the way she did in that instance, it would still be possible for us to see another decade or so of volcanic activity before she once more reverts to a relatively dormant state.'

Steve gave us a significant amount of information about previous volcanic activity. He was also keen for us to grasp that the past is the key to the present; it is not the present that is the key to the past. Eventually he said, 'OK, let's stop there and have a break.'

I was ready for a drink. He had given us lots of information, and I was beginning to feel tired from our long journey. Just as I got up from my seat, Steve came over to us. 'I've got a couple of things I need to sort out about tomorrow's transport,' he said. 'I'll hopefully be back in about ten minutes. While you're having your coffee, think of any questions you might want to ask. We'll have about an hour and a half until we have our evening meal.'

There was a coffee machine in one corner of the room and we all gravitated towards it. As we waited for those in front of us to get their drinks, I turned to Sue. 'So, what did you make of that, then?'

She had an expression on her face which I took to be a look of wonder.

'I suspect I'm going to learn a lot over the next couple of weeks,' she said.

'Had you heard any of his information before?' I asked.

'Yes, but a lot of it was new to me.' She stared across the room as she added, 'I'm sensing that this could be one of the most important trips of my life.'

'What did you think of Steve?' I asked.

She looked thoughtful. 'He comes across as a matter-of-fact professional scientist. I don't know why, but I wasn't really expecting that.'

It was our turn at the coffee machine and I prodded a couple of buttons to select a white coffee with no sugar.

'I know exactly what you mean,' I said. 'When I went to the debate in Harrow, I was expecting Kevin to be some kind of religious, scientifically backward ignoramus.'

Sue gave a little giggle. 'Yes, but it's not like that at all, is it?'

'No; far from it.'

I grabbed my coffee and stood to one side to allow Sue to make her choice.

'You seem pretty excited,' I observed.

'I am,' she said. 'Rob, as Steve was presenting us with that information, all this nervous excitement started to run through me.' She chose her coffee and then looked back at me. This time, it was no brief glance. Her eyes locked onto mine as she continued: 'I can't wait to find out what these people have got to tell us.'

I was fascinated. It looked as if she really did feel that this would significantly change her life in some way. She had a flurry of excitement about her which I shared. We moved away from the drinks machine, continuing to discuss Steve and his presentation.

Within minutes, Steve came back into the room, grabbed himself a coffee and retook his place behind his table.

'OK, folks,' he said. 'Do any of you have any questions about what you've heard so far?'

Jim immediately raised his hand. 'Steve, what's our itinerary while we're here?'

Steve picked up a sheet of paper:

'OK, tomorrow, we will be taking you to have your first look at Mount Saint Helens. You will also be visiting the Johnston Ridge Observatory where you'll see a video and receive information on the eruption on 18 May 1980. When we return to the hotel, I'll be giving you additional details on that eruption and we can discuss it further.

'On Monday, we'll be visiting sites where rock strata have formed very rapidly. Tuesday we will be concentrating on canyon formation in the area. There's currently a bit of a question mark over Wednesday's activities. Originally, we were going to visit some sites where steam explosion pits had formed, but the forecast looks horrendous. We may well have to reschedule that one.

'On Thursday and Friday, we hope to be turning our attention to Spirit Lake, just north of the volcano. We'll be studying the logs which are still floating on the lake.

'Next Saturday, we'll be looking at the effect the eruption had on the local forests and also looking at the regrowth. Then, next Sunday is the day that you'll probably remember for the rest of your lives, because that's the day you'll be hiking into the crater.'

A buzz of excitement went around the group. Sue grabbed my forearm and gave a little squeal. 'I didn't realize we'd actually be able to go into the crater,' she whispered, excitedly.

As for me, I had mixed feelings about this news. I was pretty sure that they would not take us somewhere they felt would be dangerous but, after all, this was an active volcano.

I looked at Sue with some amusement. I could not ever remember seeing someone over the age of ten show such unadulterated joy. She was one happy bunny, and I loved her enthusiasm.

My thoughts then turned to Sam back in Britain. I wondered what we would have done if Sam had been interested in coming on the trip. It sounded as if some of our excursions would involve terrain that might have proved to be a bit of a challenge for someone with a prosthetic leg.

Steve cut into my thoughts:

'On the second Monday, you'll have the opportunity to look around the other visitor centres. The Tuesday is currently set aside for us to review the things you've learned and to ask any additional questions. However, after what I've just said, it's possible that we may rearrange the trip to the site of the steam explosion pit if our trip on Wednesday is washed out. We're then hoping to take you to an area where we'll show you some of the research we're doing.

'So, that's a very quick run through of what you'll be doing while you're here.'

Given the way my thoughts were running, there was one question which was foremost in my mind and I raised my hand.

'Steve? How do we know Mount Saint Helens isn't going to blow her top while we're here?'

He smiled. 'Under the circumstances, Rob, that's a very understandable question. The honest answer is that we can't say with one hundred percent certainty that there won't be any activity at all, but the chances of that happening are tiny. Mount Saint Helens is currently in another quiet phase, although you can often see steam rising from the newest of the lava domes. If the volcano were to erupt in the near future, we should have plenty of warning from a number of strategically placed and very expensive instruments designed to identify any tell-tail volcanic activity.'

'And what kind of activity would indicate that another eruption was imminent?' I asked.

'We'd expect any significant eruption to be preceded by several days and more likely weeks of seismic activity. If a significant amount of magma rises towards the surface, you'd expect some kind of ground deformation or increased volcanic gas emissions. These kinds of events might indicate that an eruption was getting closer.'

'And if we don't see those things, are you saying that it's perfectly safe to be around the volcano?'

Steve didn't respond immediately. 'There are certain smaller volcanic events which could occur without any significant warning. For example, it's possible to have small explosions of steam or volcanic gases within the crater. Mount Saint Helens has occasionally displayed this kind of behaviour since the eruptions in 1980. A number of such explosions did occur between 1989 and 1991, at a time when the volcano was not actually erupting. It's also possible to have limited rockfalls within and around the crater.'

It was Sue's turn to ask a question now. 'Steve, is the general public able to access the whole of the Mount Saint Helens area?'

'No. Actually, that's a good point, and it's something I should explain to you. The Mount Saint Helens' National Volcanic Monument is within the Gifford Pinchot National Forest and is managed by the USDA (U. S. Department of Agriculture) Forest Service. There are certain areas, especially around Spirit Lake which are out of bounds to most people. Only geologists with a permit are allowed to access these areas. Having said that, we will be taking you into some of those areas.'

'So how have you managed to wangle it for us?' Jim asked.

'I have a friend who works for the USDA Forest Service. He's arranged it so we can have a special permit to visit some of these areas. However, we will have to abide by the conditions he has stipulated. Also, he has arranged for us to be accompanied by two of his colleagues. They won't be with us all the time, but they have a lot of knowledge about Mount Saint Helens and will be a great addition to our team. We have an agreement that a member of our team must always accompany any visitor at all times.

'So, this is a very opportune moment to tell you never to go off on your own. Should you wish to look at something we've not yet viewed, let us know and we can all go and have a look. In the unlikely event that someone becomes separated from the main group, you'll all be supplied with a whistle so you can send a signal to others. However, we don't want that to happen. If you wandered off and something were to go wrong, we could get in quite a bit of trouble.'

There, then, followed a few questions about our upcoming trips, but Steve did not want to say too much about them. He said that he'd rather we came to the subjects fresh, not having too much prior information. In no time at all, the session was over, and Steve informed us that we would be going in for our evening meal.

'I'm guessing you guys who have come over from England will be feeling pretty bushed,' he said. 'Afterwards, Jenny and I will be around if you have any more questions, but it might be an idea to get an early night so you're relatively fresh for the trip tomorrow.'

When we were back in the restaurant, Sue and I sat with Steve and Jim. The atmosphere was relaxed and we had a pleasant chat, finding out a bit more about our new friends.

Remembering a comment that Steve had made a bit earlier I

asked, 'Steve, you said there would be another couple joining us. Are they colleagues of yours?'

He shook his head. 'No, the Austins are a couple from Florida. Actually, we don't know a great deal about them. We do know that they are a husband and wife from near Miami and, like Jim and Sue, they're both involved in science education. We know they've been to Mount Saint Helens before, but they're very keen to understand our take on the geology in the area.'

'Are they Christians?' Jim asked.

Steve nodded. 'Oh, yes, I think so. However, we don't know that much about them. Really, it was a last-minute arrangement but, being keen to spread the word as much as possible, we accepted them on the trip.'

Jim glanced around at the other members of our group and a slight frown appeared on his face. 'Steve, isn't this a fairly costly trip to put on for so few people?'

Steve looked slightly frustrated. 'Originally, there were supposed to be another five people coming on this trip but, for various reasons, they all had to pull out. It's almost as if someone didn't want anyone to hear our information. However, don't forget that we also have the research side of the work. We would be in the area even if we had no guests here.'

I smiled. 'Well, you obviously feel it's all worth it.'

Steve nodded. 'Absolutely. We need to get this information to as many people in education as we can.'

Chapter 4
Mount Saint Helens

Stretching out in the king-sized bed with the early morning sun streaming through the window, I felt a surge of excitement about the day ahead. I'd slept like a baby, felt refreshed and ready for the first full day ahead of me.

The Christian members of our team had gathered for an early-morning service in the meeting room. After breakfast, we would be receiving a presentation on the eruptions before making our first trip to the volcano. As I stood in the shower, I felt like a little boy getting up on Christmas morning and anticipating the excitement of the coming day. At breakfast, those of us who were visiting the volcano for the first time were unsurprisingly animated, and the energy in the room was palpable.

However, those who would be our guides and teachers seemed equally enthusiastic. They were delighted to have the opportunity to show us all the geological sites.

When breakfast was over, we all congregated in the meeting room to listen to Steve's presentation. We learned that this would cover details of the main eruption on 18 May 1980. I noticed with some amusement that we all occupied exactly the same seats as on the previous afternoon. On the screen were the words 'Mount Saint Helens' along with a captivating photograph of the mountain.

Steve took his place behind the console. 'As before, please feel free to interrupt me at any time if there's something you want to ask.' He glanced down at his notes.

'OK, I believe that when people look back at the twentieth century and consider which geologic events did most to challenge the dogmatic teaching of evolution, the eruption of Mount Saint Helens will be right at the top of the list.[6] If a creationist had tried to devise a geological occurrence to support his beliefs about our planet, it's hard to come up with a better one.'

That was setting the bar pretty high, I thought. If someone talks something up and it fails to meet their lofty claims, I sometimes struggle to believe anything else they have to say. I sincerely hoped that was not going to be the case in this instance.

'It sounds as if the eruption was a big one,' I said.

Steve looked over at me. 'Actually, Rob, no. In fact, it was relatively small when compared to other volcanic eruptions that have occurred. As you'll find out, it's not the size of the eruption that's important here. It's the geological features that were created as a result of that eruption. It was almost as if someone wanted Mount Saint Helens to set up a natural laboratory for us to study those events. The fact that it was a relatively small event is even more significant when we try to imagine the massive upheaval which would have occurred during a global catastrophic Flood.'

Out of the corner of my eye, I noticed Sue briefly glance sideways at me. Although I had not known her long, I was pretty certain I knew what was going through her head. I smiled inwardly. Unlike Sue, I had been in this situation before. I had been on an expedition where I had thought that what I was being told was nonsense, only to discover later it had been completely accurate. As a result, I was probably a little more cautious about questioning Steve's facts on this occasion.

He went on. 'One of the things we want to show you is that the evidence we see here at Mount Saint Helens can help us to understand other geological features around the world. For example, the Grand Canyon, Yellowstone, coal deposits, and many others.'

Steve then began the story of the eruptions of Mount Saint Helens by going back to the middle of March in 1980. At this time, radio reports had stated that an earthquake had occurred directly under the mountain and, within a week, the volcano had started to vent steam. At the end of March and during April there had been some small volcanic ash eruptions. Steve displayed a slide showing one of these events.

As he turned back from the screen, he continued, 'During the two months between the start of these fairly minor steam and ash eruptions until the main eruption on May 18, geologists noticed that the north slope of the mountain was swelling at a rate of between 3 to 5 feet a day. In fact, on the last three days, on May

15, 16 and 17, they measured that this expansion had increased tenfold. It was obvious to everyone that something significant was about to take place. They didn't necessarily expect the events which actually occurred, but they knew something major was about to happen.'

Steve showed a slide of one of the last profile shots of Mount Saint Helens from before the main eruption. It was a beautiful and symmetrical mountain of 9,677 feet. We could also see a body of water called Spirit Lake just northeast of the mountain.

At just after 8:32am on 18th May 1980, Mount Saint Helens had blown her top. It had been a catastrophic geologic event—one which Steve asserted had challenged evolutionary theory right at its foundation.

He then showed us a slide of Mount Saint Helens after the eruption. The volcano was now only 8,365 feet high. It had lost 1,300 feet from its summit as over half a cubic mile of material had slid off the top and the northern slope of the mountain. One eighth of a cubic mile of landslide material had gone down the northern slope into Spirit Lake. Steve told us that this had resulted in a series of massive waves washing 860 feet up the hillside on the northern shore of the lake. The waters had sloshed back into the lake basin which now had a natural dam at the southern end.

At the same time that this debris had gone into the lake, three eighths of a cubic mile of landslide material slid down the western slopes of Mount Saint Helens into the Toutle River drainage area and blocked that drainage area.

We were told that a 5.1 magnitude earthquake immediately

under the summit of Mount Saint Helens had caused the summit and northern slope to slip from the top of the mountain. Superheated water had produced a steam explosion equivalent to 20 million tons of TNT blast energy. This blast was not directed upwards as is normal with volcanic eruptions, but horizontally over the landscape in a northerly direction. It had levelled 150 square miles of forest in six minutes.

Steve continued to describe the event. 'This eruption occurred on a beautiful sunny Sunday morning. Because of the changes noticed by the geologists in the activity at the volcano, there were a number of people who were interested in studying that activity. In fact, the eruption at Mount Saint Helens was one of the most photographed geologic events in history.'

Steve put up an aerial photo showing a view of the crater from above. 'One couple were flying over the summit and the north slope of the mountain in a light aircraft at the time the eruption started,' he said. 'Here you can see the first evidence of rock fall in the summit crater.'

It was not particularly clear on the slide, and it is not easy to determine rock movement in a still photograph. Nevertheless, it did appear as if there could have been rock fall in the crater.

Steve went on. 'The couple in the aircraft took this photograph as the earthquake energy reached the summit of the volcano and rocks began to fall. They were making their third pass when they saw the beginnings of the eruption.'

Steve displayed a new slide showing the beginnings of the lateral blast from Mount Saint Helens [see image 2]. 'This cloud

Image 2: Mount Saint Helens erupting across the landscape
Public domain.

of ash and steam was at a temperature of around 600 degrees Fahrenheit and was moving at a velocity of around 200 miles per hour,' he said. 'A photographer was on the ground and took some of the pictures I'm about to show you now.'

There followed a number of images of the volcanic cloud heading towards the camera.

Jim seemed to read my mind as he asked, 'Steve? What happened to the guy with the camera?'

Steve laughed. 'Don't worry, Jim. He made it. I think it was a near thing, but thankfully, he survived to share these photos with the rest of us.'

Steve then displayed an image from a weather satellite around 22,000 miles in space. It showed a ring-shaped cloud revealing the atmospheric effects of the event forty-three minutes after the start of the eruption.

During the afternoon, the volcanic ash cloud completely covered eastern Washington State. It reached into Northern Idaho and even into Western Montana.

Steve displayed another slide. 'In Yakima, Washington, it became so dark at midday that the streetlights automatically turned on.'

For nine hours, Mount Saint Helens had erupted violently and had built a huge plume of volcanic ash which hung over the summit. In that nine-hour eruption, Steve told us that Mount Saint Helens released the energy equivalent to 400 million tons of TNT blast energy. That, in turn, is apparently equivalent to one Hiroshima sized atomic bomb per second for nine hours.

'When geologists visited the area the following day, the surface of the earth looked like the moon. The ground was covered by volcanic ash at a temperature of around 500 degrees Fahrenheit. They needed special shoes just to walk on it.'

The pictures were amazing. The area had been completely devastated [see image 3]. Everyone was studying the images in awe.

Steve continued: 'Huge areas of forest were completely levelled by the steam blast.' Another slide went up: 'It took less than a minute to flatten the area of forest you can see on this slide [see image 4, p. 90]. Remember, this was a mature forest. It was completely devastated by the blast.'

Steve turned from the screen to face us—his voice more solemn.

'A total of fifty-seven people died as a result of the eruption. All of these deaths were avoidable. All these people knew that Mount Saint Helens was about to erupt. They had gone into areas where there was reason to believe that there was significant geological danger. All these people died having received a warning.

'Probably the most famous person to die in the eruption was a man called Harry Truman; obviously not the president, but an eighty-year-old man of the same name who lived at the south shore of Spirit Lake.'

Steve showed a photo of the man at his lodge before the

Image 3: The devastated landscape following the eruption
Public domain.

Image 4: The devastated forests following the eruption
Public domain.

eruption. 'The authorities went to him to warn him to leave as he was in a highly dangerous position. However, he refused to listen. He wouldn't leave his home and, as a result, he was buried under 100 feet of landslide material and another 100 feet of volcanic ash.'

I noticed Sue's face drop in sadness.

Steve's next few slides showed the extensive damage that had been caused by the mud and water.

'On six major rivers in the Mount Saint Helens area there was very severe damage from mudflows. There was actually more financial damage caused by the mudflows than from the steam blast—even areas a long way from the volcano where people assumed that they would be safe from the effects of the eruption.'

Another slide went up. 'This logging camp was destroyed by the force of the mud.'

He then showed further slides displaying how mud had swept through valleys to a depth of 30 feet. One of these valleys was half a mile wide. You could tell how far up the mud had reached because it had left a clear mark on the trees at the valley edge.

Next, Steve turned to Mount Saint Helens itself. 'Geologists have spent a tremendous amount of time studying the crater of the volcano.' He clicked from one slide to another.

'Here you can see the way the crater looked in the mid-eighties. Notice we have this great dome-shaped structure. This is rock that sits in the neck of the volcano and it acts in a similar way to a cork in a bottle of champagne. Just as a champagne cork holds down the fizzing pressure in the bottle, so this structure holds down pressure from within the neck of the volcano. Molten material has been squeezed up there, forming that dome-like structure. This is what we call the lava dome'[see image 5, p. 92].

The room was silent, except for the faint whirr of the computer's fan as he continued to his next slide, showing the structure from above.

'This is one of the earlier domes. There have been a number of different lava domes formed since the eruption in 1980. This

Image 5: Lava dome within the Mount Saint Helens' crater
Photo by Steven A. Austin PhD. Used with permission.

earlier one was blown out by a subsequent volcanic eruption. As you look down on the lava dome you might be able to see areas of hot molten rock which has been forced into some of the cracks.'

Steve told us that most of the time it was relatively safe to go into the lava dome to collect samples. It did not sound particularly safe to me, but I guessed they knew what they were doing.

As the images reeled by, a vague recollection of something that had been said at the debate before we had gone on our expedition to the Congo came to mind.

'Kevin? Didn't you mention something about the Mount Saint Helens lava dome in your presentation at the debate in Harrow?'

Kevin smiled. 'Well remembered, Rob. Yes, I mentioned that

samples of rock had been taken from the lava dome and dated. The results returned from the dating of those samples proved that the assumptions used to acquire dates from these techniques are highly flawed.'

I turned back to Steve. 'Did you have anything to do with that work?'

'No. But the dating of the lava dome is only one of the pieces of evidence that Mount Saint Helens has yielded which exposes the unreliability of the radiometric dating methods that the evolutionary geologists trust.'

Steve looked back at the screen. 'Anyway, these lava domes kept being destroyed and then rebuilt as further eruptions occurred. Sometimes, eruptions don't result in any lava flows; they only result in dome building and dome cracking events.'

Steve put up a new slide. 'OK,' he said. 'Let's have a look at Spirit Lake. Spirit Lake was devastated by the landslide material that got dumped in the lake. But, in addition to the landslide material, the lake ended up half full of logs.'

Startled at the image which looked like a whole load of logs laying on the ground, I studied it more carefully and noticed water between the logs, confirming Steve's details.

He continued.

'Spirit Lake covers an area of 4 square miles and, after the eruption, around half that area was covered by logs. Indeed, it has been estimated that immediately after the eruption in May 1980, there were up to half a million logs floating in the lake. This log mat moves around the lake depending on wind direction [see

Image 6: Log mats floating on Spirit Lake
Public domain.

image 6]. In the next few days, we're hoping to take you out in a boat to see the condition of the lake today. Anyway, let's look at where most of those logs came from.'

He then displayed a number of slides of the north shore of the lake. As a result of the landslide material that had crashed into the southern end of the lake, the gigantic waves he had mentioned before had crashed up onto the north shore ripping up trees as they went. As the water had sloshed back into the lake, it had taken all the uprooted trees with it. The incredible images caused a ripple of whispered chatter among the viewers.

Still trying to assimilate all the information, I wanted to slow Steve down, but he continued to the next part of his presentation, showing us slides of some of the rock layers which had formed at Mount Saint Helens during the more recent eruptions.

'You'll have the chance to see some of this evidence tomorrow,' he said, as he worked his way through these slides. 'In fact, over the next couple of weeks, you'll be visiting most of the sites I'm showing you in this presentation.'

As he displayed the next image, he said, 'Having said that, the next few photos are of features which no longer exist as you're going to see them on the screen.'

He showed us a slide of what he called a secondary steam explosion event.

'Large masses of glacial ice from the summit of Mount Saint Helens were buried under 550-degree-Fahrenheit volcanic ash. Because the ice was buried under something that hot, within days it was venting to the surface as steam. This created these enormous steam explosion pits.'

Another slide: 'This photograph was taken on May 23,' Steve told us. 'This was the largest steam explosion pit. It was situated near the southwest corner of Spirit Lake. Steam is forcing its way to the surface and creating a hole 125 feet deep, 2,300 feet long and 1,000 feet wide. So, this feature was all created by steam five days after the eruption on May 18.'

After giving us a moment to study the image, he went on. 'This is a photograph taken from the reverse angle on June 18, 1980, one month after the eruption. The steaming had stopped and you can see about 25 feet of deposits in the bottom of the pit.'

The slides were fascinating. If his details about the dimensions of the pit were accurate, this was a massive hole.

'Please notice the rim of the pit,' Steve went on. 'This is similar to the bad lands of South Dakota, or the desert terrain in the southwest United States. We're told that this kind of feature forms slowly, from gradual erosion over hundreds of thousands of years. But we know that this all formed very rapidly in five days, not by water erosion at all, but by gravity collapsing the lip of the pit.'

Steve then displayed a slide showing one of the steam explosions in progress.

'These pits no longer exist as you see them here, because they've been filled in by material from subsequent eruptions.'

Steve moved on to display slides showing canyons, which he claimed had formed very rapidly at Mount Saint Helens. Finally, he ended the presentation by presenting evidence which he claimed might lead to the rapid formation of coal, after which, he asked for questions.

Maybe because we knew this was just an overview and that we'd be looking at these subjects in much more detail, or maybe because we were still processing the information, but no one appeared particularly inclined to ask questions. However, another distinct possibility was that we were all impatient to set off to see Mount Saint Helens for ourselves.

With the build up through the presentation, the anticipation was now tangible. We all seemed to act as one, grabbing our rucksacks and making a beeline for the carpark. A number of dusty, beat-up Land Rovers had been provided for the duration of our trip. A couple of these were only two-seaters, but others had additional seating in the back. It was one of these to which Steve led Sue and me. I clambered in and sat in the back, while Sue took the front passenger seat next to Steve, and it felt like we were heading off on safari.

When the whole group had boarded the vehicles, we once more joined Interstate 5, the road on which we had arrived from Portland, and again headed north. After about 7 or 8 miles, we left the I-5 at Junction 49, at a place called Castle Rock, and turned east onto State Route 504.[7] Steve explained to us that, further on, a large section of this road had been devastated by the eruption in 1980 but had since been rebuilt. The road was now called Spirit Lake Memorial Highway in remembrance of the fifty-seven people who had lost their lives in that eruption.

After a while, Steve informed us, 'In a couple of minutes, if you look to your right, you'll see the Mount Saint Helens National Volcanic Monument Visitor Centre.'

'Are we likely to get the opportunity to go in at some point?' I asked.

Steve nodded. 'There are a number of very interesting visitor centres along this stretch of road. Although much of your time will be mapped out for you, you'll certainly have the chance to go into these places and we'd encourage you to do that. Apart from anything else, it'll also give you additional confidence in the information we're giving you.'

Both Sue and I looked to our right as we passed the centre.

Just beyond this, there was a sizeable body of water. 'Nice lake,' I observed.

'That's Silver Lake,' Steve offered. 'We'll be running along its north shore for a while.'

I turned to Steve to make another comment and noticed a faint smile on his face.

At the same instant, I heard a slight intake of breath from Sue in the front. I noticed that she had also finished looking at the lake and was now staring almost straight ahead. I leaned to my left to see what had caused the reaction and immediately understood. There, still some way off, but clearly visible through the windscreen was Mount Saint Helens. No one spoke, and a reverence settled on us as we all studied the volcano.

'Is that what you were grinning at, Steve?' I asked finally.

He gave a short nod, keeping his eyes on the highway. 'This is the first place where visitors usually get their first good look at the volcano. I was wondering how long it would be before you spotted it.'

I looked back at Mount Saint Helens. 'How far away is it?'

'In a vehicle, it's just over 45 miles to the Johnston Ridge Observatory,' he said. 'However, the road is anything but straight. I'd guess it's quite a bit less as the crow flies.'

The next landmark we got to was a small community called Toutle.

As we passed through, Steve said, 'In a minute we'll be crossing the Toutle River. To the right, there are two forks of the river that come together before flowing under the highway. Both the main river and its north fork were overwhelmed by those mudflows I was telling you about after the 1980 eruption. You'll be hearing more about that later.'

'We're still some way from the volcano, aren't we?' Sue asked. 'How far did the mudflows reach?'

'Almost 60 miles downstream. It actually got as far as Interstate 5.'

I whistled. 'That's amazing.'

'Incredible, isn't it?'

A few minutes later, we came to a junction.

'This is the road you'd come down if you were visiting from Seattle,' Steve informed us.

We continued along the SR 504, running through a small settlement called Kid Valley. Steve mentioned that we would soon be joining the section of highway that had been built following the 1980 eruption.

'You'll notice that we're starting to climb,' he said. 'This newer section of road follows the ridges above the northern fork of the Toutle River. We'll be crossing some pretty high bridges over creeks running out of a number of narrow canyons. All these creeks empty into the Toutle River.'

There was silence again as Sue and I took in the amazing scenery.

After a while, Steve informed us that we'd soon be passing another visitor centre. However, his next comment was not quite so welcome.

'At some point over the next few days, we'll be taking you up in a chopper,' he said. 'Some of the helicopter trips take off from near here.'

Immediately, the familiar feeling of panic ran through me. 'Wonderful,' I said through gritted teeth.

Sue laughed. 'He doesn't like flying,' she told Steve.

Steve gave a brief chuckle. 'I'm sure we won't force you to go if you really don't want to.'

Over her shoulder, Sue urged me, 'Rob, you must go. It'll be a fantastic experience.'

I knew she was right. I hated the idea of going up in a helicopter, but this was a once in a lifetime chance, and I suspected I would probably later regret it if I chose not to go on the trip. In any case, deciding not to respond, I did my best to put helicopter rides out of my mind.

My fears receded as we approached the visitor centre and a majestic view of Mount Saint Helens filled the windscreen. In fact, it was beginning to look like the impressive volcano I had imagined.

For a while, we continued east along the SR 504, just enjoying the views.

Eventually, Steve broke the silence. 'The bridge we'll be crossing in a minute is the longest span we'll have to go over. It crosses Hoffstadt Creek. Not only is it the longest, but it's 370 feet above the valley floor.'

This was another detail I could have done without. On approaching the bridge, I told myself, 'Don't look down. Just keep looking straight ahead.'

‘This is where we enter the “blast zone”,’ Steve said as we left the bridge. ‘This is the furthest point where trees were damaged or levelled by the blast.’

He suddenly gestured towards the right. ‘If you look out there, you’ll get a fantastic view of the north fork of the Toutle River Valley.’

Looking down from our fairly lofty elevation was not my cup of tea. My stomach turned as I peered across the vista, but the views were breath-taking. My fascination increased as Steve continued to supply us with further information about how the 1980 eruption had devastated the area. Some of this damage was clear to see.

The SR 504 continued through a section where Steve told us that millions of seedlings had been hand-planted in a successful attempt to reforest the area. As I studied the landscape, I considered that the rapid growth of the trees made it very difficult to believe such devastation was caused to the area as recently as 1980.

After continuing on for some time, Steve suddenly dropped his speed. ‘This area is called Coldwater Ridge. There’s a science and learning centre here, but it’s only open at weekends at the moment. We’ll hopefully get you in there at some point.’

After a while, Steve announced, ‘This is where we officially enter the Mount Saint Helens National Volcanic Monument.’

‘How much land does it cover?’ I asked.

‘It’s around 110,000 acres.’

As we crested the ridge, the highway began to lose elevation.

Steve continued his tour guide commentary of the journey. 'We're now heading down to run alongside South Coldwater Creek. Many people expected this whole area to be a total wasteland for decades. Within this area known as the Mount Saint Helens National Volcanic Monument, no one is allowed to do any replanting of trees. They wanted to see what would happen to the land if they just let nature take its course. It's true, some areas are still pretty barren, but in other places the vegetation has re-established itself quite rapidly. Many are amazed at how quickly this has happened.'

After completing a hairpin turn, the SR 504 rose steeply.

'This is the final climb up to the Johnston Ridge Observatory, or the JRO, as we call it,' Steve informed us.

The climb certainly was a steep one and the engine roared as we made our ascent. We all fell silent as Spirit Lake Memorial Highway made its final climb up to Johnston Ridge.

My ears popped a number of times as the air pressure changed. 'How high are we?' I asked.

'When we reach the ridge, we'll be a little over 4,200 feet above sea level,' Steve informed us.

The road finally bent around towards the south and, a few minutes later, we were arriving at the car park in front of the Johnston Ridge Observatory Visitor Centre. Mount Saint Helens was standing magnificently due south of our position with Spirit Lake directly to the east.

We all got out of our vehicles. Sue and I immediately raced round the Land Rover and stood staring at the volcano. It was absolutely stunning. Standing there and studying it in the late morning sunlight, it seemed so peaceful. It was almost impossible to believe that this amazing geological feature could have been responsible for such devastation just a few decades ago.

Steve broke the spell as he beckoned us. 'OK, please gather round.'

We obeyed.

'Well folks, this is your first close-up and personal view of Mount Saint Helens. We're going to take a short walk so you can get an idea of the area. We'll stop and have our packed lunch before coming back and going into the visitor centre.'

'How far are we from the volcano?' Jim asked.

'About 5 miles,' he said.

'It's stunning,' Sue said with wonder in her voice.

There were murmurs of agreement from others in the group as phones came out of pockets to take pictures.

A few hundred yards into our walk, I stopped to take a couple of photos too, and also to take in the atmosphere of the place. It had an aura of peace and tranquillity, and I soaked in the wonder and let my senses savour the surroundings. As we continued to stroll along the top of the ridge, we shortly came to a stop at a position which had yet another stunning view of Mount Saint Helens. It was there that we decided to have our packed lunches. Steve continued to point out various areas of interest as we munched our way through our food. The view was idyllic and I could have spent hours in total silence just taking in the landscape.

During a lull in conversation, while everyone was eating and continuing to study the volcano, I sent a message to Sam, giving a report of the day so far. I took another snap of Mount Saint Helens and attached it to a brief message. A few seconds later, I got his response.

'Hi Bruv, that's stunning. Maybe I should have come after all.'

I imagined him sitting at home and wondered if he really was regretting his decision not to come. From my point of view, I would not have missed it for the world.

Steve allowed us to take in the view for a few more moments and then announced, 'In a minute, we'll go back and enter the Johnston Ridge Observatory Visitor Centre. We'll be viewing a video which will give you a good understanding of what the May 1980 eruption was like.'

There was a reluctance to leave but the Visitor Centre was very instructive. The video gave an amazing insight into the eruption, as well as its effects on the surrounding area. One thing I was pleased to note was that the details we received from the JRO very much confirmed the information we had already learned from Steve.

Sue was brought to tears by the personal accounts of those who had been caught up in the May 18 eruption. Some of these testimonies were tragic, but others were much more up-lifting. I was certainly grateful that I had not been there to witness the event first hand; it had been quite an emotional afternoon.

As we came out of the Observatory, for the first time it struck me that the 1980 eruption of Mount Saint Helens was becoming very real to me. Hearing the personal testimonies from those who had witnessed the event had had a profound emotional impact on me too. Standing just a few miles away and actually looking at the volcano responsible for all the mayhem felt surreal. It stood so still, so silent, and yet the devastation was inconceivable. This gave me plenty to ponder on the journey back to Kelso, and Sue felt the impact too. It was a quiet, contemplative journey back to the hotel.

After our evening meal, as promised, Steve gave us the opportunity to discuss and ask questions about the day. Unfortunately, although I had very much enjoyed our first trip to the volcano, a wave of tiredness had got the better of me. The long flight over the 'Pond', or the emotional day, or a mix of both, had taken its toll on many of us in the group. Everyone seemed subdued and sluggish.

I managed to muster up one question to which I was keen to get an answer.

'Steve?' I asked, 'this may be more related to the presentation you gave yesterday, but is what you've learned at Mount Saint Helens going to be helpful when you're asked to predict future volcanic events?'

'Actually, Rob, that's a really good point. More and more, geologists are being asked to predict what might happen in the future. They're beginning to appreciate that past and present geologic events might have a big part to play in answering these kinds of questions. But if people are really being honest, there are certain questions that we can't answer with any degree of certainty. For example, we don't really know if the intermittent activity we've seen since 1980 is truly over. We don't know if another large explosive eruption similar to that of May 18, 1980, is likely to take place within the next few years or decades. And nor can we be sure if significant lava flows will accompany any future eruptions. All these things are important to try to discover but, if we're being honest, really, we can't be certain.'

He looked around the group expectantly. 'Does anyone else have a question?'

No one seemed inclined to ask anything, and I think Steve recognized that a number of us were quite tired.

He stood. 'OK, folks, I think that'll do for today. You've had a lot to take in. In the morning, we'll start to look at individual aspects of the evidence from Mount Saint Helens. Tomorrow's subject is going to be the rapid formation of rock layers.'

By that time, I was finding it difficult to keep my eyes open. Sue, Kevin and Jim also looked as if they were in need of sleep. So, after saying 'good night', we all retired to our rooms.

Chapter 5
Rock Layers

On waking that Monday morning, I felt refreshed and ready for the new day. I had slept well again and was grateful for the big, soft comfy bed. My thoughts turned to Sue as I made a cup of coffee and began to get out some clean clothes. I wondered how she was feeling after yesterday's revelations and felt a thrill of anticipation as I contemplated another day in her company.

After breakfast, everyone was energized and eager to set off on the day's adventures. We were headed for an area where Mount Saint Helens had deposited a significant amount of volcanic material in a very short space of time.

When our vehicles came to a halt, Steve explained that we would have to leave the Land Rovers at that point and walk the rest of the way. We all grabbed our rucksacks and set off. but I could not help noticing how unusually quiet Sue was that morning.

Arriving at the first site, Steve turned towards us and announced, 'OK, folks, I'm going to ask Steph to give you a very brief introduction to the history of geology. It's very important you understand how people's thinking has changed in the past. This will give you a much better chance of understanding how different people interpret the evidence you'll be viewing over the next few days.'

Steph detached herself from the group and after taking a few steps towards the cliff wall, she turned to face us.

'Thanks, Steve. OK, folks, before I get into the history, I'd like to spend a few moments explaining how most secular geologists think today. They believe that we can only explain what has happened in the past by studying the events that happen in the present.'

Steph spent a couple of minutes explaining how geologists have noticed that, most of the time, erosion and sedimentation happen very slowly today. As a result, they make the assumption that this is the way these processes have always happened in the past.

Some of Steph's introduction I had heard before. Prior to my previous adventure, in Kevin's debate with an evolutionist, this view of the rocks had been discussed. I listened carefully as Steph delivered the information with care.

'It's this mindset that convinces most geologists that the rock strata were laid down very slowly over huge periods of time,' she said. 'However, notice that I said it's the way "most" geologists think. There are a growing number of secular geologists who are beginning to recognize that the physical evidence doesn't fit that belief. I'll let Steve tell you more about that later. So, let's go back and take a look at how we got to the position in which we find ourselves today.'

Steph removed her rucksack, opened it and withdrew a number of sheets of paper. She stepped towards us and handed sheets to each of the members of the group who were there primarily to learn. There were three landscape sheets of A4 stapled together at the top left-hand corner. On the sheets were timelines. Everyone leafed through the pages taking a look—the breeze ruffling the papers as we studied the contents.

Steph retook her place. 'Until the late 1700s, the traditional biblical view was the majority position.[8] Most believed that the Bible gave an accurate account of the beginning of the universe which they dated to about 4,000 years BC. They also believed this was followed over 1600 years later by a global catastrophic Flood in Noah's day. Your first sheet is a timeline which represents this view.'

I studied the sheet. There were other events on the timeline which looked as if they too had something to do with biblical events. There were also a number of lines of text. Although I did not have time to read them at that moment, they appeared to mainly relate to the six days of creation and Noah's Flood. After giving us a few moments to study the sheet, Steph spent some time explaining their belief that most of the fossils were formed as a result of being buried rapidly in sediment at the time of the Flood.

Steph then moved on to the second theory. 'That view was replaced in the first part of the nineteenth century by what is known as the catastrophist view. This is represented by the timeline on your second sheet.'

There was more rustling of paper as we all obediently flipped over to the second page.

'The catastrophists tended to believe in a supernatural beginning, but they didn't believe the biblical account of history. They believed that over millions of years, every now and again there would have been a regional or global catastrophe that destroyed much of the earth and much of the life on the earth and then, after each catastrophe, survivors would repopulate the earth or God would supernaturally create new forms of life to replace those that had been wiped out. Things would continue for millions of years until the next catastrophe occurred. Believing that these catastrophes were entirely natural, they couldn't rule out future events on a similar scale.'

As I studied page two of the handout, I could immediately see what Steph was describing. She spent a few minutes giving us further details and mentioning individuals who had subscribed to that way of thinking. Eventually, she explained, 'This view ruled in geology for about thirty years but, by around 1830, it was replaced by what has become known as the uniformitarian view.'

We all flipped over to the third timeline.

'I need to briefly discuss two of the individuals who were influential in promoting this idea. The first of these was James Hutton.[9] He was a wealthy landowner in Scotland who was trained in medicine, but his real love was geology. He believed that his land was being eroded into the river, and the river was transferring those sediments down to the estuary where it would be laid down in layers of mud. He believed that as further layers were formed, the bottom layers would be solidified by the heat of the earth and, later, these would be raised up to form new land masses which would eventually be eroded into the sea.

'As a result, in 1795, he published a book called *Theory of the Earth*, in which he viewed earth's history as cyclical. He made a famous statement saying that he could see 'no evidence of a beginning' in the rock record.

'Then there was Charles Lyell. Lyell built on the ideas of James Hutton who died in 1797, which was the year of Lyell's birth. He insisted that not only were the processes of sedimentation and erosion uniform, but that they had worked at the same rate of energy and frequency throughout earth's history.

'Notice that there are no catastrophes marked on this timeline. The uniformitarians would accept local floods similar to those we see today. They would also allow for volcanic action in the past, but again, only like those eruptions we see today. So, basically, they were saying that we must explain everything by present processes operating at present intensities and frequencies. Those promoting this view insisted that no regional or global catastrophes could be used to explain the observable evidence.

'A phrase that is often used to convey this way of thinking is '*the present is the key to the past.*' In other words, we can only use geologic events we see in the present to explain what has happened in the past. This theory became known as uniformitarianism, and earth's history became even longer.

'From around 1840, this philosophy became the ruling dogma in geology. Ever since that time, people have been trained in schools, colleges and universities to view the rocks using this uniformitarian view of earth's history. All the science journals and the geological associations were controlled by this uniformitarian view.'

I felt I was beginning to gain a greater understanding of some of Steph and Steve's comments. They were always keen to point out that everyone had the same physical evidence to study. It was the different beliefs people held about the world which caused them to interpret that evidence in different ways. As I flipped back through the various timelines, I was fascinated to see how different theories could be proposed by looking at exactly the same physical evidence.

As Steph folded her own sheets and returned them to her rucksack, she said, 'OK, folks, I hope that brief look at the historical position will help you during your time here. It's absolutely crucial that you understand there's more than one way to view the physical evidence.'

'Thanks very much, Steph,' Steve said, as he swapped places with her. 'Please keep those timelines and Steph's words in your minds as we investigate this area over the next few hours.'

Everyone folded their sheets and there was a moment's pause as we all put the papers in our bags.

Steve began:

'During the eruption in May 1980, this location north of Mount Saint Helens was a site of intense geologic activity. Since the start of that eruption, up to 600 feet of deposits have formed at this spot.'

I was staggered by this figure and tried to do some rapid mental arithmetic. I knew that the ceiling in my lounge at home was 8 feet high. So, 600 feet was seventy-five times higher than that. It seemed a ridiculous amount of material, but in all the dealings I'd had with the creationists to date, their facts had always turned out to be accurate. Everyone else was listening intently to Steve.

'Since the layers were laid down, this area has been eroded to reveal some of those 600 feet of deposits.' He half turned and waved a hand at the cliff face behind him.

He spoke for another few minutes about the rocks in front of us, before we moved to a new area.

On arriving at a sheer wall of rock, Steve explained, 'As you can see here, there is minute layering in some of these deposits'[10] [see image 7, p. 114].

On the video Steve had shown the previous day, we had seen images of these layers, but to see them in the flesh had a much greater impact on me. Some of the layers were very thin indeed. However, that raised a question in my mind.

'Steve? How can you be sure that these layers were laid down as you claim?'

Steve nodded. 'Thanks, Rob. It's important I explain that. We have historical observation and eyewitness reports and photographs of this area repeatedly between the eruptions showing the sequence in which these deposits formed. I can show you some of that documentation later.'

Steve went on to point out different areas of the rock wall. He then led us some distance to a different area of cliff face. We

Image 7: Fine rock layers deposited in hours at Mount Saint Helens
Photo by Steven A Austin PhD. Used with permission. JHW DSc_4958 Edited 7-17-2009 (002).

walked and scrambled over some undulating terrain until we reached the site he wanted to show us.

'One of the most interesting layers is this one,' he said, pointing at a particular area of rock. 'It was deposited on June 12, 1980. Hurricane velocity flows came surging down from the crater over this area and deposited 25 feet of minutely layered strata in three hours.'

Steve turned to face us. 'Now, we might assume that when a volcano throws out a significant amount of material in an eruption, it would appear in a cliff as one single thick layer of rock. In other words, that volcanic material would have been all mixed together in a single mass. But here we can see that the deposit has separated itself into multiple individual coarse and fine layers.'

I went right up to the rock so I could closely study the fine layering in the cliff. It was staggering to think that a single volcanic eruption had resulted in all these different layers. Jim joined me, running his hands slowly over the rough surface of the cliff face.

Steve went on: 'Obviously nobody actually saw these layers form, but we believe it only took minutes for each of these individual layers to be laid down.'

I shook my head in disbelief. The layering was incredible, and Jim and I shared a look of wonder as we continued to examine the rock.

'Most people think layers like this form slowly over long periods of time,' Steve continued, 'but here we have 25 feet of layers formed in just three hours.'

After a pause, Steve said, 'I think it would be good to give you all a few minutes to have a look around this area on your own. But again, please keep in mind the various timelines Steph showed you earlier. It will help you understand that this issue is one of belief rather than scientific fact.'

Jim was still standing next to me. 'So, what do you make of all of this?' I asked, gesturing at the rock face.

Jim looked thoughtful. 'When I signed up for this trip, I was genuinely interested to hear what they had to say, but I never really expected to change my view on the age issue. As far as I was concerned, the billions of years of geological time was a fact. Even when Steve gave us his presentation yesterday morning, although I found the details interesting, I was still sceptical about his interpretations.'

‘And now?’ I asked.

He did not answer immediately but looked up at the wall of rock in front of him. When he did respond, he said:

‘Assuming their information on this layering is accurate, their arguments are compelling. Having said that, these days, strata tend to be dated using radiometric dating techniques. So far, I’ve not heard them say very much about that. If these guys can convince me that those dating methods are unreliable, I’d have to seriously reconsider my stance on the age of this planet. In the absence of that data, I guess I’m still currently in the old-earth camp.’

As we continued to study the area together, I thought back to my first encounter with this man in the Congo.

‘What about evolution?’ I asked. ‘Have you shifted at all on that subject?’

He glanced briefly in my direction before apparently becoming fascinated by the fingernails on his left hand.

‘It’s interesting,’ he said. ‘Since returning from the Congo, I’ve had a number of discussions with Kevin. He also sent me links to some very interesting articles which highlight serious problems for Darwinian theory. Initially, I was highly sceptical, but I’ve since discovered that those issues are real ones. It took some time, but I now believe evolution to be completely false.’

That really surprised me, and I would have cause to remember this little exchange a few days later. As it was, I was just about to respond to him, when Steve asked us all to get together again.

We obediently regathered in a semicircle around Steve.

‘OK, we’re now going to look at what a prominent, British,

old-earth geologist has had to say about some of the geological formations around the world.'

Steve handed out his own stapled sheets of A4 paper to each member of the group. On the front sheet was a picture of a book and its author. The man's name was Derek Ager, and the title of his book was *The Nature of the Stratigraphical Record*.

When we had all received our sheets, Steve picked up from where he left off.

'Dr Ager was a very experienced geologist, having studied geological formations in over fifty countries. He was professor and head of the Geology Department at Swansea University in Wales. He wrote four books on geology and over 200 technical papers. In two of his books, he was clearly hostile towards the Bible and young-earth creationists, whom he called 'the lunatic fringe'. In fact, he warned creationists against using anything he wrote to support their view.

'Now isn't that interesting? He was aware that his comments might very much interest people like me. But if what he says in his book about the geology of the earth is true, and if there are young-earth implications which come from the details he's giving, then anyone ought to be able to quote him. It's my own view that everyone should hear many of the things he wrote.

'In his book, Dr Ager wrote a chapter on the history of geology in the early nineteenth century. On your second sheet there's a quote from that chapter. I'll give you time to read the whole quote, and then I'll pick out certain statements for comment.'

We all turned to the second page. For a few moments, the only sound was a gentle flap of the papers in the breeze as everyone read the sheet Dr Ager had written:

My excuse for this lengthy and amateur digression into history is that I've been trying to show how I think geology got into the hands of the theoreticians, who were conditioned by the social and political history of their day more than by observations in the field. In other words, we have allowed ourselves to be brainwashed into avoiding any interpretation of the past that involves extreme or what might be termed catastrophic processes.[11]

Steve waited for all of us to finish reading before he continued.

'OK, let's break this down. When Ager says that he thinks "geology got into the hands of the theoreticians", he's referring to the uniformitarian or old-earth geologists of the early nineteenth century: men like Charles Lyell and James Hutton.

'Then he says that he believes these people were "conditioned by the social and political history of their day, more than by observations in the field". Now, this is really important. He's saying that, in his opinion, these people had been controlled and influenced in their interpretation of the rocks more by social and political ideas than they had by their own careful examination of the physical evidence. But now notice how he ends this statement written to his fellow evolutionary geologists: "... we have allowed ourselves to be brainwashed into avoiding any interpretation of the past that involves extreme or what might be termed catastrophic processes."'

Steve glanced around our group.

'Isn't it interesting that a geologist who believes in millions of years should tell his fellow evolutionary geologists that he believes they have all been brainwashed. This is very, very significant. You see, Derek Ager realized that all the way through his education, he'd been taught geology by people who believed in uniformitarian or slow and gradual principles. This would be true of his high school, undergraduate and PhD studies.

'The problem is that following all this training—eventually, Derek Ager went out into the field as a qualified geologist, as he did in over fifty countries—the more he looked at the rocks, the more he recognized that many of these geological features had been formed by *catastrophic processes in hours, days, weeks, or months, not over the course of millions of years as interpreted by other geologists*. He began to realize that the way he'd been trained to think throughout his geological education was wrong. In his own words, he realized that he had been brainwashed. The evidence for catastrophe had been there all along, but he'd not been able to see it because of this brainwashing.'

I glanced again at Sue who was looking very thoughtful.

Steve gestured towards the finely layered rock:

'Someone coming across this feature and not knowing how it had been formed might assume that these layers had taken a huge period of time to be deposited. But we have the evidence that these layers were laid down rapidly and catastrophically. So, we're back to the same old issue. We all have the same facts. The creationists and the evolutionists all have the same physical evidence to study. But it's the way that evidence is interpreted that causes us to reach the conclusions we do. And it's our presuppositions and assumptions which determine how we view the evidence.

'Derek Ager had been trained to believe in slow and gradual processes over millions of years. He had been trained to dismiss the idea of catastrophic events. So, when he went out to study the rocks, initially, he didn't see the evidence for catastrophe. But more and more observations of the real world began to show him that the assumptions he'd been trained to accept were wrong. If you don't start by ruling out catastrophe before you've even seen the evidence, you'll see the evidence for catastrophe everywhere.'

I looked past Steve and stared at the layers of strata. Raising my head slightly, my eyes took in some of the layers higher up the cliff wall. It was fascinating. Although I knew virtually nothing about geology, I still found it hard to get my head around the fact that all these layers had been laid down in three hours.

'Geologists like Derek Ager are known as "neocatastrophists" or new catastrophists,' Steve said. 'They've started to return to the ideas held by the catastrophists in the early nineteenth century that Jenny told you about earlier: ideas about geological features being formed by catastrophic events. Ager realized that if he set aside the assumption that a particular rock layer had to have formed over millions of years, another interpretation became possible. He began to appreciate that there was good evidence that that layer had formed rapidly.'

Out of the corner of my eye, I noticed Sue slowly shaking her head.

As I turned in her direction, a frown appeared on her face. 'Steve?'

she queried. 'You described Derek Ager as an old-earth geologist. You also said that he still believed in millions of years. So, would it be true to say that he believed there were millions of years where there was nothing going on from a geological perspective?'

Steve smiled. 'That's exactly right. Actually, this next bit is incredibly important. Dr Ager knew that much of the geological record showed evidence for catastrophic formation. But, as Sue has just pointed out, he still believed in millions of years. So where did he put all that time? He put it between the layers. So, he believed that one layer was deposited, and then nothing would happen geologically for millions of years. Eventually, another catastrophe occurs and the next layer is laid down.'

Steve flipped over to another sheet. 'If you look at the next page, you'll see another very interesting photograph.'

We all obediently turned to the next page to see another image of rock layers.

'When you stand at the rim of the Grand Canyon, you can see all those rock layers on the opposite side stacked up on one another.[12] We can trace those rock layers for hundreds and in some cases thousands of miles. But now look at the topography of the South-West United States' [see image 8, p. 122].

We all flipped over to the next sheet where there were photographs of the Grand Canyon as well as the surrounding area.

'We obviously have this massive canyon,' Steve said, 'but there are many more signs of erosion in the area.'

This was perfectly true, but I did not immediately grasp what he was driving at.

Image 8: View of rock layers in the walls of the Grand Canyon
Photo by J. Whitmore DSC_4958. Used with permission.

Steve then flicked back a page. 'But look at those layers visible within the walls of the canyon.'

I dutifully went back to the previous sheet.

'Those layers are all completely flat,' he said. 'We don't see any erosional features in those layers. Wouldn't you expect to see some evidence of erosion if there was a massive amount of time between the deposition of one layer followed by the next?'

As I stared at the image of the layers in the walls of the Grand Canyon, the penny dropped. Many of those layers looked as if they were as flat as a billiard table. If there were long periods of time between the individual layers being deposited, surely this would not have been the case.

It was now my turn to frown. Steve's argument made a lot of

sense. I flipped back to the page showing the terrain with its erosional features. The more I compared the layers in the walls of the Grand Canyon with the surface of the ground, the more convinced of Steve's arguments I became.

When I glanced back up, I noticed Steve studying me with great interest. As our eyes met, a faint smile appeared on his face, followed by an almost imperceptible nod. I smiled in return before dropping my eyes to the images once more. Beside me, Sue was writing something down.

Once again, Steve glanced around the group.

'Now, the comments from Derek Ager are really helpful. However, in some ways, it's incredibly frustrating. The ironic thing is that he himself was still suffering from the same sort of brainwashing that he had recognized in his colleagues. He was absolutely on the right track. There's wonderful evidence in those layers that they were formed catastrophically and rapidly.

'The problem is, that's where he stopped. If he had applied the same logic to the boundaries between the layers, he would have seen things very differently. If he'd looked more carefully at those boundaries, he would have noticed that there is no evidence for millions of years there either. In fact, there's very good evidence that this sequence of layers was laid down rapidly with very little time between one layer and the next being deposited.

'Unfortunately, just like those he was trying to enlighten, he started with a set of assumptions that ruled out a global Flood before he'd started to look at the evidence.'

Steve then said something which appeared to contradict his last point:

'Now, it's true that there are places in the Grand Canyon where those rock layers are not completely flat.'

'Doesn't that negate what you've just been saying?' I asked.

Steve smiled. 'No, not at all. In fact, it strengthens the case when you really study the layers.'

He flipped over to the next sheet and we all followed suit.

'You see the middle layer? Notice the boundary between that layer and the layer above.'

There was a long smooth curve at the boundary between the two layers.[13]

'OK,' he said, 'now look at the boundary between that layer and the one below.'

The second boundary was bent in an identical manner.

'Would you agree that that middle layer looks as if it's been bent by some force pushing up from underneath?'

That was certainly what it looked like [see image 9].

'But rock is hard, isn't it? If you try to bend solid rock, it will break or fracture. But this layer appears to have been bent like a slab of plasticine. No fracturing; just a smooth curve.' He went on:

'So, in what condition would this layer have to be in order for it to be bent without fracturing?'

'Soft sediment,' Sue said thoughtfully.

Steve nodded enthusiastically. 'Exactly, Sue. This layer must have been bent before it had time to turn into rock. In turn, that implies that it was bent soon after it had been deposited.'

Once more, Steve paused to allow us to consider these facts. When he eventually went on, he said something that seemed to me to be highly significant:

'But that's not the real problem for the old-earth geologists. The real problem is that the layers above this one are also bent through almost 90 degrees.'

He turned over to the next sheet, and, once more, we obediently followed. This image showed the same layer but also included the ones immediately above.

'This whole sequence of layers is supposed to represent 300 to

Image 9: Smoothly bent sequences of rock strata
Photo by A. Snelling PhD. Used with permission.

400 million years,' he said. Again, he paused briefly. He resumed with a question:

'Are they really asking us to believe that this bottom layer stayed soft for 400 million years while all these other layers formed slowly and gradually on top of it?'

I glanced at Sue. She was standing, staring at the sheet, a look of total concentration on her face. As I watched, a frown crept onto her brow.

She asked Steve a question about metamorphism in rock that I did not understand. As he responded, my mind drifted back to the mile after mile of completely flat layers within the walls of the Grand Canyon. Once more, I compared these with the erosional features on the earth's surface. Although, as a layman, there was obviously a lot I did not understand, Steve's arguments did make sense.

As my mind returned to the discussion in the group, Steve was still explaining:

'Metamorphism leaves tell-tale signs behind. There's absolutely no evidence for any metamorphic reaction in any of these layers.'

Sue began to ask Steve more technical questions about how he believed these individual layers could have been formed. Although I heard the responses, not having Sue's background, all the geological terminology went over my head. Sue knew her stuff, that was for sure. However, my interest was retained just by observing Sue's reaction to each new piece of information. As she listened to Steve's commentary on the strata, her attention was total. She was obviously drinking it all in. As a result of her cross-examination, it was over half an hour before we moved on to another area of interest.

When we did, Steve spent some time describing and giving his interpretation of each new site as we continued the tour. There was the nine-hour eruption deposit from May 18, various mudflow deposits, and many other interesting features.

For another hour, we continued to study the various strata layers, walking around the area, studying new geological features and quizzing Steve over anything we did not understand.

Most of the time I was walking round these sites with Sue. Having done a degree in geology, she obviously had far more knowledge about the subject, and I was curious to know what she made of it all.

'It's amazing,' she said. 'It's also extremely frustrating. I spent years studying geology and no one ever told me any of this. The teaching of geology is done entirely from the point of view of millions of years of geological time.' She looked at me. 'Rob, I'm going to have to spend some serious time delving into this subject. I'll check all their details, but if it turns out that Steve's right, there will be a number of people who will have a fair bit of explaining to do.'

At 12:30pm, we found a relatively suitable area of terrain and stopped to have our packed lunch. Sue and I joined Steve and Steph on a gradually sloping and lumpy piece of ground. Although we had coats to sit on, it was not the most comfortable meal I have ever enjoyed.

As soon as we were settled, Sue began voicing her frustration to Steve over the teaching she had received on geology.

'I've never heard these details before,' she said. 'I know you've already provided us with information about Mount Saint Helens and the surrounding area, but this morning has been different. Hearing about these things is one thing but actually coming here and observing the physical evidence is something else altogether. Steve, at some point, I'd like you to explain how you believe we've got into this terrible mess.'

Steve did not reply immediately. As a rule, when someone made a comment like this, he would normally give a little smile and chuckle before responding. However, sensing Sue's genuine unhappiness about the situation, he thoughtfully paused before replying.

'You're right,' he said. 'At some point over the next few days, I'll try to get Steph to go into that in more detail. That's very much her area of expertise.'

Sue gave a brief nod and the conversation turned to details specifically relating to the evidence we had studied that morning.

As we finished our lunch and prepared to continue our tour of the area, I chuckled to myself. Sue shot me a glance.

'What's tickled you?' she asked.

'It's just amusing to hear you discussing all this with Steve,' I said. 'The comments you're making are very similar to the ones I made to Kevin on our last trip. Sue, I know exactly how you feel.'

I paused and then modified my remark.

'Having said that, I suspect it's even worse for you. Although I had a real interest in natural science, I wasn't trained to teach it. I can appreciate how that might cause you even greater frustration than I felt.'

She nodded, thoughtfully. 'Yes, you're right. I keep thinking of the comments I've made over and over again to my students. If all this turns out to be true, I'm going to feel so stupid when I see most of them again next term.' She sighed heavily. 'Rob, it feels as if I've been lying to them.'

'Well, even if all this is true, you haven't really been lying to them, have you? I mean, lying is when you tell someone something that you know is untrue. You've been telling your students details that you honestly believed to be right.'

'Right now, Rob, that's not a huge comfort. It might be true, but I entered the teaching profession to give accurate information to the young people who had been entrusted to me. I'm beginning to suspect that I've totally failed in that respect.'

She sounded and looked crestfallen: her head down and voice full of regret. This morning had had a bigger impact on Sue than I had realized.

I softly lifted her chin with my hand.

'Sue don't be so hard on yourself. It's not your fault.'

When she looked up at me, I noticed that her eyes were moist.

Coming closer, I put my arm around her shoulders and gave her a gentle hug. Her hair smelled of apples. 'Really, Sue, it's not your fault.'

She looked up at me and gave a sad smile. 'I know, Rob. Don't worry; I'll be all right.'

There were other areas that Steve wanted us all to examine, and we spent the early part of the afternoon going around these sites. Towards the end of the day, I started to get a little bored; there was a lot of information, and the technical jargon had ramped up, but Sue was in her element.

She looked around in wonder.

'This is an amazing area for the study of geology,' she said. 'I could spend weeks wandering around here with Steve and Jenny.'

'If you do, you'll be doing it without me,' I thought to myself. However, I did not share this thought with Sue.

Just after 3:00pm, we had finished our field work for that day and were about to return to base when a WhatsApp message came through from Sam.

A stab of guilt ran through me. It had been my intention to message Sam every day with an update from our end. I read his message, frowned, and then had to read it again. It said:

'Hi Bruv. Hope all is well. Don't know what's going on here. Someone seems to be showing interest in my flat. I'm sure it's nothing to worry about. Send me an update from your end when you've got something to report. Sam.'

What was that all about? I checked the time. It would be just after 11:00 in the evening in Britain. I responded straight away.

'Hi Sam. All OK here. We've had a great day studying rock layers. I'll tell you all about it at some point. What do you mean people are showing interest in your flat?'

I got an immediate response.

'Studying rock layers? Sounds riveting. I think I'll stay here and watch some paint dry. Don't worry about the flat. I'm sure there's no problem. Let you know if I get any grief.'

I was not particularly reassured, but given the lateness of the hour in Britain, I decided to leave it.

It had been a long day. After the evening meal, we all gathered in the bar to relax and discuss the day's events. In our little group, Sue continued to quiz Steve about the day's revelations.

However, after a while, Jenny yawned and glanced at her watch. 'Will you excuse me, folks,' she said. 'I was up fairly early this morning. I think I'm going to hit the sack.'

'Sure,' Steve said. 'I'll be going myself as soon as I've finished my coffee.'

When Jenny had gone, I asked Steve what we'd be doing the following day.

With a glint in his eye, and a broad grin on his face, he said, 'We'll be taking that chopper ride you're so looking forward to.'

'Great,' I said sarcastically, and Sue laughed.

'You'll see quite a bit from the air,' Steve said, "but one of the more spectacular views is of the canyons that have been formed since 1980. In the afternoon, we'll be taking a more detailed look at one of those canyons. That may be more to your liking, because you'll have your feet firmly on the ground for that part.'

As Steve and the other members of the team gradually drifted off to their rooms, eventually, Sue and I were left sitting on our own and, despite feeling the call of sleep beckoning me, I was relieved to have some time alone with her.

'So, what did you make of today?' Sue asked.

I considered her question. 'It feels very much like the other trip I went on with Kevin,' I said. 'I'd heard most of the evolutionary arguments but, until I attended that debate in Harrow, I'd never come across the alternative view.'

'I know,' she said. 'I've done a degree in geology and I've never heard any of these arguments before.' She sighed deeply. 'It's just wrong, Rob. I keep thinking about my students. If this turns out to be true, I've been feeding them a load of nonsense for years.'

I felt I needed to remind her of something: 'Just bear in mind that there's a possibility that it might not all be true.'

'I realize that, Rob. The thing is that there's more than one issue here. Whether this is true or not is obviously a really, really important point but, in a way, it's irrelevant which of these two views is true. The point is, if there are two reasonable options, our students have the right to hear both. If what Steve and Jenny believe is so obviously a load of rubbish, then surely our students are intelligent enough to make that call. However, if it's true, our students are being prevented from even hearing the arguments. That isn't teaching; that's indoctrination!' Sue gave her fist a gentle bang on the table with this last word.

I nodded thoughtfully. This was another point that had been made in the debate over Darwinian Evolution. It was a valid point then, and it was still a valid point now. Right now, though, I was too tired to think about it.

Chapter 6
Incredible Canyons

As sleep merged into wakefulness on Tuesday morning, I replayed yesterday in my mind. My eyes snapped wide open as I remembered that today I would have to face my fears—a mix of panic and excitement mingling inside. As much as a helicopter journey was not top of my list of things to do, I was excited at the thought of seeing some of these scenes from the air. Trying to put that out of my mind, I considered yesterday. It had been a long day, and the experience had been phenomenal. I thought about the brief hug with Sue and the scent of her hair lingered in my mind.

After breakfast Jenny explained that our next viewing of Mount Saint Helens would be from the air, as if I needed reminding. She had approached one of the companies who organize helicopter trips to ask if they could provide a flight to view a specific list of sites. This had been agreed and a price negotiated.

Word had obviously got around about my aversion to flying, as Jenny looked at me reassuringly.

'You have nothing to worry about, Rob. These helicopters have a wonderful safety record.'

Then, to the group, she continued, 'We want you all to get an aerial view of the volcano, including the crater, but we also want to show you the surrounding area.'

We discovered that this was to include Spirit Lake, areas of forest, canyons and a few other features. It all sounded great, but in spite of Jenny's comments on the safety record of the aircraft, my stomach was still doing backflips. My fear of flying had caused me some uncomfortable moments in my previous expedition and I wasn't in any particular hurry to repeat the experience. On top of that, I reasoned, in a fixed-wing aircraft, if the engine fails, at least you have a small chance of gliding and effecting a safe landing. If the engine of a helicopter fails, my understanding was that those things have the aerodynamics of a brick. However, it seemed that, once more, I would have to bite the bullet.

So, half an hour later, we found ourselves heading back along SR 504. As we got closer to the location where the helicopters took off, my stomach began to indulge in a full gymnastic program.

I learned that Steve, Steph and Sue would be accompanying me on my flight, while the others would be going on a second flight, taking off half an hour later. As much as I was enjoying being with Sue, I was not sure that I wanted her to be on the same flight as me. My heart was racing, my palms sweaty, and I was willing to bet I was ever so slightly green.

We arrived at the helipad at 10:30am and Steve registered our arrival with a member of staff. He returned to give us the news that our flight would be taking off in around twenty-five minutes. This was twenty-five minutes too long for me; I wanted this to be over as soon as possible. Nevertheless, they were as good as their word, and twenty minutes later, our flight was announced. We all rose to our feet and went out into the morning sunshine.

Just walking towards the aircraft my stomach was starting to churn again. We climbed aboard and strapped ourselves into our seats using the substantial safety harnesses provided. Each of us had headphones to put on. These would partly act as ear defenders, blocking out the noise of the engine, but would also allow Steve to give us a running commentary of the trip.

As Tom, our pilot, started the motor, I was surprised. The engines did not sound as loud as I had expected.

'Can everyone hear me OK?' Steve asked over the intercom.

We indicated to him that he was coming through loud and clear.

Tom ran through his safety instructions, which only served to increase my nervousness.

Suddenly, the pitch of the engine changed and I grasped the arms of the seat with clammy hands. The helicopter taking off gave me a new experience. It was similar, but not identical to the feeling you get when a fixed-wing aircraft leaves the ground. It came as no great surprise to me that I did not enjoy it anymore.

As I sat there, I identified with someone with a fear of flying who had once told me that if God had meant us to fly, he would have given us wings. I grabbed the arms of the seat tightly and closed my eyes.

Steve came back on the intercom:

'OK, we're going to start by flying along the north fork of the Toutle River.'

The heliport was near the river and it was only a minute or so before we were flying up the river valley.

Soon, Steve was speaking again:

'This fork of the river was totally blocked as a result of a landslide at the time of the May 18, 1980, eruption,' he said. 'If you remember, when we discussed the eruption on Sunday, I mentioned that over half a cubic mile of landslide material had slipped from the top of the volcano. Most people remember the material that crashed into Spirit Lake because of the dramatic waves it caused. But about three times that amount slid down the western face of the volcano into this river valley.

'The north fork of the river stayed blocked for just under two years but was unblocked on March 19, 1982. A giant mudflow from the volcano came down over this area. It cut a whole new series of channels, and the upper part of the drainage basin of the Toutle River was established once more. From the air, you can see where this breech occurred. If you look out to your left now, you can see where the mud came down through the area, breeched through a natural dam and resulted in the complex branching drainage pattern we see today.'

Steve paused in his commentary, giving us a chance to study the landscape.

Still gripping the armrests, the distraction of Steve's voice cutting straight into my ears was strangely calming. I began to relax as he continued:

'The conventional scientific community generally tells us that drainage channels are established by streams gradually eating their way into the upland area, but that's not what happened here. We know this occurred rapidly as a result of this mudflow event. At the end of this flight, we'll come back and have a closer look at some of these canyons.'

We changed course and headed straight for Mount Saint Helens. I leant to my right to get a better view past Tom. It was amazing to see the volcano filling more and more of the front windshield as we approached. In spite of the discomfort I felt just by being up in an aircraft, I was still able to appreciate the awesome spectacle of this fire-breathing edifice that we had come all this way to study.

As we approached the crater, Steve crackled on the intercom again.

'The canyon you're about to see was formed rapidly through solid rock, not through soft sediments. Following the eruptions in 1980, creation scientists were able to get into the new canyons near the crater. We have eyewitness reports as well as photographic documentation that verify none of these canyons were here before those eruptions.'[14]

Steve broke off until we had arrived at the canyon.

'This terrain consists of ancient lava flows, ancient volcanic landslide deposits and ancient volcanic ash layers. We're not a hundred-per-cent certain if this canyon was carved out by water or a severe mudflow event, but the erosion was clearly catastrophic.'

The canyon was spectacular.

After a few minutes hovering over the canyon, Tom took us to have a look at the crater. As we arrived, I immediately noticed two lava domes. I smiled at the realization I was picking up the lingo.

Once more, Steve's voice crackled in my ears:

'I'll be telling you more when we visit the crater in a few days' time, but please notice the lava domes. Also, there's a glacier inside the crater.'

Tom then began slowly flying anticlockwise around Mount Saint Helens. Now and again, he would bring the aircraft in close, giving us spectacular views of the huge horseshoe-shaped crater and the lava domes. At other times, he would swing the chopper away and take up a position at a greater distance to give us a panoramic view of the wider area.

I was fascinated to see the increased height of the southern rim of the crater. Looking down, it was possible to see the tiny figures of some intrepid explorers who had climbed to the summit. I noticed their up-turned faces as they watched us fly overhead.

When we had passed a point due east of the crater and were heading for the northern face of Mount Saint Helens, Tom stopped and began to hover, so we had the northern face of the volcano at about 11 o'clock, and the main body of Spirit Lake at roughly 2 o'clock.

'Ahead and slightly to the left of us is the north face of Mount Saint Helens," Steve said. "This is the area which had begun to swell in the weeks leading up to the eruption. As I explained a couple of days ago, at just after 8:32am on May 18, 1980, there was a magnitude 5.1 earthquake immediately under the summit of Mount Saint Helens. The summit and north face began to slide from the top of the mountain. At the same time, there was a massive steam explosion which was directed across the landscape in a northerly direction. Around a quarter of the landslide material crashed down that north slope directly into Spirit Lake.'

At this point, Tom altered the orientation of the helicopter so the nose was pointing downwards to give us all a view of the point at which the landslide material would have crashed into the waters of the lake.

While I appreciated his intentions, the manoeuvre played havoc with my stomach. Prior to the helicopter aerobatics, my fascination with the sights we were being shown, along with the information from Steve, had almost entirely overridden my fear.

'We're now going to fly up to show you the terrain beyond the north shore of Spirit Lake before we have a look at the lake itself.'

As we flew across the water, I looked down to see if I could spot any logs floating there. Initially, I could not, but then I spotted them. One or two to start with, but then there were many of them all together.

As we crossed the northern shoreline, Steve resumed:

'When the landslide material crashed into the south end of the lake, this area was completely devastated by the resulting waves. A series of massive waves smashed into this shoreline ripping out trees as they went. And these weren't saplings; they were mature trees. Because of the shape of the land here, the water, having devastated the forest, rushed back into the lake, taking most of the uprooted trees with it'

I scanned the landscape. Spirit Lake sat in a natural basin

surrounded on all sides by sloping terrain. As I glanced over my shoulder at Mount Saint Helens and then back at the north shore, I tried to imagine what it must have been like as that wall of water smashed into the forest. Having seen the destruction caused by tsunamis, I could well imagine the devastation that would have been created by such massive waves.

After a few minutes flying around various parts of the northern shore of the lake, we headed back out over the water.

I adjusted my headphones as Steve began telling us about the logs.

'Although there aren't anything like as many logs on the lake as there were immediately after the eruption, it's still pretty impressive.'

Tom took the chopper down fairly low so we could get a good look at some of the logs. As I looked down, I noticed a disturbance on the lake and, for a moment, wondered if we were about to be attacked by an American version of Nessy. I then felt rather stupid as I realized that it was the effect of the rotor blades on the surface of the water.

'The floating logs are interesting,' Steve said, 'but it's what's going on under the surface that's really important. We'll probably come to the lake a couple of times to show you the exciting news from this area.'

After another minute slowly flying over the log mat, Tom took the helicopter up and we headed for different areas of forest. Some of these were still pretty barren, but there were others where a significant amount of natural growth had re-established itself. Steve told us that, during the next week, we would also be spending some time walking through these areas to gain a better appreciation of what had occurred in the years since 1980.

Soon we were heading off to have a look at the canyons. After a couple of minutes without any commentary, Steve began speaking again as a canyon came into view.

'There are five canyons that come together here,' he said. 'Some of them are over 100 feet deep.'

As we flew around the area, I noticed that some of the canyons had noticeably different shapes to them. Some were more of a 'U' shape, while others were more of a 'V' shape. It was absolutely fascinating. Then Steve said something that I was not expecting.

'The evidence we're viewing here should remind us of the Grand Canyon. What you are looking at here is a one-fortieth-scale model of the Grand Canyon.' He paused briefly, but then he went on.

'Remember, all this geological change occurred in a single day. All these drainage channels were established by the mudflow on March 19, 1982' [see image 10, p. 142].

I heard a faint 'wow' over the intercom from Sue.

As we flew over another canyon, Steve explained:

'This one is over 200 feet wide and over 100 feet deep. And notice the stream running through the bottom. Imagine a geologist, who believed in slow and gradual processes, coming across this sight but knowing nothing about the 1982 event. He would almost certainly conclude that that stream eroded the canyon slowly and gradually over a huge period of time.

Image 10: Canyon system carved on 19 March 1982 at Mount Saint Helens
Public domain.

'But we know that's not how this canyon was formed. If you think about it, it's actually the canyon that created the conditions for the stream; it's not the stream that created the canyon. This canyon is actually a monument to a previous catastrophic event. It's no longer being formed. At least, it's not being formed in the same way as it was in the past.'[15]

Once again, Steve's arguments gave me much to consider and, as I glanced at Sue, her eyes were wide as she was taking it all in.

After landing, we all met up to have lunch in a nearby restaurant. There was an excited buzz of conversation. Being back on terra firma, I was probably the happiest of any of them. All the same, I thought Sue had been right. Having experienced the trip, I was certainly pleased that I had done it. It had been very special.

There were lots of questions for Steve, particularly about the canyons. This prompted him to tell us about someone who had been influenced by a canyon nearly two centuries earlier.

'It's interesting,' he said, 'but when Charles Darwin was on the Beagle, his ship called in at southern Argentina. While he was there, he saw the valley of the Santa Cruz River. He noticed that there was a relatively small river running through a large canyon. Now, it's important to know that, by that time, Darwin had already been convinced that the earth was millions of years old. That's because he'd just finished reading a book by a friend of his called Charles Lyell which promoted the idea of millions of years.'

Lyell—I thought I had heard that name recently but could not remember where. Sue noticed me and whispered, 'Lyell is one of the men that Steph told us about yesterday.'

'Yes, of course,' I agreed.

'Darwin actually sketched the canyon of the Santa Cruz River in his notebook,' Steve said. 'Comments he made make it clear that he was thinking in terms of slow and gradual change over millions of years. Then, he got back into his ship and sailed off to the Galapagos Islands where he studied the finches and reptiles.

'Now, there's no doubt that he got his ideas of biological evolution from looking at the finches and reptiles on those islands. However, he got his ideas of geological evolution on which he based his biological theory having read Lyell's book and then thinking about the valley of the Santa Cruz River.'

'I didn't know any of that,' I said out loud.

'No, not many people do,' Steve replied. 'Interestingly,

geologists have studied the valley of the Santa Cruz River and concluded that it wasn't eroded slowly over immense periods of time. There's evidence of catastrophic drainage from glaciers upstream.'

After this discussion, we had about five minutes before our afternoon's studies of the canyons were due to begin, so I decided to send a WhatsApp message to Sam.

'Hi Sam, how was your day? I've spent the morning up in a chopper looking at canyons. Any news on the people watching your house? Rob.'

Seconds later his reply came in:

'Hi Bruv. I've had a good day but still have the freaks hanging around. They spend most of their time sitting in a white van on the other side of the road. Don't worry about it Bruv, nothing will happen.'

I did not much like his news. Why would someone be hanging around? Sam could be right and there was nothing to worry about, but I did not want him to take any chances. I sent another text.

'Sam, I'd be happier if you gave the police a ring.'

I got another immediate response: 'Don't be daft, Bruv, I'm not going to bother them. It's almost certainly nothing. In any case, I'm keeping a record of everything.'

As on the previous day, I decided to drop it. All the same, I was still uncomfortable about the situation.

Minutes later and we were back in the dusty Land Rovers. Steve told us we were heading for a location where we could gain access to one of the canyons that we had seen from the air in the morning. After parking up, we had quite a hike to reach the floor of the canyon. There were one or two of the steeper parts of the trail where I would have appreciated a handrail. This was certainly the case when I was about two thirds of the way down and my foot slipped on some loose material. Thankfully no damage was done, but it sent a shower of stones bouncing down the steep slope to my left.

When we reached the bottom, I turned to look back up from where we had come.

Jenny was standing at my side. 'I always think it's amazing looking up at the walls of these canyons from down here,' she said. 'I never get tired of the sight.'

Personally, at that particular moment, I was anticipating what it was going to be like to climb out again, but I did agree with her. It was an amazing sight.

There was a shallow but quite fast-moving stream in the bottom of the canyon. Steve gathered us all together and began to speak:

'OK, folks. As you look around you, I want you to appreciate that this canyon was formed in a single day. That might be difficult for you to accept but remember that we have photographic evidence recording the terrain in this area over the relevant period, proving that is in fact the case.'

Steve paused to give us all the opportunity to scan round the canyon. It truly was a stunning sight. Looking upstream, there was a left-hand bend in the canyon about 100 yards away. In the other direction, it ran straight for a significant way before taking a gradual curve to the right.

'Just imagine what people would say if we didn't have that photographic evidence. If we hadn't known about the eruptions at Mount Saint Helens, we'd be told that this canyon had formed incredibly slowly as it was eroded over millions of years by this stream.'

That was almost certainly true, I thought.

He went on: 'If your worldview tells you that canyons and other geological formations have to be formed over millions of years, that's the way it will appear to you. However, if you're prepared to consider the possibility that these features can be formed catastrophically, you have another option.'

If what Steve was telling us about the photographic record was correct, it was not just that there was another option; that other option had already been shown to be true.

The gush of the flowing water was relaxing; the air smelled clean and earthy. Steve cut into my thoughts:

'I admit, this is a completely different way of interpreting the evidence but, as we've said before, people shouldn't dismiss one of the possibilities just because they don't like the implications. We know categorically that this canyon was opened up rapidly, not through slow and gradual erosion over enormous periods of time.'

Steve wandered over to the stream and tapped the toe of his boot on the surface of the water.

'Have a look at this stream,' he said. 'Then have another look at the size of this canyon. Now, think logically. Is there any chance that this stream flowing at that rate over perhaps tens of thousands of years could erode this canyon? It makes no sense at all. And yet, they want us to believe that this is the way most of the world's canyons have been formed. It's utter foolishness.'

I looked all around and tended to agree.

Glancing around, I caught sight of Sue, standing alone; she looked lost in her own thoughts. She seemed to be staring at the walls of the canyon but, as I approached her, I had the distinct impression of someone not looking at anything at all.

'You look deep in thought,' I said.

She came out of her contemplations and looked at me.

'You remember that meeting in Kevin's office?' she said. 'The one when I made that feeble crack about the evidence being "set in stone"?'

I laughed. 'Yes.'

'Well, I was just thinking that that was actually quite profound. The true history of what happened here in this canyon has literally been set in stone. Then I thought of the rock layers that we saw yesterday. That's exactly the same. Rob, it's crazy. And what's more, I'm sure Steve's right about all this. I'm having a real struggle getting my head around it all.'

I empathized with Sue. It really shook the core of what we had been taught for years. There was a sense of uncertainty—a feeling that the floor was falling out of your world when the foundations of what you thought to be true and sure, were not.

We spent the next hour and a half investigating the area. Firstly, we went upstream to a location where it was easier to see different layers of rock exposed when the canyon had first been cut. Then we travelled downstream to a place where the canyon was significantly narrower. All this time, Steve was giving us little nuggets of information about different aspects of canyon formation and the incredible erosional power of water.

When the visit was over, Sue and I travelled back to base with Kevin.

'What did you think of that?' he asked us.

Sue jumped straight in:

'I don't want to sound like a broken record, but I'm so frustrated. And not a little angry,' she added. 'It wouldn't be so bad if all the "old earth" people were unaware of this kind of evidence but, going on what Steve told us yesterday, some of them are entirely familiar with these things. It's beginning to look more and more to me as if there's intentional deception going on here. It's disgraceful.'

Kevin gave a little chuckle.

'Sue, you're partly right. There are some who are fully aware of these details, but there are many who are not. It's very likely that the people who taught you were entirely ignorant of this evidence.'

'Then they shouldn't be!' Sue said with feeling. 'It's ridiculous that there should be so much ignorance within our colleges and universities. Those who are aware of this ought to be informing those who aren't.'

'Absolutely,' Kevin agreed, 'but that's where you're right about the deception. For the most part, those who are aware of it do want to keep it quiet. When writing about the lack of transitional fossils in the rock record, one of the top geologists in the States, Stephen Jay Gould, referred to this kind of ignorance as the "trade secret of palaeontology".'[16]

Sue turned to look at me. 'Wasn't that one of the quotes you sent me just after we first met?'

'That's right,' I agreed.

'Well, at least Gould had the honesty to write about such things,' Kevin said. 'It's the ones who are dishonest about this subject that we need to hold to account.'

The conversation continued in this vein until we arrived back at the hotel.

As there was still about an hour or so before our evening meal, the three of us decided to go for a coffee. When we were seated, I turned to Kevin.

'Geology isn't really your field, is it?' I asked. 'Is some of this information new to you as well?'

Kevin shook his head. 'Not really. Because I give presentations on the subject of creation, I regularly have to deal with questions relating to the rocks and fossils. Although I'm not anything like as well informed about geology as people like Steve and Jenny, I do have to be familiar with these kinds of arguments.'

I was just about to follow up on this when Kevin's phone emitted a sound like a duck—a sound which made Sue and I look at each other in surprise.

He picked it up and a puzzled frown appeared on his face.

'What's up, Kevin?' Sue enquired.

He glanced up. 'It's probably nothing. I've just received a cryptic message from someone at home.'

I returned to the subject we'd been discussing:

'If you have to field questions on different areas of science, you must spend a heck of a lot of time swotting up on all these subjects.'

Kevin still seemed distracted by his message, but then he said, 'Sorry, Rob, yes, there is an element of that, but the same questions tend to crop up fairly regularly. Once you've mastered those, you can deal with the majority of queries.'

'I guess you need to be a bit of a jack of all trades?' Sue suggested.

Kevin laughed. 'Yes, to a degree that's true. But I hope that doesn't mean that I'm a master of none.'

Sue and I also laughed.

'But I certainly don't know anything like as much about geology, palaeontology, astronomy and so on as I do about my own subject.'

Kevin took this opening to share some of the details about his subject of microbiology which confirmed the Bible. Once again, I was amused by the level of enthusiasm he displayed as he discussed the subject. Although it stretched my own knowledge in the area, he was always happy to explain himself, and he did it in a way which never came over as patronizing. In addition, I found his information fascinating.

Distractedly, Kevin said, 'Will you excuse me, folks? I need to go and sort something out. I'll see you at dinner.' He rose and left the bar area.

Sue and I were left alone and chatted for a few minutes before she glanced up at the clock above the bar. 'Rob, I think I'm going to go for a quick shower before we eat.'

‘Sounds like a good idea,’ I said. ‘I could do with freshening up a bit myself.’

We rose and headed for the stairs. As I turned to go up the first few steps, I glanced over to my right into reception and noticed Kevin sitting on his own, staring at his phone.

After dinner, as I walked into the meeting room, I noticed with some surprise that everyone else was already there. Also, Steve appeared ready to begin his talk.

‘Right, folks,’ he said, ‘let’s get started. Earlier in the day, you had a chance to see firsthand the incredible power of mud or water to erode through solid rock as well as soft sediments. Bearing these things in mind, this evening, we’re going to think about the Grand Canyon.’

Steve displayed a slide showing a spectacular image of that amazing feature.

‘The textbooks tell us that the Colorado River carved out the Grand Canyon, but most of the uniformitarian geologists who really know about the geology of Northern Arizona admit that they have no idea how that happened. In spite of that, they still dogmatically claim that the Colorado River is responsible for the formation of the canyon.’

His next image caused a degree of amusement in the members of our group. He had inserted a photo he had taken that afternoon. It was an image of us standing in the bottom of the canyon we had visited with most of us looking down at the stream running through the middle.

He grinned, looking at each one of us.

'Earlier, I asked you if you thought that little stream could have eroded that canyon. It was clear from your faces that you didn't think any such thing was possible. So, why do they expect us to believe that the Colorado River was responsible for cutting the Grand Canyon?

'Deep down, most geologists have been mystified by the Grand Canyon for some time. Many geologists who really know about the geology of northern Arizona, have given up on the idea that the Colorado River cut the Grand Canyon.'

I noticed an expression of surprise appear on Sue's face.

Steve continued: 'It might sound like heresy—after all, that's what the textbooks tell us—but, as I say, that's not the consensus any longer.'

I kept my eye on Sue. She gave me the impression of someone who was seriously having to reassess almost everything that she thought she knew. I could almost see her mind computing the information.

'So,' Steve asked, 'what caused the Grand Canyon?'

He put up a slide. 'This satellite photograph shows the uplifted plateau in northern Arizona. And notice the canyon's position. This area here on the northern rim of the Grand Canyon is about 8,000 to 9,000 feet above sea level, and here we see the south rim of the Grand Canyon which is at about 7,000 feet. So, why is the canyon positioned there?'

He indicated a particular point on the slide:

'Some geologists who have intensely studied the Grand Canyon and the surrounding area to the north and east are suspecting that this could be an enormous, breeched dam. They think there was some kind of rapid catastrophic breeching event from lakes that were situated just northeast of the Grand Canyon. So, just as mud and water came down from Mount Saint Helens to create those canyons you saw earlier, water breached this dam and the catastrophic drainage of some massive lakes were actually responsible for carving out our Grand Canyon.'

I remembered Kevin saying something similar at the debate in Harrow. I glanced across at him but noticed once again that his eyes were fixed on his phone. In fact, he seemed to be taking no notice of Steve's presentation at all. Although I wanted to concentrate on Steve's information, I was also intrigued by Kevin's preoccupation with his phone. Shifting my position slightly allowed me to look at the screen but also observe Kevin out of the corner of my eye.

It was at this point that Sue asked Steve a question.

'Steve, aren't you comparing apples with pears? Isn't the terrain at Mount Saint Helens quite different to that of the Grand Canyon? Might it be considerably easier to erode the volcanic material at the volcano than erode the sedimentary layers deposited in the Grand Canyon area?'

Steve looked quite impressed.

'It's interesting you should suggest that,' he said. 'Many of our critics have made exactly that point. They insist that the strata at the Grand Canyon would be significantly more difficult to erode than those at Mount Saint Helens. However, remember what we discussed about Engineer's Canyon? That canyon was carved out in a single day. Why? Because the material through which it was cut had only recently been deposited.

'Those who like to sneer at our suggestion that the Grand Canyon could have been eroded rapidly, conveniently miss the point that the layers through which the Grand Canyon was cut were likely to still be soft when the canyon was eroded. It's almost certain that the drainage of the lakes which provided the water to carve out the canyon would have occurred very soon after the end of the Flood. Therefore, the relative hardness of the layers we see today is irrelevant.'

Sue nodded slowly. 'Yes, I see what you mean.'

Steve then ran a number of video clips of actual footage of some relatively small floods. He followed this by displaying still photographs of significant erosional damage caused by those flood events. Steve was an excellent communicator. He kept everyone interested and delivered the information with zeal.

I could not help noticing Kevin though, and his sudden change of demeanour was puzzling. He had placed his phone on the table in front of him, but he was now staring straight ahead, his forehead furrowed with worry lines. I wondered what could have caused his concern.

At the end of the presentation, Sue and Jenny were in deep conversation, so I approached Kevin as he was alone.

'Kevin?' I said. 'Can we have a chat?'

'Sure,' he said, and we took a seat at one of the free tables.

'What's on your mind, Rob?' he asked.

'You are,' I said.

His head jerked up to look at me. 'Me? Why's that?'

'When you were sitting with Sue and me in the bar earlier, you got a message through on your phone. It seemed to cause you some discomfort. Soon after that, you asked us to excuse you because you wanted to go and sort something out. When Sue and I left the bar a few minutes later, I happened to glance into reception and saw you studying your phone intently.

'We then come in here tonight and you spent virtually the whole session either staring at your phone or gazing into the distance with a frown on your face.' I paused. 'Kevin, it's not like you. I'm getting the distinct impression that you're concerned about something. I just want to know if it's something I need to be concerned about, too.'

Throughout my little speech, Kevin had just listened. He now looked down at the floor with a thoughtful expression on his face.

After a moment, he said quietly, 'Rob, I think it's right to share it with you, but I'd like you to keep what I'm going to tell you to yourself.'

'OK,' I said.

Kevin furtively glanced around the meeting room. 'I don't want to go into it in here,' he said. 'Come up to my room and I'll fill you in.'

We both stood and made our way to the door. Suddenly remembering something, I said, 'Last night I stopped and had a chat with Sue in the bar. I'll just go and let her know that I won't be there tonight.'

Kevin nodded.

Ten minutes later, Kevin and I were sitting in his room with a coffee.

'OK, come on, Kevin,' I said. 'What's going on?'

'When you came up to Manchester with Sue to see me before we came out here, I showed you a picture of a woman on my phone.'

'Yes,' I said. 'It was the woman from the Ministry for Education.'

'That's right. And I told you that she's part of that group of people in Westminster who aren't happy with the work we're doing.'

I nodded.

'Well, that group have been discussing our trip. They want to know those who are part of our team, and they're trying to find out what we're up to.'

'But Kevin, you said your intentions for the trip were clearly laid out in that magazine of yours.'

Kevin gave a derisive laugh.

'I know, that's the amusing part of it. They appear to think that article was published to hide our true purpose.' He laughed again. 'They're probably judging us by their own standards.'

'But they're bound to be curious, aren't they? This new information doesn't really seem to explain your increased concern.'

The smile left Kevin's face.

'No,' he said. 'That's because of the message I received when we were sitting in the bar.'

He paused for a moment. I just sat and waited.

'As I said, the message was rather cryptic. When you saw me in reception, I was attempting to get a bit of clarity. My informant had got wind of the fact that two members of that anti-creation group had flown out to the States. The thing that concerned my friend was that it was the first they'd heard of it. They're concerned that either there's an inner circle within the group that they're not a part of, or even worse, they, themselves are suspected of not being reliable.'

'Is your friend really concerned? I mean, does he feel in danger?' I asked.

'Well, firstly, I'm not sure that I said it was a man, but secondly, the person in question does feel a little nervous about the situation.' He gave a slight smile as he went on.

'As far as he's aware, he's not done anything to bring suspicion on himself, but the situation does feel a bit uncomfortable.'

So, Kevin was letting me know that it was a man.

'And do you think these people are coming out here to cause problems for us?'

Kevin looked slightly baffled: 'I don't see how they can. We should obviously stay vigilant, but really, I'm more confused than concerned.'

'Do any of the others know about this?'

Kevin shook his head. 'I've mentioned it to Steve, but that's all.'

That, really, was all there was to say. So, after another ten minutes, I headed back to my room, feeling confused too.

Chapter 7
Fossils

As previously predicted, the weather on the following morning was terrible. There was low, angry cloud wherever you looked and the rain was absolutely bouncing down. It was decided that we would spend the day going through the evidence we had seen to date and Steve would answer any questions we had arising from that evidence.

We all met up in the meeting room at 9:30 am and started to review the information we had already received. Sue, Jim and I had all been making notes on a daily basis and much of the first part of the session involved us going through those notes to remind ourselves of the wealth of data we had recorded. We had many questions and added to our reams of notes.

Following a short break for coffee at 11:00am, we had been going again for about ten minutes when there was a knock at the door of the meeting room. It opened a fraction and a member of the hotel staff tentatively appeared.

'Sorry to interrupt,' she said, 'but Mr and Mrs Austin are sitting in reception.'

Steve looked delighted.

'That's great. Thanks for letting me know. I'll be along in a minute.'

He stood up.

'Excuse me for a few moments,' he said. 'The final two members of our party have arrived. I'll get them settled in and then bring them along to meet you all.'

Steve had only been gone for around five minutes when he came back with Jack and Briony Austin. They looked as if they were somewhere in their mid-forties, Briony with a tentative smile, and Jack with a stoic expression. We all stood to greet them and Steve went through the introductions.

'Would you folks like to tell us a bit about yourselves and how you came to join us on this trip?' Steve asked them.

Although Briony looked a little self-conscious, it was she who spoke up.

'It's great to join you all, folks,' she said. 'We've come up from Miami where we're involved in teaching the sciences. We've both been to Mount Saint Helens before, but it's only within the last two years that we've come across the creation arguments. Someone at our church told us that this trip was going ahead and we were desperate to come along. I'm sorry we couldn't join you for the start of the trip, but Jack wasn't able to get that time off work.'

It appeared that Jack did not want to add anything to his wife's words, but he had given a couple of confirmatory nods as she had been speaking.

‘Thanks, Briony,’ Steve said. ‘Well, it’s great to have you both aboard. I’m afraid you’ve missed two interesting excursions, but I’ll do my best to fill you in with the things we covered on those days. I understand you’ve already been on a helicopter flight and seen most of the visitor centres on your previous trip to Mount Saint Helens?’

‘That’s right,’ she said, accompanied by another nod from Jack.

Steve then explained that, due to the inclement weather, we were reviewing the details we had covered during the last couple of days. This was a good thing, as it would give Jack and Briony the chance to catch up.

Possibly because it was fresher in our minds, we seemed to be spending more time reviewing the details we had received on canyon formation. Once again, Steve made a remark asserting that the rocks and fossils supported the biblical claim of a global Flood far better than the belief in a slow and gradual build-up of the geological record.

Sue now asked a question which totally changed the direction of the discussion:

‘Steve, I know this is taking us into a totally different area, but every now and again you mention fossils. Why do you believe that fossils are such good evidence for the creation position?’

I suddenly realized that, in spite of all I had learned on the previous expedition, I still did not know much about how fossils were formed. Like Sue, I was also keen to understand why they believed that fossils were another positive argument in favour of biblical creation, when nearly everything I had been told suggested that fossils pointed to a long history of evolution.

'Well, Sue, I would say that the fossil record is one of the most persuasive arguments for rapid strata deposition. However, before I get stuck into the process of how fossilization takes place, I'd ask you to think about this for a minute. Do you have a garden at your home in England?'

'I do,' Sue confirmed.

'OK. Imagine that you find a dead bird in your garden. If that were to happen, you'd probably wrap it up in something and put it in your garbage. But let's assume that you decide to perform an experiment. You decide to leave it there for a while to see what happens. Well, let me ask you. What do you think would happen?'

Sue considered. 'It would probably soon start to stink; it would begin to rot.'

'Precisely. And as that rotting process started, what else might happen?'

'It would attract flies,' she said.

'That's right. And after a few days, those flies would lay eggs, the eggs would turn into maggots, and those maggots would start to consume the carcass. However, there may not even be enough time for that to take place. It's quite possible that you'd wake up the next day and find that your dead bird had already been removed by some other kind of scavenger: a fox, for example. The point is that we know dead animals don't hang around for very long on the surface of the ground. Your bird certainly wouldn't lie there perfectly preserved for a few hundred thousand years waiting to be slowly covered by sediment. Even if no scavenger got to your bird, most soft tissue would break down in weeks, and some probably in only a few days.'

That made sense, and I thought I could see the direction in which his argument was going.

'In fact, even harder parts like bones would start to break down in as little as a few months.'

I was not so confident about this statement, but I certainly did not have the knowledge to contradict him.

Steve continued, 'However, the rocks of our planet are full of literally billions of fossils. In many areas, these are exquisitely preserved. And, by the way, that even includes the soft tissue.'

I did decide to challenge that one.

'Is that true?' I asked. 'I thought most fossils were pretty fragmentary. Even the more complete ones I thought only consisted of the hard parts of the creature.'

'Well, you've made two statements there. Let me deal with them one at a time. As far as the first one is concerned, of course, in the majority of cases, you're right. Most fossils only include a handful of bones. However, I wasn't talking about most cases. What I'm saying is that there are plenty of instances where fossils are fairly complete. So, to deal with your second point, yes, in some of those cases, it's entirely accurate to say that soft tissue has also been exquisitely preserved.'

'OK, so, what in your view is your explanation for that level of preservation?'

'Ah,' he said, 'now we get to the real crux of the matter. Just consider for a minute what it takes to preserve a body. Normally, you would have to keep it in very cold or extremely dry conditions. The problem is that most creatures don't live in such conditions.

'However, there is another possibility. That possibility is rapid burial. If a body is cut off from oxygen, and if it's also kept from being reached by scavengers, then it has a much better chance of turning into a fossil.

'Now, it's important to recognize that, these days, it's unusual for a body to be rapidly buried. However, in the fossil record, there is abundant evidence of mass burials. Not only does this burial protect the body from scavengers, but the sediments in which the body is buried are also full of the minerals necessary for the fossilization process to take place.'

'And how long do you believe it takes to form a fossil?' Sue asked.

Steve smiled. 'That, Sue, is another great question.'

He grabbed his laptop which, up to this point, he had not used.

'Let me see if I can quickly find a couple of quotes for you.'

He opened up his computer and turned it on. 'Bear with me for a moment,' he said. 'I think you'll find this informative.'

There was a pause as he studied his screen. After some clicks of his mouse, he announced:

'Ah, here it is.' He looked up at us.

'Now, the quote I'm about to read to you comes from a book on dinosaurs written by evolutionists. So, these guys are no friends of creationists. They say this: "Fossilization is a process that can take anything from a few hours to millions of years."'[17]

He looked up from his screen, scanning the room.

'Now, please think about that statement carefully. They are actually making two claims there. They are saying that it's possible to form a fossil in just a few hours, but they are also claiming that a fossil can be formed over millions of years. But which of those two claims can be verified through observational science?

'How can they possibly know that a fossil can be formed over millions of years? Has any geologist lived long enough to verify that through empirical observational science? No. In fact, the science of geology has only been going for just over 200 years. So, even if we pieced together the scientific observations of geologists over that time, we still wouldn't be able to verify that claim. You see, this claim has nothing to do with observational science and everything to do with their beliefs.'

I noticed Sue frown again. 'OK, Steve, I understand that, but do we know that fossils can form rapidly?'

'Absolutely,' he replied assertively. 'That's exactly the point. That claim can be tested empirically. This statement goes on to say: "The amount of time that it takes for a bone to become completely permineralized is highly variable. If the ground water is heavily ladened with minerals in solution, the process can happen rapidly. Modern bones that fall into mineral springs can become permineralized within a matter of weeks." So, we know this process can happen rapidly.'

I glanced at Sue. She was sitting looking at Steve with a shocked expression on her face.

Steve noticed her inward struggle:

‘I know, Sue. You’ve asked me before why we don’t get to hear any of this. Well, here’s yet another instance where the public are told one thing, but many geologists are fully aware that the truth is very different. If you ask any child in school in Europe or the States how long it takes to form a fossil, they will nearly all say millions of years. But here’s an evolutionist saying that it can happen very quickly indeed.’

There was silence in the room as Steve allowed us to process this fact.

Then Jim joined the discussion: ‘And I suspect you believe that a global Flood would result in conditions which would be ideal for this process to take place?’

‘That’s right. If there was a Flood like the one described in the book of Genesis, we would have a heck of a lot of ground water which would be heavily laden with minerals.’

Sue looked thoughtful. ‘Steve, I don’t want you to go into it now but, at some point, can you or Jenny explain in greater detail the processes you believe were at work during the Flood?’

‘Certainly,’ he said. ‘One of us will grab you later.’

‘Thanks,’ Sue said. ‘Also, can you let us have the source of any quotes you give us while we are with you on this trip?’

‘Of course I will.’

Personally, I was keen to get back to the information on fossils. ‘Steve? Can you show us some more evidence confirming that fossils form rapidly?’

He smiled. ‘Absolutely.’ He turned back to his laptop:

‘In fact, let me display some of these images on the screen.’

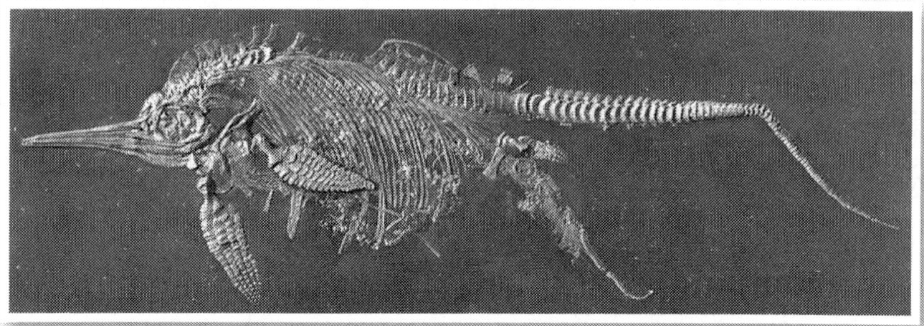

Image 11: An ichthyosaur fossilized in the act of giving birth
Photo by Creation Ministries International. Used with permission. Creation Magazine, Vol 23:1 (Dec 2000–Feb 2001), pp. 10–11. Web address for the article https://creation.com/the-earth-how-old-does-it-look.

After a few seconds delay as he connected up with the system, he displayed his first slide.

'Here's an interesting piece of evidence,' he said. 'This is an ichthyosaur fossilized in the act of giving birth' [see image 11].

He displayed the image on the screen; it was incredible. Every head leaned forward towards the screen, scrutinizing the strange image.

'This creature was, presumably, happily swimming along looking forward to her new baby ichthyosaur when a wave choked with sediments buried her alive and cut her off from scavengers. Those sediments solidified and the creature immediately began to fossilize. To preserve a creature in the act of giving birth proves that it has to be a rapid burial.

'What about this one?'

Steve put another image up on the screen. This was a picture of a fish which appeared to have been buried as it ate its lunch [see image 12].

Image 12: A fish fossilized in the process of eating its lunch
Public domain.

'Fish decompose very rapidly,' Steve said. 'And yet, we can find fossils like this one. Not only do we have the bones preserved but we also have the soft parts, including the fins of the fish, fossilized intact. Again, this can only happen if the animal is buried in an instant.'

'That's amazing!' Sue said in astonishment.

'But we also have fossilized jellyfish,' Steve continued. 'These creatures don't have any hard parts at all. So, if these creatures are going to be preserved in the fossil record, it has to be a rapid process. There is no other possible explanation.'

Again, there was a period of silence as we considered the implications of what Steve was telling us, all eyes on the image on the screen.

Sue had another question: 'Steve, how long would you say that it takes rock to form?'

‘That’s another surprising detail,’ he said. ‘Let me find another comment from an evolutionist.’

He spent a few moments searching around his files looking for the relevant quote. Eventually he found it.

‘Here we go,’ he said:

‘This is taken from an article called “Magic in the Marsh”. This involved some geological research which was going on in Norfolk in the east of England. It said this: “Without any regard to the laws of geology, mud on the marsh is hardening into stone in a few years, rather than the thousands it usually takes.”[18]

‘Now, let me stop there for a moment, because here we have the same problem that I pointed out before. How do they know that it usually takes thousands of years to form rock? And the answer is that they don’t. It’s just an assumption on their part. But now, we’re going to see that their assumptions are absolutely wrong.

‘The article goes on to say: “The rock was forming faster than anybody had ever believed possible, with one stone creating itself in just six months.” So, can you see what the problem was? It was their beliefs, and that’s what they’re admitting here.

‘This quote ends with this statement: “They often contain beautifully preserved fossils where the details of the soft flesh of the creature are caught as well as the bone, as it had no time to rot before the rock formed around it.’ So, hopefully you can see that it doesn’t take thousands of years to form rock. It just takes the right chemical conditions in the sediments.’

This was mind blowing. Rock forming quickly? I shook my head in bewilderment as Steve continued: ‘But there’s additional evidence which supports the Flood model of the creation of fossils. That is the fact that many of these fossils are found in fine sediment layers. Fine layers don't usually last that long in the present, because burrowing animals disrupt those layers as they dig for food.

'However, that's really interesting because, in the fossil record, these disrupted layers are rare. But you see, that's precisely the point. If these layers were laid down quickly in a global Flood, this is exactly the pattern we would expect to find: mineral-rich water rapidly laying down many layers over a wide area. But, additionally, it's not what we would expect to see if the present is the key to the past. Why? Because the processes we see at work in the world today are not reflected in the evidence we see in the rocks. We have now found literally hundreds of millions of fossils. And yet, there are many of the more honest evolutionists who will admit that the transitional fossils, which are so crucial to the theory of evolution, are still missing from the fossil record.

'When Darwin was doing his work in the 1800s, it was reasonable to point out that not many fossils had been found, so it was understandable that they hadn't found these transitions. However, we're now well over 150 years after Darwin wrote *The Origin of the Species*. So now, this is not a reasonable position to take.

'If evolution were true, we should have found hundreds of thousands of fossils which are clearly transitional between one kind of creature and another. Although, over the years, there have been many confident claims made about certain fossils, evolutionists of a more honest persuasion have admitted that there is significant doubt about all of these.'

Steve then told us about creatures, alive in our world today, which have also turned up as fossils in dinosaur layers.[19] These include marine invertebrates, amphibians, reptiles, birds, as well as various types of mammals.

'Incidentally,' Steve continued, 'that's another interesting point. Evolutionists will occasionally admit that mammals have been found in the dinosaur layers, but they'll say that they were small; something like a shrew. However, this is totally misleading.'

I was shocked: 'So, are you saying that there have been many different kinds of modern creatures found in those same rock layers that contain dinosaur fossils?'

'Absolutely,' he said. 'Now, again, it's true that some of those fossils are fragmentary, but others have been found which are pretty much intact. Also, many of them look virtually identical to their modern relatives.'

Sue looked incredibly frustrated, fist clenched again as she said,

'If that's the case, how can they insist that evolution is so certain?'

Steve gave an ironic laugh.

'Mystifying, isn't it? But you see, in almost all cases, the fossilized creature is given a different genus and species name to its modern relative. This, in spite of the fact that the fossilized creature appears almost indistinguishable from its living counterpart. The naming of the fossils in this way allows the evolutionist to give the impression that evolution has happened, even though, really, it hasn't. Just because the fossils have been given different taxonomic names, doesn't mean they should have been.

'By the way, this is also an issue for animals alive in our world today. There are animals that have been assigned to a different species, but they can interbreed and they have fertile offspring. So, should they really be considered different species?'

There was a pause; Jack shifted in his seat.

Steve went on: 'But this problem also works in reverse. There are creatures whose skeletons look quite different from each other, but which they say are the same genus and species. Think about our domestic dog breeds for example. They all come under the taxonomic classification *Canis familiaris*, but the skulls of many of these dogs look completely different from each other. If you compare the skull of a boxer with the skull of a German Shepherd, you would be forgiven for considering them to be completely different animals. Nevertheless, we're confidently told that these breeds are the same species. And by the way, I would agree with that.'

Steve turned to his computer, and the momentary pause gave Sue an opportunity to interject another thought.

'So, you seem to be saying that the people who named these fossilized creatures have got it wrong. Many of the creatures found in these dinosaur layers are actually just the same as the ones we have around today?'

'Exactly right,' he said, straightening up. 'At some point I'll show you some photographs of the living creatures alongside their fossilized relatives. I think the similarity will be completely obvious to you.'

I was shocked by the possible implications of this.

'In that case,' I said, 'the whole evolutionary paradigm could just be an illusion based on incorrectly named fossil creatures.'

Steve gave a short nod. 'Amazing, isn't it? But as I keep saying, very, very few people are aware of any of this. The general public is never given these details. So, is it any wonder that most folk think people like us who question evolution are completely nuts?

'Unfortunately, these modern creatures are very rarely displayed alongside dinosaurs in the museums of the world. You have to assume that this is a conscious decision taken by the museum authorities. After all, what would the general public think if they saw all these modern creatures living alongside the dinosaurs?'

Steve's revelation left me dumbfounded. If I had any remaining thoughts of support for the evolutionary position, they were slipping away fast. As a layman, with my limited knowledge of the subject, to me, a global Flood seemed like a much better fit with the physical evidence than the slow and gradual explanation proffered by the secular world. Sue's mental wrestling was written all over her face. Lunch was a welcome break; my head was positively spinning.

In the afternoon, we returned to reviewing the previous day's work. Although a day in the classroom was not really what I had wanted, by the end of the day I reasoned that it had been extremely helpful as a means of reinforcing those things I had learned over the last two days and hoped it would help me to retain it.

When our discussion finally came to an end, I decided to nip up to my room to get the leaflets I had picked up from the Johnston Ridge Observatory. The details we were receiving from Steve and Steph interested me greatly, and I was very keen to understand as much as I could about the volcano and its recent eruptions.

Although my intention had been to go straight back down to the others, I took the opportunity to send Sam a quick message.

'Hi Sam, how are things? It's chucking it down with rain here, so this morning we had a session on fossils. However, what I'm really interested in is about you and your unwanted friends. Any update? Rob.'

There was no response. I waited, confused, as Sam always had his phone to hand and nearly always responded immediately. A few more minutes passed, but still nothing. I told myself that we all have those times where responding is impossible. All the same, given some of Sam's previous news, I was a little concerned.

As I rejoined the others in the bar area, Sue was on her feet and staring resignedly through the window, her back to the room.

Standing just behind her, seeing her reflection in the window, I asked, 'What's up?'

'I was going to ask Steve about some of the comments I'd jotted down on canyons,' she said. 'I left my notebook in the door of Kevin's Land Rover.'

She motioned towards the window: 'Look at it, Rob'.

I looked out at the heavy driving rain. It was a dismal day.

I decided to play the gallant young gent: 'I'll nip out and get it for you.'

'Oh, no, Rob, you'll get soaked. I'll ask him about it at some other point.'

'It won't take a couple of minutes,' I said. 'They'll probably have an umbrella in reception.'

I asked Kevin for his keys and left the bar.

As I approached the desk, the receptionist was already talking to another customer. Not wishing to eavesdrop, I hung back a bit and waited.

The girl suddenly announced, 'Yes, sure. The rest rooms are round that corner just before you get to the restaurant.' She waved an arm in the general direction.

The man hurried off, promising to return shortly.

The receptionist looked slightly puzzled as she watched the man disappear round the corner. Then, noticing me she turned to deal with my query, offering me a warm smile.

I explained the situation and asked if she could lend me an umbrella.

She glanced through the hotel entrance:

'Not very nice, is it, sir?'

She reached under her desk and produced a large golf umbrella.

'Will that do?' she asked.

It would do very nicely. I thanked her and promised to return it shortly.

As I ran out of the front door of the hotel, I was hunching forward and holding the umbrella almost directly in front of me to protect myself from the driving rain. As a result, I almost ran headlong into the side of a battered old army jeep. It had been abandoned just a few feet away from the hotel entrance in a most inconvenient spot.

A couple of minutes later, brolly returned and notebook in hand, I re-entered the bar and handed the book to Sue.

Sue's book and the questions therein guided the conversation for the next couple of hours. At the end of that time, the discussion seemingly having reached a natural end, Sue was looking thoughtful.

'You alright?' I asked.

She visibly returned from wherever her mind had taken her.

'Yes, fine, thanks. Excuse me, Rob, I need to go and have a chat with Jenny.'

I remembered her earlier desire to speak to Steve or Jenny about the Flood. I smiled inwardly, thinking how appropriate that was given the current weather.

'OK,' I said, 'I'll see you in the restaurant.'

She smiled and headed in Jenny's direction.

As I had still heard nothing from Sam, I excused myself from the rest of the group to return to my room to send him another message. As I stood and turned towards the stairs, I nearly bumped into Steve. He was standing looking towards reception with a puzzled look on his face.

'Everything OK, Steve?' I enquired.

'Oh, hi, Rob. Sorry, I was miles away. Yes, I'm fine, thanks. It's

OK, I've just seen someone who I think I recognize, but I can't think where I know him from.'

I nodded and continued on my way to my room.

Although it would be late in Britain, given my growing unease, I told myself it was completely justified to attempt to send Sam another message.

I sent it and waited. Nothing. I frowned. What was going on? He had not mentioned going out anywhere. Not, of course, that he had to keep me informed of all his plans, but this was particularly unusual for Sam.

After our evening meal, Sue and I met up in the hotel bar. We spent some time going over the afternoon's discussion. However, after a while, Sue sensed that I was distracted and asked me if there was anything wrong.

I told her about the lack of response from Sam and explained how out of character it was.

'Maybe he's out with someone,' she said. 'Is he in a relationship?'

I shook my head: 'Not as far as I know.'

At that moment, I spotted Jack and Briony coming into the bar.

'Oh, look who it is,' I said. Sue turned and looked over her shoulder. and I gave them a little wave; Jack noticed us and gave Briony a nudge. I stood as they walked in our direction.

'Hi guys,' I said. 'Can I get you a drink?'

Briony glanced at Jack who gave a short nod.

'Thanks, Rob,' she said, 'that would be nice.'

As they sat down at the table, I went to the bar to order a pineapple juice for Briony and a coke for Jack. When I returned,

Sue was explaining her background in geology and how fascinating she had found our first couple of trips.

Although we were all sitting at the same table hearing the same words, the conversation was very much between Sue and Briony. I glanced at Jack out of the corner of my eye and got the feeling that he was used to listening to Briony's conversations rather than participating in them. I chuckled to myself inwardly, wondering how many husbands might be able to identify with that situation. I attempted to engage him in conversation.

'So, Jack,' I said, 'Briony said that you'd only recently been exposed to the creationist arguments. Can I ask how you first came across them?'

I was half expecting a protracted period of silence as he tried to muster the courage to produce some kind of verbal response. However, to my surprise, he answered immediately.

'It all happened completely out of the blue,' he said.

I was shocked. Not just over his willingness to speak, but also over the strength and tone of his voice. To be honest, I had half expected him to respond with a nod. However, his words came out confidently and firmly. There was absolutely no trace of the timidity or hesitancy I had expected.

'One of our friends at church asked me if I'd watch a DVD with him,' he said. 'He explained that it involved the creation/evolution debate and was presented by a biologist who believed in a literal six-day creation about 6,000 years ago. I told him that I'd watch it with him, but that it sounded like a lot of nonsense to me. He said, rather thoughtfully, that that had been his initial reaction too. His comment suggested to me that, at least in part, he had changed his mind.'

I had been so surprised by Jack's response, that it took me a couple of seconds to find my own voice. 'And I'm guessing it changed yours too?' I questioned.

So as not to completely disappoint me, Jack gave one of his nods.

'Rob, I couldn't believe it. Although I've been a Christian for years, I'd never heard anyone in the Church speak on the subject. It's as if the Church has totally handed all things scientific over to the secular world. But as I listened to the details on the DVD, I realized that I knew virtually nothing about the subjects being discussed.'

'And what were those subjects,' I asked.

'Oh, all sorts of things. Design features in the animal kingdom for which evolution has no explanation, radiometric dating, the process of fossilization, the creation of proteins; all sorts of different problems for Darwin's theory.'

I had encountered some of these subjects on my last trip with Kevin, so I did have a certain amount of limited knowledge. However, I was keen to learn about Jack's own experience.

'OK, you say that you didn't have much knowledge in these areas. So, what happened next?'

'Well, I tried to correct that. In fact, that's where things started to get a bit strange. It's funny; I'd never really been convinced about Darwinian evolution. I had asked myself if God might possibly have used evolution as his means of creation, but I didn't think that likely. However, I had very definitely been convinced about the billions of years of earth's history; I thought the idea of a young earth was totally ridiculous.

'As a result, this was the area where I felt I really needed some answers. I thought I had the perfect solution to that. One of my friends at the church was a geologist. I was pretty sure he'd be able to tell me if the information I'd obtained from the DVD was accurate.'

At this point, Jack paused in his account.

'Presumably you asked him about it?' I prompted.

'I did.'

There was another pause. 'And?'

He looked at me with a confused expression on his face.

'I'll never forget it,' he said. 'One of the details on the DVD concerned creatures called crinoids. I hadn't got a clue what a crinoid is. However, the point was that the guy on the DVD had described them as little marine animals. Well, my geologist friend wasn't happy. He said that if this guy on the DVD was really a biologist, he'd know that a crinoid is a plant.'

"And is it?" I asked.

'I'll get to that in a minute,' he said with a wave of his hand. 'The point is that, at the time, I was really pleased. As far as I was concerned, here was something I could check up on. Anyway, I went onto the net to do a bit of digging. Half an hour later, I had my answer. I printed off a whole A4 sheet of information on crinoids. At the top of that sheet was a single line stating that crinoids are categorized as zoological, not botanical. The guy on the DVD was right; they are animals.

'So,' he said laughing, 'perhaps he was a biologist after all. I've never had the guts to ask my friend if that meant he wasn't really a geologist.'

I smiled. 'That was probably wise. Did you present your friend with the sheet?'

'I did but, to be honest, I'd rather not go into that. Let's just say that I wasn't very happy with the response I got.'

'So, what happened next?' I asked.

'I started to gather information on the creation/evolution subject from various sources. I approached my geologist friend to see if he'd help me out with it, but he refused. He said he didn't have the time. He wouldn't discuss it at all. I hope, one day, our relationship can get back to what it once was. However, unfortunately, I won't be holding my breath.'

He shrugged his shoulders and we glanced at the girls. They were still deep in conversation.

After a short silence, he went on: 'The tough thing is that I miss the guy. We had a really good relationship, but I'm afraid I can't see that being restored any time soon. Apart from anything else, his theology is very much at the liberal end of the spectrum. If anything, my own theology is going further in the opposite direction.'

'Hmmm,' I said, 'I can see how that might create a bit of friction.'

Jack shrugged helplessly. 'Oh well, there's not much I can do about it.'

'So, what's the situation now?' I asked. 'What's your current position on the age issue?'

'Oh, I'm almost totally convinced of a young earth. I still have one or two small queries, but they're not that significant. I'm guessing this week will strengthen that position even further.'

It was fascinating to hear his experiences, but I did find the account rather baffling.

Jack then asked me how I'd become involved in the subject. So, for the next hour or so, I told him about my trip to the Congo. Not surprisingly, he spent most of that time staring at me with his mouth agape. But I really appreciated the opportunity to have that chat with him and begin to get to know him.

As I headed to my room that night, I checked my phone again. Still no reply from Sam.

Chapter 8
Spirit Lake

After breakfast on Thursday, 8 August, we set off for our first visit to Spirit Lake. It was a beautiful morning, and the ground was nearly dry, despite the torrential rain yesterday.

I was very much looking forward to hearing about the logs. The ghostly sight of them on Tuesday had really piqued my interest. Having parked up, we strolled down to the shoreline where we prepared ourselves to receive our next lot of information. Steve turned to face us with his back to the lake.

'OK folks,' he said, 'this morning, we're going to be discussing logs. Some time ago, a creation geologist did some fantastic work here at Spirit Lake.[20]

'He noticed a number of sticks floating horizontally on the surface of the water. In fact, if you look over there, you can see some floating sticks today. Anyway, as he looked a bit more closely, he noticed two sticks floating upright. They were floating off the bottom and there was an inch or so sticking out of the water. Next, he noticed some sticks standing in an upright position actually on the bottom of the lake. Then he noticed that there were a number of sticks lying prone on the bottom.

'As he considered the sticks, he began to formulate a theory. He imagined the wind blowing these sticks over to the edge of the lake and becoming grounded. Then he began to wonder about the logs. He knew that there were an estimated half a million logs floating on Spirit Lake at the time, and he wondered if it was possible that some of them could also have moved into an upright floating position. He reasoned that, having to bear the weight of the tree above, the base of the tree would probably be denser wood. If that were true, the root end would be heavier and sink; whereas the upper part of the log could float, and the whole log could go into upright floating position in the water. Subsequently, he reasoned that, sometime later, the whole log could become waterlogged and sink to the bottom of the lake. If this were the case, it might be possible to find upright logs deposited on the bottom of Spirit Lake.

'Well, in the mid-1980s, this scientist took a boat out onto Spirit Lake. It was kitted out with sonar equipment which enabled them to read the profile of the bottom of the lake. The sonar reflector readings confirmed the geologist's suspicions. He estimated that there must be around 20,000 upright objects standing on the bottom of Spirit Lake.'

Steve looked around our group.

'In a few minutes, we will also be taking a boat out on to the lake. It won't be equipped with sonar, but it'll allow you to see the logs. The horizontal logs will be easy to spot, but the logs which have gone into upright floating position won't be quite as obvious.'

As Steve finished his introduction, I noticed Kevin studying his phone. He probably sensed me looking at him as he briefly flicked a glance in my direction. After returning his concentration to his phone for another few seconds, he looked at me again and gave a brief nod, but did not say anything.

Soon enough, after a brief safety run through, we were all aboard a small boat and heading out into the centre of the lake.

'We want you to have a firsthand viewing of these floating logs,' Steve said. 'Hopefully, we'll be able to find some that have swung down into an upright floating position.'

And that is exactly what happened. We chugged along until we began to see some of the logs ahead of us. The note of the engine dropped and we started to slow a little. The skipper turned slightly to starboard so we had the logs on the port beam. It was fascinating. Although we had already seen the logs from the helicopter, viewing them from the boat was somehow more satisfying. While there was a steady low throb from the diesel engine, this was much more peaceful than the clattering of the chopper two days previously. Being among the logs was both eerie and tranquil at the same time.

Steve pointed out an area of water where two logs were floating side-by-side. One of them was almost completely submerged, while the other still had a significant amount of the tree showing above the surface of the water.

'You see how some trees have become more waterlogged than

others?' he said. 'The one nearest to us may only be a few days from going into upright floating position.'

We gently moved forward past the edge of the log mat.

All of a sudden, Jenny gave an excited shout and pointed across the water.

'Look!' she said. 'Isn't that one of the upright logs?'

After a quick request from Steve, the boat changed direction and slowly headed towards the area of the lake that Jenny had indicated. Sure enough, there was the top of a log sticking up above the surface of the water [see image 13]. This caused a stir of excitement and it gave Steve the opportunity to give a further

Image 13: Vertical logs floating in Spirit Lake
Public domain.

explanation of how the logs found their way to the bottom of the lake. The boat trip and our instruction continued for another hour.

When we broke for an early lunch, I took the opportunity to send Sam another message.

'Hi Sam, how are things? When we get back, I'm going to have loads to discuss with you. We're having some amazing info today about logs floating on Spirit Lake. However, I'm a bit concerned. You didn't respond to my messages yesterday. Everything OK? Rob.'

I waited. Again, there was no reply. My stomach lurched. I couldn't understand it. Why the silence?

My concerns about Sam were interrupted by Kevin who now strolled across to me.

'I received another message from my friend earlier,' he said.

'I guessed you had.'

Kevin looked out across the lake. 'I'm even more confused. The people who I was told had flown out to the States haven't followed us up this way; they've gone down to Florida.'

'Florida? Why on earth would they go down there?'

Kevin shrugged: 'No idea. Maybe they've got friends this side of the pond they need to speak to. My informant says he'll let me know if he gets any further information.'

When our afternoon session began, I had still heard nothing from Sam.

Steve looked round our group:

'OK, folks, I want you to use your imagination for a minute.

What do you think Spirit Lake might look like if you drained it?' He waved a hand towards the water and said: 'Might it look like a forest of trees that had grown at that location at some point in the past?'

He paused for us to consider his suggestion, so I did. I supposed it was possible.

'But we know how these trees found their way to the bottom of Spirit Lake. They may give the appearance of having grown here, but we know they were ripped out of the ground somewhere else and then deposited at this new location. The observational science is absolutely undeniable. But remember I said that there was quite a bit of sedimentation going on in the lake. Well, because this is still occurring, the root ends of the trees get buried at different levels. Those trees that drop down first are buried at a lower level than those which dropped down later.'

That all made sense.

Steve continued: 'Now, imagine a couple of thousand years go by. During that time, further erosion and sedimentation occurs. Also, there are further eruptions from Mount Saint Helens. The resulting layers of strata completely bury those trees that have dropped to the bottom of Spirit Lake. Imagine geologists coming across this scene. Because so much time has passed, they're completely unaware of the eruptions and subsequent events in the 1980s.'

Steve looked around the group: 'Is it possible that those geologists might consider that those trees once grew in that location?'

Again, he paused to give us time to consider the question.

I was struck by a possible problem with his theory. If the trees were complete with branches, I could see how the ancient forest idea might be a reasonable conclusion. However, all the branches appeared to have been ripped off, either by the initial waves or as the logs had rubbed together in the lake.

'Steve, if these trees had grown here, wouldn't they have branches on them?'

Steve gave a slight smile. 'That's a reasonable question.'

He scanned round the faces in the group.

'I'd like you all to keep that thought in the back of your mind as we go on here. As you will all be aware, the scientists within the conventional scientific community always think in terms of millions of years of geological time. There is no room in their minds to even consider an alternative. In fact, not many of them are even aware that a credible alternative explanation exists. Part of our job is to do our best to educate them.'

He looked over at Sue, and then to where Jim was standing next to Kevin. 'Sue, Jim, you're both involved in education in Britain.'

He shifted his attention to Jack and Briony. 'And you guys are involved in education in the U.S. Our greatest hope from this trip is that you begin to understand just how much the general public have been brainwashed into accepting the huge period of time that this planet is supposed to have existed. As I hope you're beginning to appreciate, this idea about how logs might float and then get buried is completely different to the conventional way of thinking.'

Steve paused as he scanned round the group again.

'Now, wouldn't it be amazing if we discovered a place on earth where this kind of evidence could be found? What if we found somewhere which had fossilized tree trunks buried in the ground? Imagine that these trees were buried with their root ends at different levels. Furthermore, wouldn't it be great if these trees happened to be buried in volcanic strata? If we found such a place, surely that would be great evidence suggesting that a similar catastrophic event may have happened in the past? Well, I'm now going to tell you about just such a place.'

He reached into his bag and produced some sheets of paper; these he now handed out to the group. As with the handout Steph had provided a few days earlier, there were a number of sheets of A4 stapled together.

This time, the heading on the front sheet was: 'The Fossil Forests of Specimen Ridge'.

As Sue spotted the title, she gave a little gasp, causing me to glance in her direction.

'You OK?' I enquired.

She was staring at the title, her hand covering her mouth.

For a moment, she did not say anything, her eyes wide as she looked down at the paper. 'Rob, this is crazy.'

'What do you mean?' I asked.

'I think I know where Steve's going with this.' She looked up at me. 'I've heard about these fossilized trees. They're supposed to represent multiple forests which supposedly grew at Yellowstone Park over millions of years.'

Steve overheard Sue's remarks and beamed with delight.

'Praise God,' he said. 'It sounds as if Sue is already aware of some of the information I'm going to give you now.'

Sue whispered, 'We'll chat about it later. Just listen to this.'

Steve looked down at his own sheets and began to speak:

'There's a sign at Yellowstone National Park describing the fossil forests in the Specimen Ridge area. The words are printed on your first sheet. I'll just give you a moment to read them.'

I looked down at the front sheet. The sign said:

Across the valleys rise the slopes of Specimen Ridge. But the forest you see there today is only the latest chapter in a remarkable story. Buried within the volcanic rocks that compose the mountain are 27 distinct layers of fossil forest that flourished 50 million years ago. Yellowstone's fossil forests are unique. Many stumps still stand upright in the same sites where they grew millions of years ago.

'Please note that the sign keeps referring to millions of years,' Steve said, 'and the fact that the trees actually grew at that location.'

On some of the other sheets there were photographs of beautifully fossilized logs standing up out of the hillside. Steve explained that natural erosion had removed the volcanic strata from around some of the upright stumps.

'You can see the modern forest growing there today,' he said, 'as well as what we're told is the ancient forest or series of forests that are supposed to have grown there in the distant past. According to the evolutionists, this is categorical proof of millions of years of geological time.'

Steve gave us a few moments to study the photographs and read the accompanying blurb.

Everyone was looking at their papers.

'If Mount Saint Helens erupted again and swamped the Spirit Lake area with vast amounts of volcanic material, the logs currently standing on the bottom of the lake would be completely covered. Wouldn't this perfectly match the evidence from Yellowstone?'

Sue and I looked at each other. I suspected we were having identical thoughts.

But Steve was not finished.

'There's another fascinating detail about these trees. We've been able to dig out some of the logs in Specimen Ridge, and we find that the roots often terminate abruptly about 3 feet from the base of the trunk. The roots don't taper to a point as roots normally do; they've been broken off. Isn't that interesting? This suggests that the trees have been uprooted and redeposited. When you add this to Rob's observation of there being no branches, the evidence becomes even more interesting.

'However, there's an even more compelling aspect of this evidence. We've done studies of the tree rings at Yellowstone, and logs buried at different levels have a correlating sequence of tree rings, indicating that the logs which now have their root ends fossilized at different levels grew at the same time. Although I'm sure the evolutionists would deny it, this data falsifies the

"Petrified Forest" interpretation and makes a mockery of some of the signs that we see at Yellowstone.

'Each of these twenty-seven distinct layers of petrified forests are supposed to represent huge periods of time, so we're told that the whole thing must represent a massive amount of time. It's ironic really. Creationists are accused of being ignorant and uninformed because we don't accept that this cliff at Yellowstone is proof of millions of years. However, the boot is firmly on the other foot. It's the evolutionists who are displaying their ignorance. If they would only take an objective look at this evidence from Mount Saint Helens, they may also have their eyes opened to the truth at Yellowstone.

'Really, it should be obvious to anyone displaying any degree of honesty that there's another perfectly reasonable interpretation of the evidence.'

Sue and I were just left staring at each other. For my part, I was absolutely amazed that so much physical evidence existed that appeared to support a young earth.

On the way back to base, I travelled in the same vehicle as Jim Redfern. Apart from our discussion during our excursion to view the rock layers, I had not really had a great deal to do with him. However, we now found ourselves chatting away as if we had known each other for years. In spite of our differences on the previous expedition, we seemed to be developing an easy-going relationship.

On the face of it, as far as science was concerned, Jim's views appeared to be experiencing a 180 degree about turn. Most of the journey we chatted about the evidence and the creationist interpretation of that evidence. While he was not totally convinced about all their claims, bearing in mind his previous stance, he was remarkably open to Steve's arguments.

Although Jim's main area of expertise was in genetics, and in spite of the fact that he had come on this trip to learn more about geology, I discovered that he also had a tremendous interest in zoology. In fact, he told me that if he could have his time over again, he would have pursued a career involving the study of the larger mammals. He confided that he was very much hoping to see elk on this trip, as he was aware that they were commonly sighted in the Mount Saint Helens area. Admittedly, I would quite like to see one too.

On arriving back at the hotel, Steve came to find Sue and me before we went in for our meal.

'Hi, folks,' he said. 'Tomorrow morning, we're going back to Spirit Lake.'

This surprised me. I had got the impression that we had finished discussing the logs and mentioned this to Steve.

He nodded as he explained, 'Well, yes, in a way, we have. Tomorrow we're going to be considering a slightly different subject. However, it's still related to the logs.

'This is something I should have mentioned before,' he added, 'but can I ask if either of you folks have any experience of diving?'

Sue shook her head. I, on the other hand, did have a little experience. I had gone through a phase of being fascinated by the sea floor. I had done some snorkelling on family holidays and had wished to take it a step further. As a result, for my twenty-first birthday, my parents paid for me to have some lessons in scuba diving. However, it had been a fleeting interest and I had done no further diving for nearly a decade.

I mentioned this to Steve.

'Why do you ask?' I said.

'Well, normally there is no swimming or diving allowed in Spirit Lake. However, when it comes to scientific research, people are allowed to go and have a look around. It just so happens that we have a couple of divers who are scheduled to gather some samples from the bottom of the lake tomorrow. In the past, we've helped out these guys by sharing some of our research with them. A little earlier, I contacted them to ask if it would be possible for one of our team to go down with them. I've just received a message confirming that they've obtained permission to take a third diver. However, they do require an assurance that that person has experience.'

'I did receive a certificate,' I said, 'but I obviously haven't brought it with me. I'll probably need reminding what to do.'

'I'm sure you'll be fine,' he said.

It was, therefore, decided that I would go down with these two divers to get some firsthand knowledge of the bottom of the lake. What an unexpected turn of events. I thanked Steve very much for giving me the opportunity. Diving, I can cope with; just do not ask me to go up in a chopper again!

After the evening meal, Sue and I were just about to leave the restaurant when Briony called out to Sue. We had not spoken to

Briony or Jack that day and we strolled over to their table to have a chat.

'Hi guys. Had a good day?' Sue enquired.

Briony was beaming. 'It's amazing,' she said enthusiastically. 'When Steve told us about those trees at Yellowstone, we couldn't believe it. There's all this incredible evidence, but no one knows about it. It's scandalous!'

Briony talked with her whole body, her hands always on the go and her face awash with expression. Quite the contrast to Jack who appeared to have retreated back into another bout of nodding as his sole method of communication. He seemed focused on the conversation but satisfied to listen to the views of others rather than share his own thoughts. I surmised that he was a bit of a thinker. I also suspected that maybe he was happier to open up in a one-to-one situation than contribute in a group setting. So, I tried to encourage him into the discussion.

'What did you think of it, Jack?'

He glanced up at me. 'Like I said last night, when I first came across this creation stuff, I thought it was total garbage. As you know, I've already done some of my own digging, but today's information takes it on to another level.'

'We're going for a chat in the bar,' Sue said. 'Would you like to join us?'

Briony smiled. 'That's very kind of you, but we've got an online meeting with some friends back in Florida this evening. Some visitors have come out from the UK to speak to a group we're members of.'

Briony glanced down at her watch. 'In fact, Jack, we better move it.' She looked back up at Sue. 'Because of the time difference, the meeting has already started, but we said we'd join them after our meal to hear these speakers.'

Bidding them goodbye, Sue and I headed for the bar and looked for a place to sit.

As soon as we were settled, Sue asked me if I had heard anything from Sam.

'No. I sent a message again earlier but haven't heard a thing.'

'I'm sure he's alright, Rob. Maybe his phone is on the blink or something.'

I did not respond. It probably appeared to Sue as if I was worrying unnecessarily, but I knew Sam and she did not. Even if there was a problem with Sam's phone, I was sure he would have found some way of letting me know.

I decided to tell Sue what Sam had said about people watching his house. 'He's been making light of it,' I said, 'but he wouldn't normally say anything unless he was fairly concerned.'

She looked thoughtful. 'I'd give it another day or so, and if he's still not been in touch, maybe you need to speak to the police. Is there anyone else you could contact to check up on him?'

'Not really,' I said. 'We don't really have mutual friends. I've met a few of his mates, but I don't have contact numbers for them.'

We sat in silence for a few moments considering the situation. Then I said, 'You're probably right. I'll give it another day and then contact the police.'

I did my best to put Sam out of my mind and enjoy Sue's company.

Sue and I began discussing the evidence we'd seen on the trip so far, as well as the information Steve had given us the day before. Sue was completely riveted over the geology—much more so than myself—but I was still finding it interesting. Given her much greater knowledge on the subject, I quizzed Sue over the evidence we had already studied. Sue took the opportunity to run through all the evidence again.

A quizzical look suddenly appeared on Sue's face. 'Rob, you will be straight with me about all this, won't you?'

I was slightly taken a back. 'What do you mean?' I enquired.

'I'm not used to people being quite so interested in my subject.' She paused for a moment and looked me straight in the eyes. 'I don't want you to pretend to be interested just because you think it will please me.'

I grinned at her. 'Do you think that's what's going on?'

She flushed slightly. 'I hope not. It's nice to meet someone who takes an interest in the same things as you. But it's more important to me that my friends are honest with me. I'm not just talking about my interests, either. I want my friends to be honest with me about everything. Is that a promise you feel you can make to me?'

Our conversation appeared to have become a little more intense. I was not sure where it was going.

'I think so,' I said.

'Just "think so"?' she queried.

I laughed. 'OK,' I said, 'I promise.'

She smiled faintly but continued staring into my eyes. I had an uncomfortable sense that she was staring deep into my soul. As the moment lengthened, my feeling of unease grew. It was almost as if she were capable of seeing all my secrets.

I laughed, slightly uneasily. 'What are you looking for?' I asked.

'Integrity,' she said.

She was certainly brutally honest, I thought. 'And did you find any?'

Sue smiled mysteriously. 'Wouldn't you like to know,' she said. 'Anyway, at least to some extent, trust has to be earned.'

Smile or not, I was not exactly thrilled about Sue questioning my honesty.

'Well, whether you believe me or not, I am interested in the information we have received. I'm probably not as riveted as you, but nevertheless, I do think it's fascinating.'

In fact, the information we had received earlier that day about the trees in Spirit Lake had really impressed me. It certainly did appear to replicate the fossil-tree evidence from Yellowstone Park.

We had been discussing the trees for a while when suddenly, Sue stopped, staring straight ahead.

'You OK?' I asked.

She closed her eyes. A tear squeezed out from the corner of her right eye. A split second later, a matching tear from the corner of her left. Both started running slowly down her cheeks.

'What's wrong, Sue?'

She did not reply. More tears followed the original ones until there was a steady stream cascading down her face.

I did not know what to do or say. I did not want to see Sue upset, but I did not know how to respond. One minute she had been talking normally and the next ... I did not understand.

I sat and waited, hoping she realized I was giving her time and being a proverbial 'shoulder to cry on'.

Eventually, Sue opened her eyes. She bent down to her handbag and rummaged around, bringing out a tissue. She delicately blew her nose. Then, she said just five words: 'Rob, I think it's true.'

I frowned, wondering what she meant. 'What's true?'

She bowed her head and the tears came again. It was some time before she answered.

This time, it was only two words: 'The Bible.'

That threw me. I had expected her to say something about rock layers or fossilized trees. However, after a few moments thought, I realized that the two things were probably connected. All the same, that did not explain the tears.

'I know Steve's information is pretty compelling,' I said, 'but why has that upset you?'

Sue looked up. There were still tears running down her face but, somehow, I did not get the impression of someone experiencing great sadness.

'You don't understand, Rob,' she said. 'I'm not talking about rock layers, canyons and fossilized trees; I'm talking about the Bible. The whole thing.'

My confusion turned to astonishment. My face said it all, as Sue gave a short laugh through her tears. ‘Rob, I haven’t just turned into a mass murderer.’

I made a conscious effort to change the expression on my face.

I looked down at my drink. ‘Sorry,’ I said. ‘I’m a bit confused. Your tears have taken me by surprise, that’s all.’

Sue found another tissue and wiped her eyes. She then picked up her drink, drained the last few drops of wine and got to her feet. ‘Rob, I’m afraid I’m going to have to go.’

I also rose from my seat. ‘OK,’ I said, hesitatingly. I was unsure about what had just occurred and was a little concerned. ‘Are you going to be all right?’ I asked.

Sue seemed slightly distracted as she said, ‘Rob, I’ll be fine, but I need to go and have a word with Jenny.’

When Sue had gone, I drained my own glass and then went to the bar for a refill. I am not normally someone who particularly enjoys drinking on my own, but I had got much to ponder and I did not feel like doing that in my hotel room. Although there were only a handful of people in the bar, and none of them appeared at all interested in me, I was somehow comforted by their presence.

As I cradled my glass, my thoughts returned to Sue and our recent conversation. The information we had received about the trees in Spirit Lake was certainly suggestive. Also, the arguments put forward by Steve and Jenny made a lot of sense, especially the fact that the roots of the petrified trees in Yellowstone National Park terminated 3 feet from the trunks of the trees. I could see how these details may have had a significant effect on Sue. All the same, I was not sure that was enough to convince me to accept the Bible in its entirety. That was a big leap.

As the minutes passed, my reflections turned to Sam. I had told Sue that I would give it another day before contacting the police and I would do that, but I was very concerned now. Sam never took long to respond to a message, so I was certain something was wrong. Sue had suggested that there could be a problem with his phone. This was a possibility but, knowing Sam as I did, he would have sent me a message from someone else's phone to let me know the situation. Another option was to contact my parents. The problem with that was the chance of causing them unnecessary stress. In spite of my concern, there was still a chance that there was a perfectly rational explanation for Sam's silence. The last thing I wanted to do was worry my parents unnecessarily.

I wracked my brains to see if I could think of any of Sam's friends that I might be able to contact. But, as I had told Sue, I did not know any of his friends particularly well—certainly not well enough to have their phone numbers. I wondered if I could get hold of the number of any of the band members with which Sam had gigged. It was a long shot, but maybe I could contact them through one of the pubs in which Sam had played.

I was about halfway down my pint and still pondering these things when my mobile gave a ping. In spite of the fact that it would be the middle of the night in England, hope rose in my heart. Excitedly, I grabbed my phone. However, when I saw the name displayed, that hope was extinguished. It was Sue. Not that I did not want to speak to her. If I had seen her name come up on my phone at any other time, I would have been delighted. My reaction just went to show how concerned I was about my kid brother. I read Sue's message:

'Where are you?'

'Still in the bar.'

Two minutes later, Sue came bouncing into the bar with a massive smile on her face. In spite of my thoughts of Sam, her smile was infectious.

I grinned back at her. 'What's up with you?'

She came over to me, put her arms around my neck and gave me a kiss on the cheek.

'I'll get a drink and then I'll tell you. Can I get you another?'

I looked down at my remaining half pint. 'I think I'll have a coffee if that's OK.'

I sat back down as she went up to the bar, beaming all over her face.

What on earth is going on, I thought to myself. I did not have long to wait.

As she sat down opposite me, she joyously declared, 'Rob, I've just become a Christian.'

I smiled at her. This was more for her benefit than because her news had made me happy. I actually felt rather deflated.

'I'm not quite sure what the correct response is to that,' I said, with an awkward smile. 'Do I congratulate you or something?'

She laughed. 'I don't think congratulations would be inappropriate,' she said. 'Actually, it feels amazing.' She had a sip out of her wine, before she continued. 'I'd like to explain what happened to me if, that is, you're happy to listen.'

I shrugged. 'OK,' I said slightly uncomfortably. 'Feel free.'

During our earlier adventure in the Congo, I had understood Kevin's arguments about the problems for evolution being support for the Bible. However, unfortunately for Kevin, that had not caused me to reach the conclusion he wanted me to reach. The way I saw it, just because Kevin could present some, admittedly convincing, arguments and serious problems for both the origin and subsequent evolution of life, that did not mean that the Bible's account had to be correct. It certainly did not logically follow that all the stuff about Jesus must also be true. As I had mentioned to Sue before, I had been resistant to taking the step of faith which I had been assured would result in me being 'born again', as they put it.

Sue's announcement bothered me. I liked her. In fact, I liked her a lot! The last thing I wanted was for her new-found faith to ruin the relationship I felt we were beginning to develop. As a result, I was nervous about this pending conversation. Sue obviously believed she had been affected positively by whatever it was that had just happened to her, and it was clear that she was excited by it. While I was genuinely pleased for her, I did not want that excitement to cause her to try to force me down the same track.

Sue must have sensed my unease. 'Don't worry; I'm not going to try to convert you.'

I smiled sheepishly. 'Was it that obvious?'

She laughed. 'Rob, I just want to tell someone. When something good happens in your life, you want to share it with somebody. You seemed like the obvious person.'

I nodded, feeling somewhat comforted. 'OK, go for it.'

'Well, you know the chat we were having earlier?'

I nodded again.

'As we were discussing everything we've learned, I was contemplating the shock I'd felt as Steve had presented each new piece of evidence. As you said yourself, his information has been compelling. Well, all this new data potentially completely overturns most of the things I thought I knew about geology. Can you understand how much of a kick in the teeth that felt like?'

I considered how I might feel in her position. 'Yes,' I said, 'I think I can appreciate that.'

'I don't know if you remember, but yesterday, I grabbed Jenny for a chat.'

I recalled Sue having a brief chat with Jenny and knew that they had taken themselves off somewhere.

'I remember,' I said, 'but I've no idea what you were discussing.'

'I wanted to understand more about the way the creationists explain how the rocks and fossils had been formed. They had often referred to a great Flood, and I wanted to know more about it. To me, from what I'd been taught, the whole idea of a Flood that had covered the whole planet seemed crazy. But many of the points they were making about strata deposition and canyon formation appeared reasonable. Anyway, I had my little chat with Jenny.'

She stopped.

I glanced up. She was staring straight ahead—I assumed, recalling their discussion.

'And what did you learn?' I prompted.

Sue came out of her trance. 'If you really want to understand what they believe, I suggest you have a chat with one of them. I think I grasped most of what Jenny was saying about how they think the Flood happened, but some of it is fairly involved, and they'd be able to explain it much better than I could.'

'Well, OK,' I said, 'but there must be some reason for you telling me this.'

She nodded. 'Initially, their ideas about Flood geology seemed very strange but, as I thought about the subject over the next twenty-four hours, it began to make much more sense. When we were having our chat earlier, it was as if everything fell into place. Of course, there's no doubt that part of that is their interpretation of the geological evidence and the way it confirms what the Bible says, but much more significant was a memory that came back to me from my childhood.

'I was sitting in a little chapel at the age of nine or ten. My grandma was sitting next to me, telling me that God was good. She told me that he loved me so much that he sent his Son into this world to die on a cross to pay the penalty for everything I would ever do wrong in my life. She said that He wanted me to love Him and to get to know Him.'

Sue paused and looked down, a pensive look on her face. She sighed as she said, 'It just struck me that I've done plenty in my life that I'm not proud of. There's loads of stuff I need to be forgiven for. All of a sudden, everything made sense. Jesus, His cross, our sin; in a flash of comprehension, like pieces of a puzzle being put in place, everything came together. I explained all this to Jenny and she told me that it was the Holy Spirit that had revealed that to me. She said that if I was prepared to put my faith in Jesus, I could live the rest of my life with the Holy Spirit as an ever-present companion.'

As Sue had been speaking, there were memories coming to my own mind too. My granddad telling me about his own conversion, and Kevin saying that I would never make a greater decision in my life than the decision I made about Jesus.

'What happened then?' I prompted.

Sue looked directly into my eyes. Her own eyes were starting to glisten again. 'I asked Jenny what I needed to do. She said I needed to make Jesus the Lord of my life. She said that if I was prepared to recognize that I was a sinner in need of a Saviour; that I was prepared to acknowledge that Jesus is the Son of God; that He is the only one who can save me; and that I was prepared to give Him my life as He gave His for me, I would be given a brand-new spirit. She said that didn't mean I would immediately start living a perfect life, but that a change would happen deep within me. She said that I would probably notice that I had new desires. I would probably have a wish to know much more about God and His Word, spending time with other Bible-believing Christians, and even to want to talk about my faith with others.'

As Sue spoke, there were all sorts of conflicting emotions going on in my head. One was a desire to experience what Sue had evidently experienced. Another opposing realization was that I had a natural resistance to all she was saying. It was all very confusing. I reasoned that, while Sue obviously believed that some major spiritual event had taken place deep inside her, she was probably living under some kind of delusion.

'What happened then?' I asked.

She smiled. 'Jenny explained a bit about what it meant to become a Christian. Then she led me in a prayer. She said that the prayer itself was completely useless unless I truly believed the things I was saying. She showed me a verse from the Bible which said something about confessing Jesus as Lord. But it also said that we have to believe it in our heart.'

'And did you believe it?'

She beamed. 'Yes. It's the first time I've prayed for years. I said what Jenny told me to say, and I meant every word.'

'Then what happened?'

'It was as if a heaviness had gone from my heart,' she said. 'I felt a peace like I've never felt before. And Jenny was right. I'm desperate to know what the Bible says.'

I looked down at my pint which now only had an inch of beer in the bottom. I was not quite sure what to make of it all. I did not know how, but I suspected that this change in Sue would affect our relationship in some way. Although Sue and I were not officially a couple, my thoughts had definitely been drifting in that direction. My mind went back to Sam and his reaction to Jane Walker explaining to him that she would not go out with someone who was not a Christian. I decided to ask that question.

She looked straight into my eyes and she lowered her voice, a serious look on her face. 'Listen, Rob, this is all very new to me. I don't know how this is going to affect me, never mind anyone else. I'm going to have to explore what this means in my own life. I guess I'll be speaking to Jenny quite a bit. I'll have to get some advice about how to study the Bible and what other changes I might have to make in my life.' She looked down at her glass and laughed. 'Who knows, maybe this will be the last glass of wine I ever drink?'

'Well, you'd better make sure you enjoy it, then.'

Chapter 9
Devastating News

The next morning had been set aside to return to Spirit Lake to explain the current conditions at the bottom of the lake. I got out of bed and was heading for the shower when I glanced at myself in the mirror. I looked awful. I had had a terrible night's sleep and my eyes were testament to my restless night. A ping from my phone indicated the arrival of a message. Snatching up my mobile from the bed, the screen displayed a message sent from an unfamiliar number.

Re-reading the message, I sat down on the edge of my bed in a state of shock, not trusting my legs to hold me up. It was a brief message:

'Rob, *this is important*! I've been kidnapped! Don't tell anyone else about this. Get away from everyone else in your party and message me back. Sam.'

Sam was a bit of a tease and was not averse to joking around, but not even he would joke about something like that. I felt sick. I sat staring at my phone, completely unable to take it in. It was almost impossible to believe the words so clearly visible on the screen.

As I began to respond, I stopped. Was this even Sam? My mind was spinning. With panic rising, I began to pace the room, following the line around the bed and back. I stopped, walked to the window and tried to get a grip of the situation. I tried to order my thoughts. Firstly, there were things about the text which were unusual. To start with, why was he not using his own phone? But secondly, he hardly ever called me 'Rob'. It was nearly always 'Bruv'. Had this text been dictated by Sam? Or was he trying to tell me something by using a different style? I could not be sure.

The fact that I had been asked to get away from the others to send my text at least gave me time to think. Whoever had sent the text would not be aware that I was sitting alone in my hotel room, and they might therefore expect it to be a few minutes before I responded. It would probably be best to respond in an emotional way and hopefully gain more information. Typing a message had never seemed so difficult.

'I'm on my own. I won't tell anyone about your message. Sam. 'What's going on!'

A few seconds passed and the phone vibrated in my hand.

'Your brother will be safe as long as you do exactly what you're told. Do *not* tell anyone about these texts. If you do, don't expect to see him again. We need you to find out what your party will be doing over the next three days and let us know. Make sure your phone is charged at all times. Keep it with you. We will be in touch soon to give you further instructions.'

I immediately sent another message. All it said was: 'Who are you?'

There was no response. My guts were in knots. How on earth was I going to be able to act normally with everyone else when this was going on?

I checked the charge on my phone: 48%. I plugged it into the charger and belatedly went into the bathroom, stepping into the shower.

As the water ran over my body, my mind was racing. What should I do? I considered calling the police, but the risk to Sam's safety was too much. I hoped I would wake up; maybe this was a bad dream, but it was not. No, I could not risk Sam's safety. I would have to comply with their demands. But how on earth was I going to manage to keep this from everyone else?

When I stepped back into the bedroom, I had just started getting dressed when there was another ping from my phone. Again, it was from the new mobile number.

'Rob, you need to find out all you can about their research work. They know they are doing some work relating to ore deposits. They want that information, and my safety depends on your success.'

So that was it. Sam's kidnappers must think they would be able to use the knowledge to make some kind of financial killing. All of a sudden, a penny dropped in my mind. When Kevin had initially told me about this trip, he had said something about there being an additional and unexpected potential benefit to their research. He made a comment about being able to predict the location of valuable ore deposits. I had forgotten about that. However, he had also said that the subject was technical. My heart sank. I very much hoped that I would be able to understand it enough to pass it on to Sam's kidnappers.

When I was dressed, I slipped my notepad into one of the back pockets of my jeans along with a pencil. I would have to make plenty of notes, because there was no way I would be able to keep the information in my head. I picked up my mobile and sent another message.

'Sam, I'll need time. I haven't heard anything about their work on ore deposits yet.'

I waited for a few seconds but got no response.

Ten minutes later I was down with the others. Initially, I had to put up with some mild mockery about being late for breakfast, but my prickly mood indicated that I was not much feeling like light-hearted banter.

I would have to watch that, I thought. If the other members of the group noticed a major change in my demeanour, they would begin to suspect that something was wrong. I did not want that.

There were high spirits in the group today too—quite a contrast to my own state of anxiety. Everyone else was delighted about Sue's news. She had informed them that she had 'given her life to Christ' on the previous evening. Naturally, most of the group being committed Christians, this had caused no small stir. Sue, herself, was almost glowing. Something significant had obviously taken place within her. However, given the news I had just received, it was hardly surprising that my own enthusiasm over her conversion was not quite matching up with the rest of the party.

Another problem that morning was my attitude to our morning's activities. I had been delighted when Steve had presented me with the opportunity to go scuba diving in Spirit Lake. He knew I had been excited over the prospect, but now I had lost all my enthusiasm. It was going to be a real challenge to feign interest when all I could currently think about was Sam and his predicament.

At 10:00 am, we all congregated in the meeting room. Steve began explaining about that morning's subject.

'There's another fascinating detail that has resulted because of the logs in the lake,' he said. 'As I've said before, it's almost as if Mount Saint Helens was trying to show the world that the belief in billions of years of earth's history is totally false. You see, these trees have provided further great evidence pointing to a process happening rapidly which many geologists insist takes a long period of time. Yesterday, we were discussing the petrified logs at Yellowstone Park. Well, not only are trees petrified in the earth, but they can also be turned into coal.[21] This will happen to buried wood and especially bark material when subjected to the right temperature and pressure. When you look at coal you can see the layering and banding to it in many of these coal seams'

He displayed a slide to demonstrate his point.

'It's really interesting that sheets of tree bark are very common in coal. Through a microscope you can look at coal and see the cell structure in the bark tissue.'

Another slide went up.

'OK, so let's have a look at the conventional explanation for the origin of coal. This is the idea that plants build up slowly in a swamp. As peat accumulates over a long period of time, the plant matter decays and a thick spongy layer of peat deposit is built up over hundreds or thousands of years. Later, other sediments, like sand or mud, buries the plant material and that is later converted with temperature and pressure to coal. The main problem with that explanation is that this is not what your typical coal seam looks like.'

Steve displayed an image on the screen. I tried to concentrate on the screen and Steve's words.

'Take a look at this. This is a drained swamp deposit. Coastal erosion drained this swamp and we see here over 4 feet of peat which has accumulated over hundreds of years. This is very severely decomposed [see image 14]. But also, notice the large roots hanging out of the peat deposit. Many modern swamp peats have a tremendous number of roots penetrating through them.

'However, once again, this is not what we typically see in coal deposits. As I said earlier, many coal seams look as if they are dominated by layers of tree bark. Unfortunately, as with many other geological beliefs, a significant number of people will present the swamp explanation for the origin of coal as fact. Well, it's not fact.'

Steve changed the image on the screen from the swamp peat to a picture of the logs on Spirit Lake.

'OK, so what model can we propose for the origin of coal? Well,

Image 14: A drained swamp

Photo by Steven A. Austin PhD. Used with permission.

let's call it the floating mat model. Imagine millions of logs floating in water. Those logs could jostle against one another, the bark be rubbed off and sink to the bottom where it could accumulate as a thick layer of bark peat. Imagine thick sheets of tree bark accumulating underneath a floating log mat, not in a swamp. Later, the log mat could drift away, and other sediments like mud or sand could be deposited on top. Given the right conditions of heat and pressure, it's not at all difficult to see how these deposits could be converted into coal. Incidentally, they would also look much more like the real-life coal deposits we see in the world.'

Steve now put up an image of the 1980 eruption. 'When Mount Saint Helens exploded, it created the perfect conditions to test this proposal. It turned Spirit Lake into a giant four-square-mile living laboratory for the creation of coal.'

I was taking notes determinedly to keep my mind from wandering.

'The creation geologist who came up with this idea decided to go diving in Spirit Lake to see what the conditions were like on the bottom. In many places he found a thick layer of peat. This was up to 3 feet thick and was dominated by sheets of tree bark. Now, if this was buried under temperature and pressure, it could be converted to coal. The sheets of tree bark would give that layered appearance. Unlike the explanation proffered by the secular scientific community, this is very much like what we see in coal beds today. And these sheets of tree bark are not at all hard to find. Around twenty-five per cent of the peat at the bottom of the lake consists of tree bark.'

Steve, then, began to inform us of some experiments which had been carried out to understand more about the formation of coal. Most of this involved heat and pressure, but there were also accounts of vibration sometimes appearing to contribute to the process.

These details did not hold my attention as much, and my mind began to stray onto Sam. Where was he? How was he? I did not even know if he was OK. I do not know how much of Steve's talk I missed, but I was suddenly aware of Sue's hand on my arm and turned to look at her.

She looked concerned. 'Are you OK?' she whispered.

I was annoyed with myself. With some effort, I dragged what I hoped was a cheery, carefree expression onto my face and smiled at her.

'I'm fine,' I said. 'Sorry, I was miles away.'

She seemed partly convinced, but there was still some uncertainty in her eyes. I would have to be much more careful. I turned back to the screen and attempted to concentrate on what Steve was saying. He appeared to be bringing his talk to a close.

'Something incredible has happened here,' he said. 'Folks, there are vast amounts of coal all around the world. What if that was formed as a result of this kind of process? That would mean there must have been a huge number of logs and other plant material floating in oceans over virtually all parts of the world. What would an ocean be doing covering all these different areas? Now, this obviously sounds completely ridiculous to most people in the world today but, for the sake of argument, what if we consider for a moment that the Bible might actually be giving us an accurate account of an event which could explain all this? What if a global catastrophic Flood really did occur about 4,400 years ago? The Bible says that all the high hills and the mountains were covered by the Flood waters.'

This was very difficult for me to believe. I realized Sue had come to the conclusion that the whole of the Bible was true, but I could not convince myself that the biblical Flood was anything other than a fairy story. No matter how hard I tried, I could not think of Noah's Ark as a real boat.

On our arrival at the shore of Spirit Lake an hour or so later, we were greeted by a couple of men with diving equipment. Looking at their kit, I recalled my diving training, but my heart really was not in it. As the equipment was set down, and the men were discussing the details and giving me instructions, a wave of helplessness washed over me. I tuned back into the conversation; listening to the lapping water in the background, I realized that this dive might be the best thing I could do. Firstly, I would have to concentrate on what I was doing. This might take my mind off Sam and his plight for a while. The other benefit related more to my fellow members of the team. I realized that I would not have to worry about them wondering about my sombre mood, as I was finding it impossible to act naturally.

There were going to be three of us going into the lake. My two diving buddies were Chuck and Billy. They were both far more experienced divers than I. They assured me that they would be sticking very close and would make sure no harm came to me.

As we entered the water, I was surprised to notice how cold it was—certainly much colder than I had anticipated. Glancing back over my right shoulder, I waved at the rest of our team standing on the lakeside. Sue waved back and I gave her a warm smile.

We were about ready to dive. Chuck placed a hand on my left shoulder. 'Rob, we're going to be swimming in that direction.' With his hand, he indicated that we would not be heading straight out into the lake, but significantly to the right of that. In fact, it almost looked as if we would start swimming parallel to the shore.

'The water's not that deep there, but there's a decent amount of bark peat, and that's one of the things we want to show you.'

'OK,' I said.

'For most of the time we'll swim at a fairly shallow depth. This will give you a great view of the floating logs above you. After swimming under the log mat, we'll briefly take you down to have a look at some of the logs standing upright on the bottom. Visibility isn't great down there, but we've got flashlights to help us with that.'

I nodded.

'Remember to keep to my right and just behind me. Billy will swim to your right and slightly further back.'

Once more, I nodded.

'Right, ready to go?'

'Yep,' I said and gave a thumbs up.

We pulled down our masks and began swimming in the direction Chuck had indicated.

After approximately 100 yards, Chuck dropped to the bottom and I followed. The depth of the lake at that point was only about 10 feet or so, and there was still a reasonable amount of light. Chuck and Billy lifted some sections of bark to show me and encouraged me to hold a piece. As I took it, I noticed that our actions, disturbing the bark on the lake floor, had caused a cloud of sediments to rise, slightly reducing the visibility.

Some of these sheets of tree bark were really quite big. I remembered Steve's comments on the formation of coal. I would be checking Steve's details, but if his information turned out to be correct, this evidence was certainly interesting. I placed the bark back on the floor of the lake and Chuck indicated that we should move on.

We now swam in a direction which would take us out towards the centre of the lake. We appeared to be maintaining a depth of around 7 or 8 feet. After about 30 yards or so, I noticed that we were approaching a long dark shape on the surface which was running perpendicular to our current course. As we approached, Chuck began to angle his swim upwards towards the surface. Dutifully, I followed.

We broke surface about 2 feet from the log. It was massive. The vast majority of the tree was submerged, but a small, curved portion was still visible above the surface for its whole length. I noticed that, at one end, there were truncated roots. I was interested to note that this was the end of the log which was more completely submerged. This, I reasoned, is exactly what one would expect if Steve's theory was right.

My two diving companions were treading water next to me. 'What do you make of this?' Billy asked. He stretched out his hand and ran it over the surface of the log.

For a moment I did not grasp his point but, all of a sudden, the penny dropped.

I looked at him and grinned. 'No bark,' I said. 'On the bottom?' I suggested.

He smiled back at me and nodded.

'It's amazing,' I said in wonder.

There had been times when I had wondered if the creationists were just a little strange. That thought had now been completely dispelled. As I gazed sightlessly at the bark-stripped tree in front of me, I had a growing sense that Steve's theory about these trees was completely true.

Before leaving the tree, we swam to the root end so I could see close up how the roots terminated about 3 feet from the trunk. Again, I thought of the information Steve had given us the previous day about the fossilized trees at Yellowstone Park. His arguments were compelling, and the evidence appeared to fit his theory perfectly.

Our next task was to check out the bottom of the lake. This was the part of the dive I was most interested in. I was intrigued by the idea of these massive trees becoming completely waterlogged and being deposited in upright position on the bottom.

In the time I had spent with these creation scientists, I had developed a growing confidence in the facts they were presenting. All the same, it seemed almost inconceivable that these massive trees could be ripped from their original position in a forest, swept into a lake, and then drift to the bottom where they had effectively been replanted.

As we swam to the next area of lake, I noticed that there were many more logs floating on the surface above us. As we swam around the lake, Billy took photographs with an underwater camera.

Looking up, I could see the underside of the log mat really clearly. It was awe-inspiring. I suddenly realized that there must be thousands of tons of logs floating above us. Suddenly, Chuck signalled that we were going to change direction and head to the left of our present course. I did not immediately know why this was, but as I looked past Chuck's swimming figure, I understood.

Ahead of us was one of the logs. However, this log was not floating horizontally on the surface but hanging down from the log mat above. It was a truly amazing sight. As we drew closer, again, I was struck by the absence of bark on the tree. I looked up to where the top of the log reached the surface of the lake. There were many other horizontally floating logs but, just to the right of the vertical log, I spied a small patch of open water. I managed to get Chuck's attention and tried to convey my wish to swim up to check out the top of the vertically floating log. After a slight hesitation as Chuck and Billy briefly conversed with some signals which meant nothing to me, they indicated that we could swim up to the surface.

As my head came out of the water, I immediately saw that there was only a couple of inches of tree above the surface. In fact, the top of the log was irregular; the top of the tree having been snapped off, there were only a few small sections of the top of the log still visible above the water. I thought about our trip on the boat the previous day. If we had come across this log, we might not even have noticed it. It was certainly much easier to see the upright floating logs from underneath the log mat.

Billy had also broken surface just to my right. 'I reckon if we returned in a couple of days' time, we'd find that this tree would be on the bottom,' he told me.

I glanced at Billy and gave a short nod. It would not surprise me either. It was fascinating to see all these trees in different stages of their journey to the bottom of the lake.

After another few minutes studying the top of the log, we were off again. This time we were heading for an area of lake which was over 30 feet deep. At that depth there was almost total darkness.

It was not long before we found our first upright tree standing on the bottom of the lake. As we followed the log down to the floor of the lake, we found that its base was buried in some kind of peat deposit. With all the sediment in the lake it was incredibly dark and Chuck used a flashlight to illuminate the scene. Billy positioned me on one side of the tree and indicated that we were going to try to move it. He moved around the other side of the tree and we attempted to tip the tree. We had no success. The log was stuck fast. It appeared to be buried in at least 3 feet of sediment which had formed around the base of the tree. After another couple of minutes trying to coax some movement out of the log, we gave up and moved on.

Chuck and Billy led me to a second upright log around 20 feet away. We repeated the exercise. This time, however, the log appeared to have dropped to the bottom more recently, because we could get it to sway slightly. They also brought to my attention that the sediment in which the tree was buried consisted predominantly of tree bark.

Suddenly I had a revelation. Mentally, I had understood Steve's argument about the logs dropping down at different times with the root ends buried at different levels, but it had still seemed like a theory. Now, seeing the physical evidence with my own eyes, it all made total sense. I did not just believe it was possible; I knew it was true.

Each new piece of evidence Chuck and Billy showed me added more credibility to the theory Steve had presented to us. All the same, it was easy to see how scientists believing in an old earth could come across this evidence in the future and reach a faulty conclusion. These logs might give the appearance of being multiple forests which had grown here over an immense period of time, but the undeniable truth was that this had all happened within a matter of just a few decades.

We spent a few moments checking out some logs which had sunk to the bottom and then fallen over. Again, some of these had obviously just recently arrived on the floor of the lake, as the whole of the log was visible, but others were almost entirely covered with sediment.

This was the last of the evidence that I was to view and we set off to rejoin the rest of the team.

While I had been diving with Chuck and Billy, the others had been given further information about coal deposits. This included additional details which Steve insisted caused problems for the traditional explanation of the origin of coal. He assured me that he would give me a couple of sheets containing the information he had passed on to the others. However, Sue did briefly have the time to tell me about one of his arguments.

He had brought up the subject of trees buried in the ground which ran vertically through many different rock layers [see image 15]. These had been termed 'polystrate fossils' because they extended

Image 15: A tree stump running vertically through rock layers
Photo by A. Snelling PhD. Used with permission.

through many different geological strata. Some of these had been shown to run through multiple coal deposits. Steve's argument was that, if all the layers took millions of years to be deposited, the trees wouldn't have lasted long enough for the various layers to form around them. As with many of his other arguments, I could not immediately see anything wrong with his logic.

Throughout our lunch, I was wondering how I was going to bring up the subject of the work they were doing on mineral deposits.

I knew there would be no problem in getting them to discuss it but, up until that point, I had shown zero interest in the topic I was terrified that my change in attitude would arouse suspicion, so I was having to analyse every word and action. My fears were allayed when I did eventually bring it up with Jenny, as it provoked no comment at all. She was delighted that I had asked and said that she would be very happy to furnish me with the information.

I suddenly remembered the instruction to pass back details on our itinerary.

'Jen, can you remind me what we'll be doing over the next few days? At some point soon I'd like to start hearing about this mineral deposit stuff.'

'This afternoon, we're going to be having another review on the trip to date,' she said. 'If you feel up to it, we can start going through the mineral work this evening. Tomorrow we're going to have a look at forests, and the following day we're scheduled to take a hike into the crater of Mount Saint Helens. Monday has been set aside so you can explore some of the visitor centres. Now you've seen some of the physical evidence, I think Steve and Kevin want you to hear what the secular world says about things and compare that with the details you've learned from us.'

I was still discussing these things with Jenny when Sue joined us.

'Rob, have you managed to get hold of Sam?' she asked.

I could have kicked myself. Why had I not thought of that? It was a natural question for Sue to ask. She knew how concerned I was about my inability to contact him.

‘I’ve still not been able to get him,’ I said feebly. I glanced down at my watch. ‘I’ll try him again now.’

‘Is there something wrong?’ Jenny asked.

‘I’ve just been having a few problems contacting my brother,’ I said hurriedly. ‘I’m sure everything will be fine.’

I tapped in a message to Sam that I was sure would receive no response; it did not. However, about five minutes later, I did get a message. It was from Dad. It said, ‘Hello, Robert. I hope you are well and your trip is as interesting as you were expecting. Have you heard from Sam? He had been relaying your messages to us, but we’ve not heard anything from him in the last couple of days. We are a little concerned. Do you know if there is any kind of problem? Love, Mum and Dad.’

Great, I thought. That is all I needed. It was hard enough keeping a lid on my own doubts and fears, without having to also deal with those of my parents.

I decided that I needed to keep this as close to the truth as I could without divulging the news about Sam’s kidnapping.

I responded: ‘Hi Dad. I’m fine thanks and hope you and Mum are too. My trip is fascinating. I’ll look forward to telling you all about it. I’ve not been able to get Sam either, but I’m sure all will be OK. I’ll let you know when I manage to get him. Love, Robert.’

As Jenny had mentioned, that afternoon we had a further review of the trip to date. I found it very difficult to feign interest. Although I tried hard to concentrate on the subjects being discussed, Sam’s situation constantly forced its way into my mind—the waves of panic and helplessness repeatedly rising and falling. Once or twice, I caught Sue looking at me with a concerned look on her face.

After our evening meal, Jim, Sue and I joined Steve, Jenny and Kevin in the meeting room to learn about their research work.

Jenny, with her usual sparkling smile, could not have been a greater contrast to my gloomy mood. She stood next to the table on which she had placed her laptop.

'OK, folks, this group of sessions will hopefully give you a high-level understanding of the research work we're currently involved in. I'll start by running through how radiometric dating methods are supposed to work and we'll have a look at different dating techniques.[22] I'll then speak more specifically about uranium-lead dating, which is the method relevant to the work we've been doing.'

I noticed that there was no mention of any ore deposits. I slumped in my chair and worry knotted my stomach.

Jenny began by telling us that radiometric dating was the process of estimating the age of rocks from the decay of their radioactive elements. She explained that there are certain kinds of atoms in nature that are unstable and spontaneously change into other kinds of atoms. These unstable atoms are referred to as being radioactive, and the changing process is known as nuclear or radioactive decay.

Although I already had a sketchy awareness of some of these details, I was scribbling away like mad, attempting to record all her information. I realized she was probably pitching this at my level, as Sue and Jim were not taking any notes.

Jenny gave us an outline of how the methods were supposed to work, sharing information about the equipment used to measure various elements within rock. She explained that there were a number of assumptions that geologists had to make about the starting conditions before they could obtain any results from these methods. She also made it abundantly clear how she felt about the reliability of those assumptions.

Jenny then began to speak specifically about the uranium-lead process. She told us that this involved unstable uranium atoms decaying down through a series of steps into stable lead atoms. She took some time in explaining about protons and neutrons in the nuclei of atoms, giving us an understanding of the difference between alpha and beta decay, and telling us what alpha particles were.

As she continued to provide these details, my brain began to hurt. This was now definitely not pitched at my level! As I sat listening, not even knowing what to write down, I became more and more concerned about the complexity of the subject and my own ability to understand it.

Jenny moved on to give us an overview of work done by creation scientists in recent years which had called the beliefs of the conventional scientific community into question. She told us that these details seriously challenged the evolutionary claims of millions of years.

'The work we're doing now is building on the work which began over two decades ago,' she said. 'It's the potential this work has to undermine the 'old earth' claims that we're most excited about.'

In spite of my all-consuming concern for Sam and my need to understand Jenny's information, I did allow myself a quick glance at Jim. He had expressed a desire to understand the creationist take on the dating methods. I wondered if these sessions would provide him with the answers he was looking for.

Jenny began to wrap up the session. She finished by saying, 'I suggest we meet up again tomorrow evening. In that session we'll move onto radiohalos. I'll explain what they are and why they're so significant.'

As the session broke up, I was just leaving the meeting room when Sue lightly tapped my forearm. She did not look at me but turned left and headed in the direction of the bar. I briefly spoke to Jenny to thank her for her information and say good night to everyone. A few seconds later, I too was heading for the bar.

I immediately saw Sue sitting on her own at a table at the far end. She was looking very thoughtful and I sincerely hoped that this discussion was not going to be too challenging.

'You OK, Sue?' I asked. 'Can I get you a drink?'

She shook her head. 'No thanks, Rob. I don't think this will take long.'

'OK,' I said. 'I think I'm going to have a coffee, anyway.'

Once the coffee was ordered, I was back and pulling out the chair opposite Sue. As I sat down, I said, 'So, what's this all about, Sue?'

She looked up at me. Her expression was hard to read. She did not seem annoyed or upset, but I could sense this was not a light-hearted chat.

Before she spoke, she looked down at her hands which were clasped together on the table in front of her. 'Yesterday, you promised me you'd be honest with me.'

'Yes, I did.'

She looked up at me and held my gaze for some seconds, before once more looking back down at her hands. 'And will you?'

'I'm not entirely sure I know what you're getting at,' I said.

She looked up again, and this time, held my gaze.

'Rob, I think you do. However, just in case you're not quite as intelligent as I've given you credit for, please will you explain what was going on in that session? I know you've shown a reasonable amount of interest in the work these people are doing but, overnight, you seem to have morphed into someone who's so committed to geology that you're scribbling down every little detail. In addition, the subject of dating rocks is much more technical, and I'd suggest is far less interesting for a layman than the information we've had previously. Why the sudden desperation to understand this particular subject?'

It was my turn to look down. I sighed deeply, really wanting to keep my promise to Sue. Looking into her eyes, a jolt of electricity buzzed through me. I needed to be honest.

'Look, Sue, I'm currently dealing with a really tricky issue. There's a good reason why I don't want to involve others at the moment, but I promise I'll tell you when I can.'

'Have you ever heard the saying, "A problem shared is a problem halved"?'

'I have,' I said. 'But unfortunately, at the moment, it's not really an option.'

'Of course it is, Rob. It's always an option.'

I could feel my stress levels rising. 'Sue, you don't know what you're talking about. You have no idea what the situation is and, whether you like it or not, for the time being, you're not going to find out.'

My concern for Sam and my frustration over his situation had resulted in these words coming out more harshly than I intended. In the fog of emotion, I could immediately tell that I'd hurt Sue's feelings.

'Look, I'm sorry, Sue. I shouldn't have spoken to you like that, but I'm dealing with a really tough situation, and it's hard work.'

'OK,' she said quietly. 'I guess you'll have to deal with it in your own way. Let me know if you think I can help.'

She rose from her seat and I also stood. We shared a fairly frosty 'good night' and she left for her room.

I would have left myself, but as I watched Sue's retreating back, I noticed one of the bar staff heading in my direction with a cup of coffee.

When I eventually got back to my room, I sent a brief text to the kidnapper's phone. Absolutely no niceties, just a curt message explaining that I had had my first session on their technical work, and that this was just explaining the relevant terms to us. I told him that I'd send another text when I had further information.

As soon as the message was sent, I remembered the instruction to inform him about our plans for the next few days, so I sent a second message containing the details I had been given from Jenny earlier about our future movements. When the second message was on its way, my mind returned to Sam. There were surely a limited number of people who would know where Sam lived, and also that I was part of this trip. Had members of the Westminster group that Kevin had mentioned been busy gathering intelligence on all Kevin's acquaintances and their families? And, if so, might this group be our best chance of discovering where Sam was now?

Something else was starting to bother me. Jack and Briony Austin; were they what they claimed to be? I remembered standing next to a puzzled Kevin the previous day as he had given me an update on the two people from the Westminster group who had come out to the States. He said that they had gone down to Florida but could not think why they would do that. It now struck me for the first time that we had accepted Jack and Briony into the group and they just happened to come from Florida. Also, on the previous evening, they had both disappeared to take part in an on-line meeting with people in Florida. By their own admission, this had included visiting speakers from the UK. Was that just a coincidence? I was not so sure. Questions whirred through my mind; the coffee was a poor choice, I mused. As I looked in the mirror, I felt another sleepless night was on the cards.

Chapter 10
MISSING

In the morning, I woke up sweating. The night had consisted of hours of wakefulness, punctuated by short periods of restless sleep. I decided to avoid the mirror as I headed down to meet the group. Today, our main objectives were to explore two areas of woodland which had been devastated by the 1980 eruption. One of these sites was within the Mount Saint Helens National Volcanic Monument where the land had been left to regenerate naturally. The other site was further away from the volcano and had received human assistance in its bid to recover.

After our breakfast, we gathered in the hotel foyer where we were introduced to two men who we had not previously met. Ron Carter and Cecil Bennett led regular hiking trips into the Mount Saint Helens crater throughout the year, and we learned that they would be guiding us into the crater the following day. However, these two men also knew a lot about local forestry, so they were also highly qualified to provide us with additional information on our current quest.

Unfortunately, the weather forecast for the afternoon was not great, predicting three hours of steady rain from around 3:00 pm. Taking this into consideration, Steve and Jenny said that we would stay out until the rain arrived, and then come back and discuss any observations we had made.

At 9:30 am, we got into our vehicles and headed for Spirit Lake. Sue and Kevin were chatting excitedly in the front, with me in the back in a trance, worrying about Sam. On arriving at the north shore of Spirit Lake just before 10:00 am, I was suddenly spellbound. I was standing facing the lake and looking south across the water towards Mount Saint Helens. I remembered what Steve had told us about the tsunami type waves that had come crashing into the northern shore of the lake, where I was now standing. I swung around to look at the site where those waves had ripped hundreds of thousands of mature trees from the ground in seconds. There was something about this place that was almost mystical. It was captivating, and it absorbed the attention and the senses. As I stood there, I tried to imagine the area covered by a mature forest and then tried to visualise all that water in gigantic waves ripping those vast trees from the earth. The power of those surges must have been absolutely incredible.

After allowing us a little time to take in the scene, Cecil gave us some additional information on the destruction caused by the waves.

Then Ron chipped in: 'The 1980 eruption caused a massive disturbance around here from an ecological point of view. It's interesting,' he said. 'In some areas, life was almost entirely wiped out. However, in others, there was an extremely high survival rate.' Ron spoke very fast and had a heavy southern drawl.

'The biological response to the disturbance began almost immediately, but the rate of change has been different in different areas. For example, lakes, streams and forests have all responded at different rates. As you know, this area was a forest and is still quite badly affected. But in a few minutes, we'll take you to an area where the recovery has been much faster.'

Ron and Cecil spoke to us for another ten minutes or so, pointing out various differences in the terrain. After this, as promised, they led us to an area where there had been a significant amount of regrowth.

'Within the Mount Saint Helens National Volcanic Monument, there are some areas of amazing biodiversity which have recovered naturally,' Cecil told us. 'We refer to these areas as biological hotspots,' he added.

In this particular area, I could not see any trees, but smaller shrubs and other plants had taken root and appeared to be thriving.

Ron and Cecil acted as a tag team, one picking up where the other left off. It was Ron who was speaking now:

'Some of these hotspots developed relatively quickly.'

'Why has there been so much new growth in this particular location?' Briony asked.

'There are a number of reasons why these hotspots develop,' Ron said. 'Both living and dead organisms, left behind after the eruption, have probably played a part. We term these things "biological legacies" and they almost certainly assisted the accelerated regrowth. Another factor is erosion. People often assume that erosion is detrimental to the growth of trees and shrubs, but in some areas at Mount Saint Helens, it's exactly the opposite. Erosion has actually assisted new growth by removing volcanic deposits to reveal mineral-rich soil.'

Despite everything, being on site again had alleviated some of my mental turmoil, and I found myself immersed in the wonder of the catastrophe and resulting landscape.

Cecil took his turn: 'Although these hotspots make up a tiny percentage of the National Volcanic Monument, they contain a large percentage of the areas' total biodiversity.'

I noticed Sue standing with Jenny a few yards away and wondered what was going through her head.

Next, they took us to see an area where some trees had seeded themselves since the eruption. To my amazement, some of them had achieved an impressive size.

'What are these trees?' Sue asked.

'Red alder,' Ron answered. 'This species is pretty good at re-establishing itself following a major disturbance.'

It was incredible. It was difficult to comprehend how so much regrowth had occurred in the few decades following the 1980 eruption. Much of the land was still barren but, all the same, where growth had taken place, it did seem mighty impressive to me.

After spending half an hour in that location, we moved on to visit a small lake which had formed as a direct result of the eruption.

'Events like volcanic eruptions can create habitats as well as destroying them,' Cecil told us. 'This lake didn't exist before the May 18 eruption.'

He and Ron explained that colonies of different creatures had established themselves in this new lake. This took us up to lunchtime and we stopped to have something to eat.

In the afternoon, we moved to an area outside the Mount Saint Helens National Volcanic Monument. This was to visit an area of forest which had been badly affected by the blast, but which had had a significant amount of assistance in re-establishing itself.

As our little convoy reached its destination and we began to disembark, I recognized that this was much busier than the area we had visited in the morning. I mentioned this fact to Steve.

He nodded. 'Thousands of tourists come to the area each year to view the volcano and surrounding countryside,' he said. 'Access to the site we visited this morning is highly restricted, but there is no such prohibition in this area.'

As he was speaking, as if to prove the point, another couple of vehicles swept into the carpark and pulled up about 50 yards away from where we were standing.

As we left our Land Rovers and entered the forest, the difference between this and the area we had seen in the morning was quite noticeable.

Jim appeared especially interested in the forest. 'Ron? You said this area has received a lot more help when it comes to restoration. What was their approach? What did they do initially?'

Ron stopped to answer Jim's question: 'Right from the

beginning, there was a real desire to salvage as much of the downed timber as they could.[23] The work to do this began almost immediately. The government first carried out a study to ensure that it would be safe for people to work in the ash,' he explained, 'but once that study was completed, their work started in earnest. They needed to recover the timber as quickly as possible, because they didn't want insects or anything else to damage the wood.'

'Does anyone have any idea how many trees they were able to recover?' Jim asked.

'Oh, hundreds of thousands,' he said. 'They were removing hundreds of truckloads each day, and the work went on for about two years. I heard it reported that they reckon they recovered enough timber to build something like 85,000 three-bedroomed homes. That's a lot of wood.'

Jim was on a roll: 'Once they'd shifted all that timber, what happened then? he asked.

'Their next job was to get millions of saplings planted. They dug down through the ash to the mineral-rich soil and hand planted about 18 million saplings.'

'18 million?' I queried in disbelief. 'That sounds incredible.'

'I know,' Ron said. 'It was an amazing effort.'

After this little exchange, we moved off again.

Every now and again, we would come across other groups intent on investigating the forest. Nearly all were wearing rucksacks and, like our group, a number of them had binoculars hanging around their necks.

As we continued to stroll through the trees, Ron and Cecil

passed on information about the forest and the changes that had occurred over the last forty or so years. Personally, I had never really had much of an interest in trees, but having seen photographs of the devastation caused to the area during the 1980 eruption, I was dumbfounded by the amount of regrowth and the general health of the forest.

Briony also appeared captivated by the surroundings. 'What are all these trees?' she asked. 'Are they all the same type?'

'Most of these trees are noble firs,' Cecil said. 'These do better than some of the other species at this elevation. Lower down, there are a lot of red alder and Douglas firs. However, other species like the red cedar are also planted in certain locations.'

Cecil and Ron then took us over a ridge and down into the next valley to an area of the forest where it appeared that many trees had been cleared.

'This area was harvested last year,' Cecil informed us. 'Mature trees are felled and the timber sold. You can think of it as a kind of forest economy. Soon after the harvest, new saplings are planted again to ensure the sustainability of the forest.'

We began to walk along the side of the harvested area. Almost immediately, we came across a fallen tree which looked as if it had come down quite some time ago. It was lying in a thick area of undergrowth and was a contrast to the rest of the area, which was arranged neatly in comparison.

Cecil pointed it out to us. 'You see this area here?' he said. 'This has been left like this intentionally. An area like this can be very helpful to some of the smaller inhabitants of the forest. Firstly, it can be a source of food, but it can also provide somewhere to hide.'

For a while, we stopped our stroll through the forest and broke up into smaller groups, having different conversations about all the things we had seen. Sue and I were busy discussing the economic side of forestry with Steve and Ron when Jim wandered over.

'Steve,' he said, 'I'm just going to take a quick stroll back up to the top of the ridge. I'm pretty sure that I just caught sight of a deer. Don't worry, I'll stay in sight of you. Don't go without me.'

'Hold on, Jim,' Steve said. 'I'll get Ben and Steph to come with you.'

Ben and Steph were currently in deep conversation with Cecil, Jack and Briony, and it looked as if their little chat might last for a while yet.

Jim recognized this. 'Don't bother them,' he said. 'I'm only going to be about five minutes. Don't worry, Steve, I'll stay in sight.'

'Make sure you do,' Steve said with a smile.

Jim nodded. He wandered away from us through the trees and up a slight incline to the top of the ridge.

I saw him stop and turn towards us giving us a cheery wave. Then he turned away and raised his binoculars to look down into the adjacent valley.

I turned back to Sue, Steve and Ron. 'Are you telling us that none of these trees are more than forty years old?' I asked Ron.

Ron nodded. 'Yes, sir, that's right,' he said. 'All the trees in this particular vicinity are young. There are a few trees that survived the blast a few hundred yards from here.' At this point, he waved an arm towards the west. 'But all the trees in this immediate area were either flattened or had all their foliage and most of their bark stripped from them.'

'What about before 1980?' Sue asked. 'The trees that were actually flattened by the eruption. How long had they been here?'

This was one question for which Ron did not have the answer. However, he promised to find out and get back to Sue with the details. But, once again, her question propelled us back into the whole area of dating methods. In the debate I had attended before our previous expedition to the Congo, I remembered the subject coming up of dating trees by their tree rings. Not being able to remember much about it, I asked Steve to explain.

As he began to respond, a few spots of rain started to find their way through the canopy above us.

The discussion had been going for some time when Kevin joined us.

'Hi, folks,' he said. 'The rain has started. Should we soon make tracks?'

Having been absorbed by our conversation, I had not really paid much attention to the worsening weather conditions, but I now realized that the rain had become significantly heavier.

Steve looked around. 'You're right. It's probably time we left.'

'Where's Jim?' Kevin asked.

Our discussion had caused me to lose track of time. It was quite a while since Jim had left us. I turned to look up to the top of the ridge where I had last seen him, but there was no sign of him.

'He said he'd be about five minutes,' Sue said. 'That was about twenty minutes ago.'

I looked at my watch. She was right.

Steve looked distinctly unimpressed. 'Great,' he said. 'I'll go and see if I can find him.'

'Shall we all come?' Sue asked. 'It'll save you coming back to find us here.'

Steve hesitated for a minute, weighing up the matter. 'OK, that might be better.'

We rounded everyone up and set off for the top of the ridge.

Steve turned to Kevin. 'Is Jim in the habit of wandering off on his own?'

'I don't know,' Kevin said. 'We're not particularly close friends. We've had quite a bit of contact since the last expedition, but we've never actually been on a trip as part of the same team.'

As we got closer to the top of the ridge, we started to call out and blow our whistles, but no response came back.

Irritation had crept in to Steve's voice as the moments ticked by. 'Where on earth has he gone? I warned everyone about wandering off on their own.'

'Perhaps he's fallen and injured himself,' Jenny said.

Steve did not respond.

We arrived at the top of the ridge. Once more, we shouted and blew whistles. Still, there was no response.

Steve sighed heavily. 'Now what?'

Unfortunately, the heavy cloud was providing a persistent drizzle. While many of us had waterproof jackets, only Kevin had come dressed in waterproof trousers. My jeans were already starting to get damp and I was beginning to sympathize with Steve's frustration over Jim's continued absence.

It was the first time I had seen Jenny without a smile. A worry-frown lined her brow. 'I don't like this, Steve,' she said. 'I don't know Jim any better than any of the rest of you, but he seems a fairly sensible man. I don't think he'd go wandering off without letting us know what his intentions were.'

There was silence for a while as we considered Jenny's words.

'Excuse my ignorance,' Sue said, 'but do you have things like bears or mountain lions in Washington State?'

Her question gave me a jolt. I had not considered that.

'We do,' Cecil said. 'We have cougar in this area. They are the second largest species of cat in the Americas. There are also American black bears and grizzlies found in Washington State. However, if you encounter a bear in these parts, it's almost certain to be a black bear. I should also say that both these species will generally avoid contact with humans whenever possible.'

That was a relief, although I was not convinced that it helped much when it came to the whereabouts of Jim. If he had been attacked by some wild beast, surely, we would have heard some kind of commotion?

Kevin came up with a plan. 'Steve, there are a number of us here. I think we should split into small groups and search this immediate area. We know he came this way. If he's fallen or injured himself, he can't be far away.'

Steve reluctantly agreed to the proposal. 'OK folks, we'll go with Kevin's suggestion, but I don't want anyone going too far. Make sure you're within the range of the whistles.'

I teamed up with Sue and Ron. Kevin went with Ben and Steph, Steve and Jenny went as a pair, while Cecil accompanied Jack and Briony.

Sue, Ron and I began searching an area off to our right. Every fifteen minutes, each group would give two short blasts on a whistle and await a response to make sure we were still within earshot of the other groups.

As we continued our search, my mind drifted on to Sam. Up until this point, I had been absorbed by Ron's and Cecil's easy-going teamwork but now, my fears over Sam's welfare returned.

The skies had darkened, and an hour and a half had passed, but none of us had found any sign of Jim. It was almost as if he had been lifted clean off the face of the planet. I had never given any time at all to the idea of alien abduction but, at that moment, it would have been a challenge to come up with a more plausible theory.

Nevertheless, I continued to try to find one. I recalled our other expedition. Jim had been very much opposed to the work of the creationists back then. Was it possible that opposition was still alive and well? Could Jim still be opposed to Kevin's work? Even if that were the case, that did not really explain his disappearance. But, apart from that, personally, I did not believe it. I recalled the discussion I had had with him as we were studying the rock layers, five days previously. I was convinced that he was genuine in his desire to understand the claims of creation scientists. I also believed that this was purely for his own benefit, not for any questionable motives. The whole episode was so confusing; I did not know what to think.

Eventually, we heard three short blasts on a whistle. This had been the agreed signal to return to discuss the situation. We responded with our own three blasts and headed towards the meeting point.

We were all dispirited. The longer we searched without success, the more likely it was that something truly unpleasant had befallen Jim. It was hard enough dealing with the situation concerning Sam, without Jim being missing and having no idea whether or not he was OK.

When we were back together again, Steve said decisively: 'OK, we're going back.'

Jenny started to object, but Steve interrupted her.

'Jenny, we could be out here for hours and not find anything. I've had a chat with Ron and Cecil and they're going to organize a search. They have more knowledge about this area and they'll be much better equipped to look for Jim than we are.'

A stunned silence settled as we all walked back to the vehicles, where Steve had another discussion with Ron and Cecil. They assured us that they would be in touch as soon as they had any information. The rest of us climbed solemnly into the vehicles and headed back to base.

By the time we had arrived back at the hotel, ironically, the rain had stopped. We congregated in the conference room to dry out a bit and grab a hot drink. Inevitably, the conversation turned to Jim and his disappearance. It was a total mystery to everyone, with each of us dissecting our own recent conversations with him. None of us could come up with a plausible explanation as to what might have happened.

During a pause in the conversation, I wondered whether to mention the question that had come into my mind over Jim's previous anti-creation stance. It felt disloyal just having the thought. All the same, as everyone seemed to be at a total loss to explain the situation, I turned to my left and carefully expressed what was on my mind.

'Kevin, I don't think this is at all likely and I only mention it because we're having such a struggle to explain what has happened.' I paused and took a deep breath. 'Listen, Jim has come across to me as genuine in his desire to learn the truth about these geological questions. But, during our previous expedition to the Congo, he was very much opposed to the creationist way of viewing things. You don't think there's any chance that he's still an evolutionist at heart? Is there any chance he might actually be trying to undermine your work in some way?'

It went completely silent as everyone considered the possibility. However, everyone unanimously decided that Jim was acting in good faith. I tended to agree with their assessment, but I could not quite shake that tiny doubt.

I was in the middle of saying, 'I'm sure you're right,' when my phone gave a ping.

I stopped abruptly and looked down at my mobile.

The message was from a number I did not know. It said, 'Granger, we need to know about the work of your creationist buddies. I suggest you get us some information fairly soon. Your brother's time is running out.'

These words sent a shudder through me. I closed my eyes and told myself to keep calm. I almost had to make a conscious effort to breathe.

When I opened my eyes again, I realized that everyone was watching me. 'Sorry,' I said, flustered. 'As I say, I'm sure you're right.' I hurriedly shoved my mobile in the back pocket of my still-slightly-damp jeans.

'I'm sure Jim's genuine,' Kevin said.

As the conversation continued on the subject of Jim's disappearance, I excused myself and walked in the direction of the gents' toilets. However, rather than going in, I carried on into reception and out of the front of the hotel.

The rain had stopped and a weak sun was peeping through the thinning clouds. I found a bench facing the drive and felt the seat with my hand. It was already dry. Retrieving my mobile from my back pocket, I sat to read the latest message again.

On my first reading, because I had been sitting in the hotel with the others, some of the remarks had not really made any impression. Now, as I read it for a second time, suddenly, I went cold. I remembered someone calling Sam, 'Granger', when we had been in the Congo. I could be wrong, but if this was the same man, Sam was in mortal danger. Although I was extremely concerned for Sam's safety, at the same time, I was also annoyed. Did this man think I could just magic the information out of thin air? I took some deep breaths, needing to calm down before I responded with something foolish.

Having allowed my emotions to diminish a little, I began my response:

I don't know who you are, but please don't harm Sam. If you want this information, I'll get it for you. However, if you don't want me to let on that I'm receiving your messages, you'll have to let me get the information you want when I can. If I hurry them up too much, they're bound to become suspicious and start asking questions. They have started to give me the information, but it's going to take time.

I had just sent the text and had let out a long and heavy sigh when Sue sat down on the bench beside me. She said nothing but just stared in front of her. Her silence suggested that she had seen at least part of my response.

I was annoyed and scared. 'What are you doing sneaking around like that?' I snapped.

Her head dropped. There was no reply for some time. When she did speak, she said softly, 'Rob, I'm not sneaking around. You just didn't hear me. You were rather preoccupied.'

I was frustrated with myself for my lack of care. What had Sue seen?

'You are sneaking around,' I said with some force. 'You're checking up on me.'

She suddenly became annoyed herself. 'Rob, I'm not sneaking around and I'm not checking up on you! I'm concerned for you. You've been acting very strangely over the last couple of days and I'm worried about you, that's all.'

Sue's annoyance had the effect of reducing my own. I had not seen her upset like this before and I knew I was in the wrong. My fear and concern for Sam's welfare was understandable, but it had caused me to lash out at Sue and she did not deserve that. I had already had to apologize to her once that day because of our discussion the previous evening. I did not want this to become a habit.

There was silence for some time. My mind was racing. Had she seen the message? I did not think that was likely, but there had been enough in my response to allow an intelligent girl like Sue to arrive at certain conclusions. She already knew I was concerned about Sam. What should I do?

Anyway, I realized I owed her an apology. 'Sorry,' I said, quietly. 'Sue, I'm desperately worried. I need to have a chat with you.' There was another silence. Then I asked, 'How much of my message did you see?'

She looked at me sympathetically. 'I don't know. That depends how long it was. I know enough to know that Sam seems to be in danger and that someone is asking for some kind of information.'

I put my head in my hands as I wondered what to do. I did not want to share more information with anyone than I had to, but

I reasoned that if I was going to explain the message to Sue, it would probably be best to tell her everything. It meant trusting her implicitly but, in the time that I had known her, she had shown nothing but integrity.

I made up my mind. 'Sue, come up to my room and I'll show you all their texts.'

She hesitated. 'Sorry, Rob,' she said with slight embarrassment, 'would you mind if we went through them out here?'

I realized how my suggestion might be taken and grasped her point.

'It's not that I don't trust you,' she said quickly. 'It's just how others might see it.'

I smiled and nodded. 'OK,' I said, 'but I want to be somewhere where we can see if anyone is approaching.'

Sue looked a little embarrassed again, presumably thinking about her own undetected arrival.

We located a bench which was out of view of the entrance of the hotel and from which we could clearly see if anyone was walking towards us.

When we were settled, I began. 'Listen, Sue, it's really, *really* important that you keep all this to yourself. Sam's life is in danger, and I don't want me or anyone else to make the situation worse for him.'

Sue nodded gravely. 'OK, I promise I won't tell anyone.'

So, I began to fill her in. I went back over the texts I had received from Sam in which he had explained about the people watching his house. We then recalled our first chat when I had told her that

Sam had not replied to my messages. Finally, I began showing Sue the texts I had received since Sam's kidnapping, along with those I had sent in response.

'Maybe it was a good thing you didn't immediately contact the British police.'

'I know,' I said. 'Mind you, I wish Sam had contacted them when I first suggested it. Maybe all of this could have been avoided.'

She nodded and continued to browse through the texts, worry etched on her face. 'At least this explains your new-found fascination in radiometric dating.' She stopped reading for a moment and stared into the distance. 'Rob, I really think you should let Kevin know about these texts.'

'No!' I said, emphatically. 'I can't risk that.'

'Surely if you explained the situation, he'd treat the information sensitively?'

He probably would. But I still did not think it was a good idea and said so. Although Sue obviously felt differently, she agreed to drop the subject for the time being.

The pause was interrupted by a ping from the phone in her hand.

We glanced at each other before looking down at my mobile. She handed the phone back, shuffling along the seat so she was sitting right next to me. I noticed the number displayed on my phone was the same one as the previous call.

The message read:

Get on with it. We accept that it will take you some time to get the information, but if we get the idea that you're stalling, you know what the result will be. Your brother is with friends of mine who possess equipment capable of bringing a bit of symmetry to your brother's legs.

There was a shocked gasp from Sue, and I went cold. This message just about removed all doubt. That was exactly the sort of spiteful comment I would have expected Smith to make. I recognized that I had another decision to make. Should I share my suspicions about the identity of this man? Once again, I thought that if I was going to tell her anything, I may as well tell her everything.

'Sue, I'm afraid I think the man who sent that text is the same man who put a bullet in Sam's leg in the Congo.'

She was shocked. 'Oh, no! What makes you think that?'

I explained to her that it was the way that he referred to me as 'Granger', telling her how he had spoken to Sam. However, I was confused. Irrespective of whether or not this was the man who used to call himself John Smith, why, all of a sudden, would he start using a different phone. I stored the new number in my contacts list under the name, 'Smith'. As this latest message did not appear to be requiring a response, I did not bother.

After our evening meal, we gathered in the meeting room to continue our education on their research work. As we settled ourselves into our seats, Jenny began by mentioning the subject which was on all our minds:

'We're all obviously very concerned to know what has happened to Jim, but the police have advised us to try, as much as possible, to continue with our work. I appreciate that won't be easy. It goes without saying that if we receive any information, we'll be sharing it with the police, but it's important that we leave them to get on with their investigations.'

After a short pause, she went on: 'OK, tonight, I'm going to start by giving you an introduction to what radiohalos are and how they're formed.[24] We'll then be looking at some specific kinds of radiohalos and I'll explain why they're significant.'

Again, no mention of ore deposits. This was really beginning to concern me.

Jenny began her presentation. Her usually sunny smile was diluted this evening. Nevertheless, she professionally continued, explaining that as a result of the decay of some radioactive elements within rock, microscopic spheres of discolouration can form. These spherical-shaped areas of damage are known as radiohalos. She began to explain to us how uranium radiohalos were created from the decay of uranium. As she related this information, I was getting more and more stressed. Because of my frantic notetaking, I was not able to spend any time attempting to actually understand the subject.

Jenny then introduced us to some different types of radiohalos. Instead of being produced by uranium, these were formed by the decay of the element polonium. The curious thing was that these polonium radiohalos were generally found in very close proximity to those formed by uranium. This phenomenon had been noticed decades earlier but, for years, no one had been able to give a good explanation as to why this should have happened. It turned out that, as uranium decays, the last three alpha decay steps in that process relate to the element polonium.

Jenny explained that one of the reasons it was a mystery was because, while uranium decays extremely slowly, polonium decays very, very rapidly. As a result, it was a real challenge to the geologists to explain how these different radiohalos could form at the same time, and right next to each other. I just kept scribbling, and hoped I could make sense of it later.

A couple of decades ago, one of Jenny's colleagues had proposed a theory which might resolve the mystery, she excitedly exclaimed. His proposal was that during the uranium decay process, hydrothermal fluids, or hot waters, within the rock may have transferred polonium atoms from one site to the other. Over recent years, geologists had gathered experimental data which, Jenny claimed, strongly supported her colleague's theory.

All this was fine, but unfortunately, I had not understood a tenth of what Jenny had been saying most of the evening. I suspected I would have to pass all this information on to Smith, but how?

I looked down at my notes again. Because of the speed with which I had been writing, they looked a complete mess. I was not even sure I would be able to decipher what I had written. I would have to grab Sue to see if she could help me make sense of it all.

As Jenny started to wrap up the session, at last, she gave me hope that the information I so badly wanted to hear would soon be discussed.

'Our studies of these radiohalos have led us to a number of other exciting conclusions. One of these is that the hydrothermal fluids we have just been discussing may also be responsible for producing new ore deposits. This is quite an exciting possibility, and I hope to be able to tell you more about that tomorrow.'

Relief flooded my whole body. I felt the tension in my muscles ease. I suspected that Smith's patience would not last much longer.

As on the previous evening, when the session broke up Sue and I headed for the bar.

After we were settled at one of the tables waiting for our coffees, Sue said, 'You do realize that the guys in there are completely confused about your desperation to understand the subject?'

I sighed. 'Yes, of course, but what can I do about it?'

'You could tell them.'

'I can't,' I said emphatically. 'I can't risk Smith finding out that I've disobeyed his instructions.'

'How could he possibly know?' she asked. 'He's in Britain with Sam.'

'I don't know,' I said, irritably. 'Sue, this is my brother we're talking about. How would you feel if it was a member of your family?'

There was a momentary pause as she looked down at the table. Continuing to stare at the table, she shook her head. 'I don't know, Rob. It must be extremely hard for you. But I'm afraid I still think that the best thing you could do is to confide in Kevin. He's not stupid. I'm sure he wouldn't do anything if he thought there was even a chance that this Smith character would find out.'

'But he couldn't guarantee that, Sue. We have absolutely no

idea whether Smith has people in this country. For all we know, he has friends keeping an eye on us.'

Sue glanced up at me. 'I think that's pretty unlikely, Rob.'

I wondered whether or not to admit to some of my other thoughts. I conceded that I might as well be completely candid with her.

'I'm afraid I'd even wondered if he could have planted someone in our group.'

She looked at me in disbelief. 'Now you're being paranoid,' she said. 'There's no way any of these guys are working for this man.'

'Sue, I understand why you'd say that, but that's what Smith did on our last trip.'

At that moment our coffees arrived. Our conversation briefly came to a halt as a young waitress placed a cup and saucer in front of each of us with a bowl of brown sugar and a little jug of cream.

'Thanks very much,' I said.

'You're welcome,' she responded, giving me a beautiful smile. 'Enjoy,' she added, as she headed back towards the bar.

I looked back at Sue who had an amused expression on her face.

In spite of the serious nature of the discussion we were having, I could not help being affected by her look of amusement. 'What's up with you?' I asked.

'Would you like me to leave?' she asked, the amused look still in place. 'I do believe you've got a new admirer.'

'Don't be daft,' I said, picking up the jug of cream and dropping a few spots into the black coffee.

‘I think I’ll have to keep an eye on you, Mr Granger,’ she said, with a mischievous little giggle.

Admittedly, this exchange did provide a slightly lighter interlude in the proceedings, but I now brought the conversation back to the matter in hand.

I spent a few minutes relating some of the details from our previous expedition to the Congo. While I did not necessarily expect this to change her mind, I hoped that it would help her to understand why I might at least consider infiltration as a possibility.

Sue shook her head. ‘Rob, I just don’t see any of our group working for someone like Smith.’

‘What about Jack and Briony?’

‘No, I don’t believe it. They’re a lovely couple.’

Neither of us spoke. Then, as I watched Sue’s face, I saw a dawning realization.

‘He can’t have anyone in our group,’ she said, confidently.

‘Why?’

‘Have another look at your messages. If he had someone else working for him in this group, he wouldn’t be so desperate to get you to obtain the information on minerals. Just think about it. Jack and Briony have shown absolutely no interest in the mineral work.’

I considered her words. That was true. Thinking back over the messages I had received from Smith, they did not appear to come from someone who had an alternative method of obtaining the information.

‘I think you might be right,’ I said. Then I remembered something else. ‘Sue, while I was scribbling down my notes, I did not really have a chance to concentrate on Jenny’s reasoning. Would you mind going through my notes at some point and helping me to understand them?’

She smiled, ironically. ‘Yes, OK. But it would be much better if you went through them with Jenny or Steve.’

We spent another twenty minutes deep in conversation, discussing the pros and cons of sharing the information with the others.

‘Sue, I’m not telling anyone just yet. If people find my behaviour strange, they’ll just have to put up with it.’

A look of concern clouded her eyes.

‘I’m sorry, Sue. I understand how you feel, but I’m afraid I’m going to have to ask you to keep this to yourself for now. Leave it with me for a while. I promise I’ll give your comments some serious thought.’

This brought the subject to an end for the time being, but I knew it was only a temporary intermission.

When I eventually got back to my room, I sent a message to Smith. In very brief note form, I explained the limited information I could remember and hoped this would satisfy him for now.

Unfortunately, it did not. I received an almost immediate reply.

It said, ‘This is all rubbish, Granger. When are you going to get the information on ore deposits?’

Anger rose up in me again, but it did reinforce Sue’s belief that he could not have someone else in our group.

Chapter 11
The Crater

Sunday, 11 August, had the potential to be the most exciting day of our whole trip. At the same time, it was also the day about which I felt most nervous. This was the day we were scheduled to hike into the crater of Mount Saint Helens.

Until Kevin had invited me on this trip, the idea of visiting the crater of an active volcano had never been at the top of my bucket list of things to do. In fact, I do not think I had ever even considered it as a possibility. However, if it had not been for the serious situations with Sam and Jim, I would have been able to think of nothing else.

The trip was going to involve a twelve-mile hike and meant a very early start to the day. In spite of the early start, being Sunday, most of our group met in the meeting room for an early short service. Because of her recent conversion, Sue decided to join them. She asked me if I was interested in going along, but I politely declined the offer.

After breakfast, we all gathered in the hotel foyer. We were due to meet Ron and Cecil in a car park at the start of the trail at 7:00 am.

When we arrived, Cecil recognized that we were struggling and tried to raise the mood in our group a little. 'I hope you're all feeling energetic. This is likely to be a day that you'll never forget, but it's a fairly strenuous hike. You'll be ascending through about 3,000 feet of elevation. However, please don't let that put you off, because you'll be seeing some amazing sites today.'

After a few safety instructions about the day, we set off on our hike. There was a strange atmosphere. The disappearance of Jim was still very much troubling everyone, although I heard in the hum of conversations something about prayers for his safety. Coupled with the long hike ahead, the mood was a mix of determined expectation and subdued sadness. It was not that long before we found ourselves climbing steadily. I went back to the conversation in my living room on that wet April day and wished Sam had agreed to come with us. Although, as my boots crunched over the rough ground, I did wonder how he would have coped with the terrain.

We had been traversing the slopes of Mount Saint Helens for some time when Ron told us that we were walking across 2,000-year-old lava flows. I glanced in Steve's direction, wondering if this information was consistent with his assessment of the age of these deposits. However, there was no immediate indication that he disagreed with Ron's statement. I wondered at myself; in the past, I would have accepted these dates without question. Now, however, I found myself questioning everything. How things had changed!

Suddenly, Ron pointed up into the sky off to our left. Looking up, outstretched wings hovered overhead. The bird of prey appeared almost motionless, just hanging there in the sky, presumably riding unseen thermal currents.

'Bald eagle,' Ron informed us. 'You regularly see them in these parts.'

After a few more seconds studying the raptor, we continued on our way.

We had been going for another half an hour when Cecil took his invisible cue to take over. 'What we're walking over now is a Pumice Plain. This is volcanic material which was deposited by a pyroclastic flow during the 1980 eruption.'

I interrupted his explanation with a question: 'Cecil, what exactly are pyroclastic flows? I know they have something to do with volcanic eruptions, but that's about the extent of my knowledge.'

'They're fast-moving clouds of super-heated gases, steam and ash,' he said. "They can be hugely destructive and, because they travel so quickly, they've been responsible for the deaths of many a volcanologist.'

That was a sobering thought.

'Nasty,' I said. 'I can think of better ways to go.'

Ron laughed, replying, 'Actually, Rob, you probably wouldn't know much about it. It would be over in a fraction of a second.'

I guessed he was right. All the same, I still did not fancy putting it to the test.

Fifteen minutes later, I was walking immediately behind Steve when he came to an abrupt halt. I almost careered straight into his backpack.

'Have you ever come across one of these, Rob?' he asked, pointing towards some of the flowering vegetation sprouting from the pumice field.

As I looked more closely, I could see a tiny little hummingbird hovering in front of one of the flowers.

'Oh, wow,' I said. 'No, I've never seen one of those before. What an amazing little creature.'

Sue was a good few paces behind with Jenny, deep in conversation. All the same, I could not help myself interrupting them to call her attention to it.

Continuing on our journey, I was mesmerized by the landscape. After the devastation caused by the recent eruptions, there were so many signs of life in the area. It had not been what I expected.

We crunched our way over the ash layers as we continued following the trail. Although there was the constant noise of our tramping, in many ways, the scene was peaceful. As we continued the ascent with little information coming from Ron and Cecil, my thoughts ran free; it was quite hard to convince myself that I was actually climbing an active volcano.

I was still caught up in a sense of wonder, when, on turning a bend in the trail, another sight almost stopped me in my tracks. There, glistening in the morning light was Spirit Lake. I could clearly see some of the logs floating at the southern end. We all stopped for a few minutes to take in the view.

My next surprise was provided by a couple of mountain goats. I had heard a deep bleating noise from up the slope off to my right and glanced up directly into two pairs of eyes. The two goats were some way off, but they locked eyes with me, seemingly picking me out for special attention. Utterly still, as if carved out of marble, they stood looking down upon us. The only movement was their slowly turning heads as they tracked our journey along the trail.

Every now and again, we would come across monitoring equipment. These were strategically positioned to detect seismic activity which might indicate that Mount Saint Helens was preparing to indulge in a new period of destructive behaviour. Although I knew nothing about these pieces of kit and how they worked, I was somehow comforted by their presence.

We had been walking for another hour or so when Ron brought us to a halt.

'OK,' he said, 'we're going to leave this main trail now and head up towards the crater. Because so much of the northern slope was blown away in the 1980 eruption, there is now a mile-wide breach in the northern side of the crater. We're going to hike up and go through that breach.'

Despite the morning chill in the air, I was getting hot as a result of the climb. The grey terrain was punctuated by occasional patches of green shrubbery, which had become sparser as we climbed. As we set off again, Ron told us that they sometimes have to re-route their trips into the crater as the effects of further erosion often changes the landscape on the northern slopes of the volcano.

Continuing to climb, the terrain became more and more barren, those patches of shrubbery long gone. Most of the time I was looking at the ground, being careful where I was putting my feet. The rhythmic crunch as one foot carefully set in front of the other had an almost hypnotic affect. Suddenly, I almost cannoned into the back of Sue, who had stopped abruptly. Following the direction of her stare, I saw what it was that had caused her unexpected halt.

'Well, there it is,' Ron said with a grin. 'That's the lava dome which was formed during the particularly active period following the 18 May 1980, eruption.'

I glanced down at my watch. We had been walking for about five and a half hours. Now, there, in front of us, was the famous Mount Saint Helens lava dome which I had heard so much about.

Ron continued, 'It's not particularly easy to see from here, but there is a second dome behind it.'

He told us that this second dome was much newer and was formed during the more recent volcanic activity between 2004 and 2008.

When we stopped to have our packed lunch, we were near the top of Step Canyon, one of the canyons we had viewed from the air five days ago. The view we had seen from the chopper had been amazing and, in spite of my fear of flying, I was glad to have done it. However, it had not given me a true understanding of the size of the canyon.

As Sue and I began tucking into our sandwiches, Briony and Jack came over to join us. Briony started to quiz Sue about her job, asking her if she would have the opportunity to share what she was learning in the classroom. As usual, Jack was not inclined to speak for the sake of it. Along with most of us who were hiking into the Mount Saint Helens crater for the first time, he was gazing around in wonder, taking in the atmosphere of the place and enjoying the sights on view. It truly was an amazing place.

Jack looked in my direction and I thought he was about to ask me something. However, after a moment, I realized that he was looking past me and staring curiously into the heart of the crater.

'What's fascinating you?' I asked him.

He shot me a glance. 'The mist,' he said.

Following his gaze, there did seem to be a faint mist above the lava dome.

I looked across to where Ron was chatting with Kevin. 'Sorry to interrupt, guys, but Ron, can you tell us what that mistiness is in the crater?'

Ron and Kevin both turned to look towards the lava dome. 'Yes,' Ron said. 'Remember, this is an active volcano. You often get a small curtain of steam rising from the newer of the two lava domes. The amount of steam can vary, but it's often quite visible.' As he studied the scene, he resumed thoughtfully, 'Actually, you've come on a good day. That's the clearest I've seen the steam from this distance.'

Looking back at the mist, it seemed to be rising in the air. 'It almost looks like smoke,' I said.

Ron smiled. 'It's interesting you should say that. The Cowlitz Indian Tribe call this mountain "*Lawetlat'la*". That means 'smoker' in their language. I know some of you guys are very interested in the Bible's account of creation. Well, this place plays an important role in the creation story of these indigenous American people. It's actually of great spiritual significance to them.'

I could certainly understand how some could attribute spiritual qualities to this 'smoker'.

When we had finished our lunch, Cecil and Ron began to tell us a bit more about Step Canyon and how they believed it had been formed. They explained that a glacier had begun to form within the crater of Mount Saint Helens. This was a real puzzle to me. My own simplistic understanding of volcanos led me to believe that there was no way ice could form in the crater of an active volcano.

Cecil told us that the Mount Saint Helens crater glacier was interesting as it was the newest glacier to have formed in the whole of North America. It is unusual in the sense that it exists at a lower elevation than most other glaciers in the region. This is because the south rim of the crater shields it from direct sunlight. Winter storms result in significant amounts of snow falling into the crater, which is how the glacier got started. Over the years, the winter snow feeding the glacier has been greater than the melting experienced in the summers. Consequently, the Crater Glacier at Mount Saint Helens is one of the few of the world's glaciers to actually be increasing in size. We were in the middle of August on a pleasant summer's day, so perhaps it was not surprising that there was currently some melting going on. Little rivulets of water were wending their way towards the top of Step Canyon.

Having arrived in the crater, I marvelled at the sheer size of the lava dome. It was immense. Cecil told me that it was equivalent in height to a thirty-storey building.

Ron and Cecil spent some time leading us to various parts of the crater, identifying anything they felt was significant, continuing their double act of information relaying. They reminded me of Morecombe and Wise; the easy-going camaraderie was evidently based on a mutual, long-standing friendship, and they occasionally had a little joke with each other. Not to mention, Cecil was taller with darker hair, and specs, and Ron was slightly shorter with silvery hair.

Cecil cleaned his glasses as he pointed out that the Crater Glacier is horseshoe-shaped, wrapping itself around the lava domes. Although Crater Glacier is only a few decades old, it is a couple of hundred feet thick in places. Another interesting detail is that it is not immediately obvious that it is a glacier at all. There is quite a thick covering of debris on the glacier which, we were told, helps to insulate it from melting. In fact, Ron told us that the glacier is around forty percent rock.

As Ron went on speaking, I glanced around, catching Sue staring at the ground. She was not listening to Ron. This was surprising, as she would normally be drinking in any information given by the geologists.

Continuing to study her, she squatted down and dipped her finger in a little stream of water. Then, she stood up and looked towards the younger of the two lava domes.

I returned my attention to Ron and realized that he and Cecil were concluding their talks and preparing us to begin our trek out of the crater. I had climbed a volcano, and I was mentally congratulating myself at the feat and taking a final photo to preserve this memory, when I became conscious of a very faint, soft, high-pitched whistle. Turning slowly, I attempted to identify the sound.

Kevin noticed my slightly furrowed brow. 'What's up, Rob?'

'I was just trying to work out where that whistling was coming from.'

Kevin tilted his head, trying to hear the noise I was speaking about.

After a moment, he said, 'I can't hear anything.'

The sound had diminished, but I could still just about hear it.

'I think it's coming from over there,' I said, waving an arm towards the more recent lava dome.

It was difficult to get an accurate fix on the source of the sound, but I sensed that was the general direction from which the whistle was coming.

Kevin shouted over to where Steve and Jenny were studying a section of glacier. 'Steve, can I have a word?'

Steve and Jenny strolled in our direction. When they were within a few yards, Steve looked at us expectantly. 'Everything all right, Kevin?'

'Rob says he can hear a whistling sound,' Kevin told him.

'I heard it, too.'

This remark came from Sue, who appeared by my side. 'It was somewhere between a whistle and a hiss,' she added.

'That's right,' I said. 'Quite high-pitched.'

'Maybe that's why you two can hear it and we can't,' Kevin said.

'Younger people can generally hear a greater range of sounds than old fogies like us.'

'You speak for yourself,' Jenny said, with a broad smile.

We all laughed.

Steve shouted to Cecil. 'Cecil, can you give me ten minutes? I'd like to have a quick look at the dome.'

'Steve, do you think it might be safer to leave the area?' Kevin queried.

'There shouldn't be anything to worry about,' Cecil said, attempting to reassure him. 'We've had no unusual readings from any of the seismometers in the area. I'd be very surprised if there was a significant event any time in the next few weeks.'

Kevin glanced towards where I was standing with Sue. 'Well, OK, but don't forget we've got guests here.'

Cecil nodded and turned to Ron. 'Ron, will you get everyone ready to go back down? I'll go with Steve and see if anything's going on. We'll meet you at the breach when we've checked things out.'

Ron gave a brief nod as Steve and Cecil turned away to make their investigations.

'You take care, guys,' Jenny said to their retreating backs.

As I watched them go, I realized the sound had stopped. I listened intently to see if I could hear anything, but whatever had been responsible for the sound appeared to have ceased.

The rest of us donned our rucksacks and Ron began to lead us back towards the breach in the north of the crater.

As we trudged on, I had almost forgotten the whistling, when the sound came again. If anything, this time it was louder. That fact was confirmed as everyone's head jerked up to look towards the back of the crater.

'You might be an old fogie, Kevin,' I said, 'but I think even you heard it that time.'

When he turned back to me, he had a smile on his face, but I could not help noticing that there was a degree of concern in his eyes. This concern had an immediate effect on me. About ninety per cent of what I knew about volcanism I had learned within the last week, so I was certainly no expert. However, I knew enough to understand that if Mount Saint Helens blew her top while we were standing in our current position, that would be curtains.

I glanced over to where Ron was standing with Ben and Steph. Ron did not seem at all concerned, which made me feel a little better. All the same I was keen to get away from the area.

I turned to speak to Sue who had been standing to my left. However, she was no longer there. As I looked around to see where she had gone, I found her once more squatting down and staring at a small stream. She had a puzzled look on her face, so I wandered over to her to see what the problem was.

'What's up, Sue?'

She glanced up at me from her squatting position. 'There's much more water,' she said, distractedly.

I frowned. 'What do you mean?'

'When we arrived earlier, there were these little trickles of water. That's not surprising. You'd expect some melting to take place in the summer months. But there's a lot more water now. Some of it has collected in small pools, and some has formed into little streams. It's probably that we're at the warmest part of the day. If it was significant, I assume it would have been noticed by our experts. I just thought it was interesting.'

Sue was right. Thinking back, I realized that there was quite a bit more water around now than when we had arrived in the crater.

We discussed the water as we awaited Steve and Cecil's return. For some of this time, the high-pitched whistle was noticeable, then it ebbed into a distant hiss, disappearing altogether.

After a five-minute period where we had heard nothing, I had just remarked to Sue that perhaps the symphony was over, when a dramatic hissing and whistling caused us to almost jump out of our skins. As I swung around, I saw a jet of steam shooting skywards on our side of the lava dome. Faces followed the upward trail, suddenly whipping down at the sight of Steve and Cecil who were staggering in our direction. As one, we started to scramble towards them. As they drew closer, we could see Steve attempting to support Cecil. The pair stumbled and almost fell.

We were within about 15 yards of them when Ben turned towards the rest of us and shouted, 'You guys wait here. Steph and I will deal with it.'

We all stopped and let them go the remaining distance to Steve and Cecil. Ben dropped his medical bag and helped Steve to lower Cecil to the ground. Steph opened the medical bag and started removing items while Ben began to examine his patient.

Looking beyond the small group at the jet of steam, I saw with relief that it was beginning to dwindle. The whistling was still ringing in the air, but that too was reducing. After a few more seconds, all activity appeared to have ceased, except the bustle of Ben and Steph checking Cecil over.

Although glued to the spot, I looked around, desperately wanted us all to get off the mountain as quickly as possible.

As I returned my attention to the group in front of me, I tried to read their expressions to make sense of what was going on. They were not encouraging. Ben's expression was hard to read. He had a professional face on and was busy doing something to Cecil who was lying on the ground and obscured from my view. Steve was looking concerned and ashen faced. Although Steph was busy helping Ben and had her head down, I thought I could see tears glistening on her cheeks.

All of a sudden, Cecil let out an agonized groan. It sent a shiver through my body and my stomach flipped.

Ron strode over to be with his friend. There was a brief conversation, and then Steve left the group to come over to speak to us. He looked as if he were in shock himself.

'Are you OK, Steve?' Kevin asked.

Steve waved a dismissive hand. 'I'm fine; don't worry about me. It's Cecil that caught it. The steam jet hit him on his righthand side. I'm afraid he's in quite a bad way.'

Briony asked the question that was on my own mind: 'How are we going to get him down?'

'Ron's going to call for some assistance,' Steve said. 'Meanwhile, Ron will lead you guys down, while Ben and I help Cecil.'

'Is that going to be possible?' Jenny asked.

Steve gave a shrug. 'Not sure,' he said. 'Ben's given him a shot to help with the pain, but it'll still be a difficult descent. I'm sure there will be some help on its way. I just hope we can move him OK.'

'What about the volcano?' Jack enquired. 'Is it getting ready to blow?'

Steve did not seem in the least bit worried and shook his head. 'I'd expect a lot more, smaller ash and steam eruptions for some time before any major blast. We shouldn't take anything for granted, but I don't expect any major event here for quite a while. Geologists will be keeping a very close eye on the seismology readings in the area.'

A few minutes later, Ron rejoined us and we set off on our return journey. As we left the crater, I looked over my shoulder to see how the others were getting on. At that distance, it was difficult to tell, but Cecil appeared to be on his feet, so I started to feel slightly easier about the situation.

As we began our descent, no one spoke; the hissing and whistling had ceased, and our crunching footsteps on the volcanic material were the only sounds. The incident with Cecil had given us a jolt. Although, for the most part, I trusted Steve and his assessment of our relative safety, I could not help feeling a degree of alarm. We had been told that, before the 1980 eruption, there had been a couple of months of much smaller volcanic events leading up to the main blast. The problem was that I was having trouble convincing myself that any future eruption would behave in an identical way.

A couple of times I glanced behind me to see if I could spot the others. Perhaps unsurprisingly, I could not. After all, we would almost certainly be moving a bit quicker than they would.

Checking my watch, we had made another fifteen-minute journey on our descent when I suddenly heard the rhythmic throbbing of helicopter rotor blades. This alone was not especially noteworthy as there were regular flights taking interested punters like us to get a bird's-eye view of the volcano. However, this aircraft was not approaching on the usual flightpath. Looking up, I saw a chopper flying straight towards us. It flew over our heads and continued on a course which would take it towards the crater. We all stopped and watched as the chopper slowed and then began to circle a particular spot.

Looking round our group, I could not help noticing the deep concern on all the faces. As we watched, we saw a figure being winched down from the belly of the helicopter. The pilot began to adjust the position of his aircraft. From our own position, it looked as if he were about to fly into the side of the mountain, but this was just an illusion. Having traversed a couple of bends in the trail, the shoulder of the volcano was obscuring the critical area from our sight.

Kevin took out his mobile and put it to his ear. 'Steve!' he shouted. 'What's going on?'

From our own position, the helicopter's rotors were not particularly loud, but I suspected where Steve and the others were, the sound would be deafening.

Kevin listened for a moment, then he shouted, 'How is Cecil?'

There was a look of concentration on Kevin's face as he

attempted to hear Steve's responses. This time, the response was a longer one.

When Kevin did finally speak, he yelled, 'Do you want us to wait for you?'

There was another brief pause, but we heard Kevin reply, 'OK, we'll see you back at base.' And with that, he hung up.

'What's happening?' Jenny asked.

'Cecil's not great,' Kevin said. 'It was clear to Ben after only a couple of hundred yards that Cecil wasn't going to make it down under his own steam.'

When we arrived back at the hotel at about 7:30 pm, we went straight into the restaurant, after a quick freshen up. With such a long trek, we were all famished. Steve gave us an update on Cecil's condition. We learned that he had been flown to the nearest specialist burns unit which was at a hospital in Portland, Oregon. Ironically for the Christians in the team, the hospital was named 'Emanuel' which I now discovered meant 'God with us'. The doctors had said that Cecil was in a significant amount of discomfort and was likely to be spending a number of days in hospital. They were still assessing his injuries, but they had reported that the burns were serious. It was currently just speculation, but it sounded as if skin grafts would be required. Just the thought of that made me feel queasy.

Inevitably, the day's events and Cecil's accident were the main topics of conversation during our meal. However, thoughts then started to turn to our own situation.

'What implications does this have for the rest of our time here?' Sue asked.

'That's a good question,' Steve said. 'I've been in touch with the US Geological Survey and they're surprised about this activity. There appear to have been no indications which would cause them to expect such an event. Even since our unfortunate experience, there have only been minimal readings; nothing which would cause any particular concern to the geologists. There have been some very slight readings, but hardly anything really. To be on the safe side, they've put restrictions in place to limit access to the volcano, but they're saying that the chances of a major eruption in the near future are pretty small.'

I was halfway through my meal when my phone gave a ping. Unsurprisingly, when I checked who had sent the message, I saw Smith's name. The message was one short question. All it said was: 'Have you lost someone?' This was accompanied by a smiley face.

My initial response to this text was one of confusion. I spent a few moments wondering why Smith would mock me over Sam's disappearance when I was fully aware of the situation. Then, all of a sudden, I went cold. My thoughts were so dominated by Sam and his predicament, perhaps it was not surprising that I had overlooked other possibilities. As I began to think more clearly, I realized that Smith's message was almost certainly not referring to Sam's disappearance. It was much more likely to be referring to Jim. Cecil had obviously just had his own accident, but surely Smith would not be aware of that yet.

This sent my head into a spin. How on earth could he know

about Jim? Somehow, it would appear that he knew a good deal about our party. I thought back to the text messages I had received. It seemed clear to me that he was the person holding Sam. However, if that was the case, it would also appear that he had an accomplice or accomplices on our side of the Atlantic who were keeping us under surveillance and relaying information back to him. If so, maybe even more disturbingly, was it possible those people were actually responsible for Jim's disappearance?

I noticed Sue glance at me a couple of times, questioningly. I remembered my conversation with her the previous evening. She had again advised me to confide in Kevin about Sam. I had mentioned to her that Smith might have people keeping an eye on us. At the time, Sue had convinced me that this could not be the case, but the text I had just received suggested something different. What on earth was going on? Whatever the truth, and however he had managed to achieve it, I could not help feeling that in some way, Smith must also be responsible for Jim Redfern's disappearance.

My train of thought was interrupted as I glanced at my watch with a frown. It was 8:08 pm here; that made it past 4:00 am in Britain. Did Smith never go to bed?

The point was, what was I to do now? I did not want to jeopardise Sam's position. I knew Sue thought I should tell Kevin, but if there was any chance that Smith did have a spy in our camp, I would have to extract an iron-clad promise from Kevin that he would not pass on the information to anyone else. The trouble was that I did not see how he would possibly be able to give such a guarantee.

I felt a bit guilty, but I decided not to say anything to Sue about this latest text for the time being. I wanted the time to consider the text message myself before having a battle over the rights and wrongs of telling others.

Thinking about Kevin prompted another train of thought. What about his friend? Kevin had said that his contact had discovered that two people from the Westminster Group had come out to the States. Could that have a bearing on Jim's disappearance? Were they working with Smith? If so, it was likely that they also knew something about Sam's situation.

As on the previous two evenings, after our meal, we retired to the meeting room for the next session on the research work.

Jenny got up to speak. 'OK, folks. Yesterday, I said that tonight, we'd have our next session on radiohalos and these ore deposits. However, we've had a long day and we've also had the upset of the incident with Cecil. I suspect, if you're anything like me, you're feeling quite tired. So, what I intend to do is give a very brief overview of tonight's talk and then we'll pick it up again tomorrow. Is that OK for everyone?'

I had mixed feelings about this. True, I was feeling very tired, but I was also concerned about any delay in getting the information to Smith. As I weighed up the pros and cons, I noticed everyone else agreeing with Jenny's proposal.

She looked at me. 'Is that all right with you, Rob?'

I nodded reluctantly. 'Yes, that's fine.'

'Wonderful,' she said with a weary smile. 'OK. Well, members of the secular scientific community often claim that creation scientists never make predictions which are later verified experimentally. So, one of the things we'll discuss tomorrow evening is an example to show you that that claim is total nonsense. If you remember, yesterday, we looked at the possibility that hydrothermal fluids were responsible for transferring polonium atoms to allow polonium and uranium radiohalos to form alongside each other. Well, the geologist responsible for this work was also studying reactions between certain minerals within metamorphic rock. He also knew that significant amounts of water had been involved in the process. As a result, he predicted that when they took and analysed samples from the area, they'd find large numbers of radiohalos.

On carrying out their experiment, the data completely vindicated his position. Further testing provided even more support for his theory. So, this is a fantastic example of a creation scientist making a prediction ahead of time which has been confirmed by subsequent field work. We need to understand that thinking in line with the Bible can often directly lead you to making correct scientific predictions. And, in spite of assertions made by many in the atheist camp, there are plenty of examples of this.'

Although I was frantically scribbling down the information, I was still able to appreciate the significance of Jenny's words.

Jenny then briefly displayed a number of slides showing samples from different areas of the world which contained significant levels of ore deposits within them. There was granite from Cornwall in England containing large deposits of tin, uranium, copper, lead and zinc. She explained that these had formed in fractures in the rock as a result of hot waters flowing through to create these deposits. Interestingly, and completely consistent with their previous work, this area contained a huge number of uranium and polonium radiohalos.

'So again,' Jenny said, 'the more hot water you have, the more halos you find.'

Still looking up at the screen, some of her enthusiasm had returned as she talked about her specialist area.

She continued: 'It was becoming more and more obvious to this creation geologist that he could use high numbers of polonium radiohalos in granites and other rocks as a pathfinder to find new ore deposits.'

As I continued to record these details, I began to feel much more hopeful. However, I was still left with the problem of how to communicate all this to Smith. Currently, all I had was a load of scribbled notes. Furthermore, I did not know what most of them meant.

I assumed these would be Jenny's last remarks for the evening, but she had one last nugget of information to pass on.

'Now, the really exciting thing is that, up here close to Mount Saint Helens, we've recently found amazing evidence which provides us with further support for our theory. In addition, there are certain companies that extract ore deposits who are very interested in our work. They have expressed an interest in commissioning us to help them to know where they might find these minerals. These discussions have only just started, but it's a really interesting development. Tomorrow, we'll look at these subjects in a bit more detail.'

These last comments were eye opening. If Steve and Jenny were already in discussions with certain companies with a view to sharing data, and if Smith was aware of that, this might explain why he was so keen to obtain the information in a hurry.

My legs were feeling the effects of the day's exertions and, as I walked to the bar area with Sue, I was glad to sit down again.

'Sue, this has to be the information Smith is after. I'm sure he wants to know how to identify ore rich areas in order to make a killing.'

Sue frowned. 'Maybe, but I don't understand it. It makes no sense. He'd need a ton of specialist knowledge to benefit from this information.'

We sipped our drinks in silence as I considered her words. 'I'm sure you're right, Sue, but he obviously does want the information for some reason.'

Our conversation then drifted onto the power of experimental confirmation of predictions made by scientists. However, as Sue was talking, something popped into my mind, seemingly from nowhere.

Sue noticed the change in my expression and asked if I was OK.

'It's the other way round,' I said slowly.

'What is?'

'I think he's here.'

'Who?'

'Smith. I don't believe he's ever been with Sam.'

Sue looked puzzled. She said nothing but waited for me to continue.

'That's why the mobile number changed,' I said. 'I don't believe those first messages ever came from Smith. They were from whoever is holding Sam. Smith obviously knows them. I just remembered what he said on that mail that you saw.'

I got my phone out and searched for the message. 'Here it is. It says, "Your brother is with friends of mine who possess equipment capable of bringing a bit of symmetry to your brother's legs." Smith isn't with him. I suspect Smith has been over here all the time. I just assumed that he was with Sam.'

Sue nodded thoughtfully. 'Hmm. I see what you mean.'

'And that's another thing,' I said. quietly. 'When I got the message from Smith earlier, it came through at just after eight o'clock. If he'd sent it from Britain, it would have been about four in the morning.'

Sue looked shocked. 'You got another message from Smith today? Is that what you were looking at while we were having our meal? What did he say?'

I could have kicked myself. I had not intended to say anything to Sue about the message.

'It didn't make much sense,' I confessed. 'But the point is that I'm pretty sure, given the time of sending, he was very unlikely to be in England.'

To my relief, Sue did not ask to see the message.

Finishing our drinks punctuated by many yawns, the crater hike, the emotions of the day, and my last few nights of sleeplessness had caught up with me. We agreed to call it a night as my heavy eyes struggled to stay open.

As soon as I was back in my room, I sent a message to Smith. It was just a bunch of bullet points relating to the evening session. I mentioned that Jenny had begun to discuss the ore deposits but told him that I had got the information in very rough form. I promised to get it to him as soon as possible. Finally, I mentioned that they were also excited about some findings in the Mount Saint Helens area.

After sending the text I glanced at my watch. It was only 10:05 pm, but given my tiredness, I decided to hit the sack.

The next thing I knew I was suddenly wide awake. I had been in the middle of a vivid dream. It was unusual for me to remember my dreams in any detail, but this trip was a new experience in the dream department for me. In this dream I had been at the bottom of Spirit Lake with Chuck and Billy, trying to sway one of the upright logs.

I immediately sat up. Glancing at the clock on the bedside table, I groaned; the time was 1:56 am. Everything was completely dark except for the illuminated numbers on my clock and a very faint glow coming through the curtains from an external light in the grounds of the hotel.

I had no idea what had disturbed my sleep, but I felt wide awake. I was not aware of a noise or any other occurrence that might have caused my sudden wakefulness. I listened to see if I could hear anything. As I lay there, the images of the dream ran through my head. I had a picture of a tree at the bottom of a lake. Comparing that to my experience on Friday, I recalled the sudden revelation I had received regarding the truth of Steve's facts about the trees in the lake. As I half lay, half sat there in my bed, I suddenly knew with absolute certainty that the details I was learning from Steve and the others were going to change my life for ever. I had no idea how that was going to happen, but the feeling was unmistakable.

As I snuggled down in the bed and adjusted my pillow, I wondered what it was all about. I was not at all sure, but I would consider the matter further in the morning. However, I could not get back to sleep. I was well and truly wide awake. I sighed and stretched out to switch on the bedside lamp. My notepad was on the bedside table along with a pen. I grabbed them and wrote down a short account of this rather bizarre episode. Satisfied that I had recorded the relevant details, I placed the notepad on the bedside table and promptly fell straight back to sleep.

Chapter 12
A Confession

Despite the interlude in the middle of the night, I awoke feeling refreshed. As I got out of bed, my calf muscles reminded me that I was not as fit as I should be. Stumbling around like an old man, I managed to get myself ready and winced as I slowly descended the stairs, wishing I had taken the lift—or elevator as they called it here.

After breakfast, a few of us were sitting in the meeting room and preparing to head off for the visitor centres. My mind turned to Sam for the hundredth time that morning. It was incredibly frustrating hearing nothing about his circumstances or his condition and I felt the anger rise in me. I suddenly noticed Kevin looking at me intently.

'Are you OK, Rob?' he asked.

Once again, I was frustrated that my emotional state appeared to be so obvious.

'Just my aching calves,' I told him.

'I've got some paracetamol in my room. Do you want me to go and get them?'

I shook my head. 'No thanks, Kevin, I'll be fine.'

He glanced briefly at Sue, who avoided his gaze. I was just beginning to wonder where the rest of our party were, when Kevin's phone quacked at him. He looked surprised and retrieved it from his pocket. As he looked down, he frowned. Then he gave a jubilant shout: 'It's Jim!'

'What does he say?' Sue enquired.

There was silence as Kevin read. The look of joy disappeared from his face and was replaced by one of deep concern.

'What's up?' I asked.

Still Kevin did not speak but continued to read.

His silence became unbearable for Sue. 'For goodness's sake, Kevin, what does he say?'

Kevin looked up at us and then back down at his phone.

'He's been kidnapped,' he said.

I felt all the colour drain from my face. When I looked at Sue, she was staring back at me with eyes like saucers. I knew exactly what she was thinking.

A moment later and my head was in my hands. I was terrified. What on earth was I to do? The idea of there being no connection between Sam's and Jim's kidnapping did not even deserve consideration. The question now was, what was I going to do about it?

I looked up. Kevin was still staring at his phone, and Sue was still staring at me. It went through my head that now might be a good time to follow Sue's example and become a Christian. If I had ever felt like praying, now was definitely that time.

Because of Kevin's preoccupation with the message from Jim, he still had not noticed my own mental turmoil.

To give myself time to think, I asked, 'What has Jim said, Kevin?'

He tore his eyes away from his phone and stared at me. For a moment, he did not speak. Then he said softly, 'It's John Smith.' He closed his eyes and suddenly looked very tired.

'It seems that Jim's being held in some kind of shack. He has no idea where, although he says that by the amount of light coming through the window along with the sounds coming from outside, he believes he's in part of a forest. Apparently, they've left him alone for a while. He's been tied up, but he partially freed himself and managed to get hold of a mobile phone which was left on a table. He's sent this text, but he's going to delete it immediately and try to remove all visible evidence. He doesn't want anyone to respond to his text for obvious reasons. He says there are two other men with Smith, and it sounds as if they're just as delightful as Smith himself. He's been given very little food, is cold, hungry and terrified of what Smith might do.'

Still looking down at his phone, one hand running roughly through his hair, he said, 'That's where the text ends.'

Sue had stopped staring at me and was now sitting with a stunned look on her face. Kevin got to his feet. 'Wait here guys,' he said. 'I'm going to see if I can find Steve. He needs to know about this.'

He did not need to search long because, at that precise moment, Steve came into the meeting room. 'Hi folks,' he said. Then, seeing our faces he stood stock still. 'What on earth's the matter?'

‘Pull up a chair,’ Kevin said, sitting back down.

Steve was in the process of sitting in one of the vacant chairs as Kevin said, ‘I’ve just had a text from Jim.’

Steve’s head swivelled round to look at Kevin and he froze in a squatting position about two inches above the chair. Any other time it would have been comical but, in the current circumstances, no one felt like laughing.

‘Jim?’ Steve exclaimed. ‘What’s happened?’

‘He’s been kidnapped,’ Kevin said.

Steve dropped the last few inches onto his seat with a thud. He did not immediately speak, puffing his cheeks in disbelief. ‘What? What did he say in his text? Are the kidnappers making any demands?’

Kevin spent a few moments putting Steve in the picture.

Steve put his head in his hands. ‘What a nightmare,’ he said. He got out his phone. ‘I must call the police.’

My stomach lurched. That was the last thing I wanted. As far as Smith was concerned, I was the only person who knew anything about either of the kidnappings. If he or someone else was watching our group and the police rolled up at the hotel, that could result in huge problems for Sam.

Steve was already looking on his phone for the number. I needed to say something quickly.

‘Hold on, hold on, Steve,’ I said hurriedly.

He looked up at me. ‘What’s wrong?’ he asked.

I was feeling flustered, and my mouth went dry. I had not clearly thought through what I was going to say next.

'Look, Jim used that phone without them knowing,' I managed to splutter. If these people see the police coming to the hotel, they might get twitchy and do something terrible.'

I could tell that both Kevin and Steve were considering my words.

'We're going to have to tell them, Rob,' Steve said assertively.

'I know, but couldn't you explain the situation and suggest a private meeting somewhere?'

'I see your point. I'll give them the details and see what they suggest.' He dialled the number.

A moment later, Steve was pacing around, speaking into his phone. 'Can I speak to Inspector McKinley, please?'

My guts were turning summersaults as we waited for the officer to come on the line.

'Hello, Inspector, we've had a development regarding Jim Redfern.'

There was a brief pause as the inspector responded to Steve's news. Then, for the next few minutes, Steve furnished the policeman with the details surrounding Jim's text message. I was also pleased to hear him question whether, under the circumstances, it was sensible to meet with the police openly.

There was an interminable period of silence as Steve listened to the inspector's next remarks.

Finally, Steve replied, 'We're engaged in a couple of areas of work.'

For the next ten minutes, he spoke about the aspect of the work that involved Jim. He explained how important it was that the general public were given the whole story when it came to the world of science. He ran through some of the trips we had been on and the evidence we had seen.

'Jim Redfern is one of the members of the team who is keen to understand our view of the geological evidence,' Steve told the policeman. 'He, and another three members of our team, work in education and they are exactly the kinds of people who we feel need to be informed about these issues.' Steve finished by saying, 'Anyway, that's the relevant part of our work. We do have other research we're engaged in, but that has nothing to do with Jim.'

Again, there was silence as Steve listened. It seemed that the officer wanted to know what the other work entailed, because Steve spent another few minutes giving him a high-level overview of the mineralogy work and its possible significance and potential.

Again, Steve listened. This time, it seemed that he had been asked if the kidnappers might be able to benefit financially from the knowledge.

'It's possible, but you'd require a significant amount of specialist knowledge before you'd be able to take advantage of this research.'

Listening to one side of this conversation, we kept our eyes on Steve as he paced the length of the room.

'We've made no secret of it. We wrote about our intentions in one of the creationist publications, but these tend to be read by people who are already convinced of the Bible's message. Very few people outside that group will realize we exist; never mind the type of work we're involved in.'

My anxiety was increasing. Would the information Smith wanted me to pass on to him have any bearing on Jim's predicament? Out of the corner of my eye, I noticed Sue looking in my direction and guessed the same question had occurred to her. I was sure Smith would not have enough detailed knowledge of minerals to take advantage of the information I had provided so far, but maybe he would be able to acquire it somehow. Another possibility was that Smith was not even aware how much real understanding of the subject he would require to profit from it.

I remembered Kevin telling me at the start of this latest adventure that they had already announced the purpose of their trip in the magazine, *Creation Monthly*. This had included details about the mineral research. Once again, I wondered if the decision to announce these details might not have been particularly well-advised.

After another few exchanges between Steve and the inspector, the call was ended.

'So, what's going to happen now?' I asked.

Steve stopped pacing. 'Well, the first thing I'm going to do is have a word with the others. If you guys still want to head off to the visitor centres, that's fine. However, I'm going to stay here and do what I can to help the cops.'

'I don't feel like going,' I said. 'What did they say about Jim?'

'They seem to think that the work on minerals might be a motivation to "unscrupulous and greedy criminals". Personally, I doubt it, but they're the experts. He took your point about the kidnappers not being aware that Jim had sent a message. They're going to start a search in known shacks, but they're going to do it in unmarked vehicles. At some point, the inspector will want to have a look at the text Jim sent to Kevin. Anyway, I'm going to find Jenny and the others. They need to be told about this.'

I glanced over at Sue. She was staring at me and looked rather scared, and I knew she was inwardly urging me to reveal the details about Sam. She stared at me for a moment longer, then she got up and headed for reception without saying a word. I guessed she was going back to her room, and I palpably felt her disappointment with me.

When she had gone, Kevin asked, 'Have you two had some kind of argument?'

I massaged my forehead lightly with the tips of my fingers. How do I explain this? 'We've not fallen out, Kevin.'

'Maybe not, but she's spent the last few minutes just sitting and staring at you.'

Kevin was looking at me in a way which made it clear that he was expecting some kind of response. I did not want to discuss it; I did not want this conversation and could feel myself getting ever more stressed. Just ignoring Kevin's remark, I suspected, would invite further suspicion. I needed to respond with something. I was just about to speak when Kevin beat me to it.

'Is there something going on that I need to know about?'

'Kevin, I need to go and find Sue. Depending on how that goes, I might have a chat with you later, but I'd appreciate it if you didn't push it right now.'

He continued studying me, then gave a short nod. 'OK, Rob, but if this has anything to do with Jim's situation, I'll need you to say so.'

I nodded in return and then rose to my feet. 'I'll see you later,' I replied, and left the meeting room.

As I looked around, I could not see Sue. I decided to head through the front door to the area where Sue had caught me responding to Smith's text. I immediately saw her sitting on the bench we had occupied two days ago and went over to join her.

'Is it OK if I sit down?' I asked.

She looked up. I could see the tear tracks down her cheeks. After a moment, she nodded, so I perched on the end of the bench.

We sat there for some time, neither of us speaking.

Eventually, Sue said through her tears, 'Rob, you have to tell Kevin what's going on.'

I let the words hang in the air. I did not want to see Sue upset, but Sam's situation was desperate. I had to do everything within my power to ensure that he came through this without being harmed.

'You realize the more people who know about this, the more risk there is to Sam's life?' I countered, quietly.

'I understand that' she said, turning towards me, 'but how would you feel if you were a member of Jim's family? If this... this monster is as nasty as you say, who knows what he might do. Particularly if he suspects that Jim had spoken to the police about the events during your last expedition.'

That was a very fair point.

'And on top of that, what guarantee do you have that this

horrible man will let Sam go even if you do as he says? From what you've told me, I wouldn't trust him as far as I could throw him.'

That was not what I wanted to hear, but I knew as she was saying it that she was right. John Smith, or whatever his name was, was one of the nastiest people I had ever met in my life.

Sue's tears were not helping my chaotic thoughts and fraught nerves. 'Sue, I need to go and have a think about all of this. Please don't say anything until I've had another chat with you.'

She briefly glanced up at me before turning her head away and staring at the ground. We sat there in silence for another few seconds before I took my leave and headed for my room.

As I closed the door behind me, I swore loudly. I did not care who heard me. I was furious and felt completely powerless, having no idea how to change any of the circumstances I faced. I was terrified by the thought of doing anything that would result in harm coming to Sam, but aware that Jim faced danger too. By nature, I was not a violent person but, the way I felt at that moment, I could have cheerfully ripped John Smith's head clean off his shoulders.

I threw my notepad onto the bed and walked over to the window which overlooked the front drive of the hotel. The sun was shining; a peaceful scene contrasted with the fierce storm of emotions filling my head.

I moved to my right and could just make out the image of Sue, still sitting on her own with her head down and cutting a very gloomy figure. The distress she was feeling was significantly adding to my feeling of fury. She did not deserve this. In fact, I suspected that this ought to be one of the most amazing weeks of her life. I had shared her enthusiasm for this voyage of geological discovery, and I had felt a bond with her over our newfound knowledge. I had even been affected by her excitement following her decision to become a Christian. Despite my misgivings, her inner joy was infectious and I was pleased to see her so happy.

I turned from the window and threw myself face down on the bed. I felt like punching someone. I did not much care who that someone was. At that moment, I just wanted to lash out, to release some of the pent-up anger and frustration which was increasing by the minute.

An indeterminate period of time had passed when there was a soft knock at the door. That was all I needed! Still face down on the bed, I considered ignoring it but realized that whoever it was almost certainly knew that I was in there.

‘Hold on,’ I growled.

As I stood, taking a few deep breaths, I reluctantly covered the few feet to the door of my room.

Kevin was standing there. He had an expression on his face which was hard to read.

‘Do you mind if I come in for a minute?”’ he asked.

Yes, I certainly did as a matter of fact. Politely, I replied, ‘No, come in.’

Kevin stepped inside and I closed the door behind him.

‘Have a seat,’ I said, waving a hand in the general direction of the single armchair in the corner of the room.

As Kevin lowered himself into the chair, I perched myself on the edge of the bed. Not feeling much like a chat, nor being the person who had instigated this interview, I waited for Kevin to speak. He briefly glanced around before looking at me. He was quiet, calm in fact, but had a serious air about him.

'Rob, I think you should tell me what the problem is. It's obvious you've got one, and it appears to be affecting other members of the team.' As I raised my eyebrows, he gestured to the window.

'I've just been outside and found Sue sitting on a bench in tears. When I asked her what the problem was, she said that she couldn't tell me. She said that she'd promised you she wouldn't say anything.'

It was at that moment that I completely lost the plot. The pent-up emotion, the anxiety, the secrecy, the fury all became too much for me. I snatched up my notepad which was still sitting on the bed and violently hurled it across the room. Although it was thrown with some force, as the sheets opened out, its velocity reduced dramatically and, when it reached the wall, it struck with a rather unimpressive slap before sliding pathetically to the floor.

In a loud voice, I demanded to know from Kevin how many horrendous situations his God expected an individual to deal with. Unfortunately, this sentence was punctuated with a number of colourful expletives.

Kevin had never heard me venting my spleen in such a way, yet he was remarkably unmoved by my outburst. He just sat there calmly, studying me.

His reaction, or perhaps lack of one, had the effect of vastly diffusing my anger. However, that anger was immediately replaced by a different kind of emotion. There was suddenly a feeling of overwhelming sadness and defeat sweeping over me.

Seconds later, I had my head in my hands and was sobbing like a child. Kevin said nothing, giving me the opportunity to release the emotion that had been building for days.

It was some time before I felt a firm but gentle hand on one of my shoulders.

'Rob, what on earth's happened?'

I knew it was time for a confession, but I was incapable of coherent communication. Each time I attempted to speak, another wave of emotion swept over me and choked any words I attempted to say.

'Take your time, Rob,' Kevin said quietly. 'There's no rush.'

I took him at his word. For some time, I just sat letting the turbulent storm inside subside.

Eventually, I reached the point where I thought I might just about be able to construct a few sentences without collapsing into another flood of tears. I sighed deeply and blew my nose. Regaining some semblance of control, I headed to the bathroom washing my face and drying it with a freshly laundered towel. Feeling slightly better, I returned to the bedroom and perched on the edge of the bed.

It was difficult to know where to start. Should I go back and give him all the details in chronological order? One thing was certain: I was going to have to explain everything to him. I thought I may as well start with the main point.

'Sam's been kidnapped,' I stated. Then, immediately felt the tears coming again. I was getting irritated at the emotional battering to which I was being subjected. I wiped the tears away with a degree of annoyance.

'You're joking,' Kevin said in amazement. 'Are you sure?'

'Don't ask stupid questions,' I snapped, irritably. 'Do you think I'd be in this state if there was any doubt?'

'I'm sorry,' he said hurriedly, holding his hands up. 'That was a ridiculous thing to say. Rob, how did you find out?'

Going through the communications I had received from Sam, I explained the period of silence I had had to endure during the lack of contact. We then looked at the texts I had received.

Kevin had gone white as a sheet. 'I don't know what to say, Rob. Every time you get involved with me something terrible happens. To make matters worse, those things always seem to happen to Sam. I'm so sorry.'

I did not really know how to respond. I could not say, 'Don't worry about it,' or 'It doesn't matter.' I was incredibly worried, and it very much did matter! However, I did not blame Kevin for the current situation. True, it was Kevin who had asked me if I wanted to be involved in the trip but, as he had said at the start, he had expected me to say, 'No'. I certainly had not been forced into this trip; it was entirely my own choice. Unfortunately, thinking of Sam and his predicament, that was not much comfort.

When, just four months ago, I had been considering whether or not to come on this trip, I remembered weighing up the pros and cons. Although it seemed fairly predictable that John Smith would want to get back at us in some way, I had reasoned that we ought to be pretty safe in Washington State. When he had opposed us in the Congo, we had been miles from civilization, and had no way of calling for help. I had told myself that Smith surely would not try anything in America. I smiled to myself grimly as I now realized that I had been wrong—most dreadfully wrong.

'Look, what you said is true,' I said. 'However, we both know that you're not to blame for the things that have happened to Sam. The other point is that we can't undo anything that's already happened. For me, the main question is, what do we do now?'"

Kevin gave me a sad smile and a brief nod. 'Listen, Rob, it's gracious of you not to blame me for this. I truly appreciate that.' He leant towards me and went on: 'But there's something else you need to know. This is not God's fault either. I don't believe for a minute that He's responsible for this mess. If you were to get to know Him, I think you'd come to appreciate that.' He paused for me to take that in. 'Anyway, I want you to know that I won't tell anyone about this that doesn't absolutely need to know. Also, before we do tell anyone, I'll make it perfectly clear that they're aware of the situation and insist on their complete discretion.'

I nodded. 'Thanks, Kevin.'

The things he said next not only took me by surprise, but they gave me reason for more hope than I had felt in days.

'I wish you'd told me about this earlier,' he said. 'We should be able to give you the information you need to feed back to John Smith about ore deposits.'

This stopped me in my tracks. I had not even considered that. Why had I not considered that? 'I'll have to put it in my own words,' I said. 'If you write the responses, he'll smell a rat. He knows I know virtually nothing about geology. If I start using technical language and present the data as a PhD geologist would ...' I trailed off, allowing Kevin to choose his preferred ending to my sentence.

'You're right,' he agreed. 'Don't worry about that; that'll be easy to sort out.'

Instead of the terror I thought I was going to feel after telling Kevin about the situation, a swell of hope began to grow. It was a welcome feeling. Far from increasing the danger to Sam, it might even reduce it.

Kevin looked thoughtful. 'I tell you what,' he said, 'why don't we provide you with a handout for a layman. After all, it's not just Smith who isn't an expert. If we're providing you with information so you can understand the subject, you could pass that straight on to Smith.'

I was shocked. It was so simple. Why on earth hadn't I thought of that? I mentally berated myself for not thinking of this earlier.

'Kevin, you're absolutely right. I've been so stupid. Sue told me straight away that I should confide in you. I'd have saved myself so much grief if I'd listened.'

'When did you last communicate with Smith?' he asked.

'Last evening.'

'Did you get a response?'

'No.'

Kevin nodded. 'OK,' he said. 'Rob, we'll work together on the messages we send to Smith. We'll only send them when we're both completely happy with the content.'

He ran his hand through his hair, then continued: 'After Sue and you left the meeting room, I went to find Steve. I told him the sort of person we were dealing with in John Smith. Rob, I think we need to find a way of meeting up with the police. I'll give Steve a ring and ask him to join us.'

Just minutes later, there was another knock on the door. I let Steve in and Kevin spent the next few minutes briefly filling him in.

Steve looked horrified—a stunned silence falling.

Eventually, Kevin broke that silence. 'I think we should let the police know about this, but Rob's very concerned about saying anything which may endanger Sam's life.'

Steve put his palm to his forehead. 'Naturally,' he said. There was another extended pause, then he shook his head and sat down heavily on the side of my bed. 'This is getting worse and worse,' he said. 'We certainly need to let the cops know about this. I'll give them a call, explain the situation and see what they suggest.'

I was concerned. 'Steve, don't say anything about Sam.'

He hesitated. 'Rob, they're going to have to be told at some point.'

'That may be,' I conceded, 'but I don't want Sam's situation discussed without being able to have some input myself.'

Steve sighed wearily. 'OK, I'll give them a ring and try to arrange some kind of private meeting somewhere.' He produced his mobile and made the call.

'Can I speak to Officer McKinley?' My heart was hammering in my chest as Steve was waiting to be put through. 'Officer McKinley. Is there anywhere we can meet without advertising the fact?'

For the next few minutes, the conversation continued. Kevin and I could only hear Steve's end of it, but it was obvious that the policeman was trying to extract from Steve the reason for the request. Listening to another one-sided phone call, I drummed my fingers on the mattress. Eventually, it appeared that Steve was able to convince the lawman that the meeting was important without divulging the details.

He hung up. 'He's going to come over with a colleague in an unmarked car. When they get here, they'll ask reception to call this room. I'll go down and bring them up. We can discuss things in here.'

I was happier with that arrangement. At least we would be away from prying eyes.

I made coffees while we waited; thankfully the wait was not long. Around twenty minutes later, we heard a car crunching up the gravel drive. We all went to the window, Steve getting there first.

'I think this is them,' Steve said. 'I'll go down. If reception call, tell them I'm on my way.'

As he left the room, I took his position at the window to see if I could catch sight of the policemen. I heard two car doors slam then saw two men carrying what looked like overnight bags towards the hotel entrance. Assuming this was indeed our visitors, at least they were taking some care to conceal their true identity.

A long ten minutes passed before Steve knocked on the door and I let them in.

When the door was closed, Steve began introductions. 'This is Dave McKinley from the police department,' and he gestured towards the taller of the two men. 'And this is his sergeant, Mike Zimmerman.' He indicated the other man who nodded at us. 'They're the cops who have been given the task of looking into the disappearance of Jim Redfern.'

Kevin and I introduced ourselves and we thanked them for coming.

'Do you want to sit on the bed?' I asked the policemen.

Officer McKinley shook his head. 'You guys sit there.' He grinned, then added, 'I'll have the chair and Mike can sit on the floor.'

We all laughed, even Mike.

When we were all settled, Dave McKinley began his inquiries. 'You folks are all friends of Jim Redfern, is that right?'

We all confirmed this.

'OK,' he said, 'so what can you tell me? I assume that this has something to do with his situation.'

Steve briefly glanced at me with an eyebrow cocked.

I nodded in response to the unspoken question.

'I called you earlier to let you know about the text message from Jim,' Steve said. 'Since then, Rob has informed us that his brother has also been kidnapped.'

The two policemen shifted their attention to me. It may have been my imagination, but I got the distinct impression that they felt I should have mentioned this earlier.

'I was told that if I said anything to anyone, I wouldn't see my brother again,' I said defensively. Officer McKinley nodded in acknowledgement, then spent a few seconds staring at my bedside light.

'OK,' he said, slowly. 'I think we need to start by understanding more about what you people are doing and why someone might think it worth his while to kidnap two of your friends.' He shifted slightly in the armchair. 'So, firstly, I need you to tell me what Mr Redfern's role is in that work.' He looked at me sharply. 'Additionally, I'll want to know how your brother fits in to all this.'

Steve kicked this off, including the details which he had not given on the earlier call with the inspector. Every now and again, Kevin would interject with comments explaining how important it was that the public, and particularly those involved in education, were made aware of some of this information. When the inspector had obtained all the details he required about the work, he turned to me.

'Mr Granger, how did you discover that your brother had been kidnapped?'

Once again, I went through the whole sequence of events. I explained about my texts to and from Sam; Sam's period of silence; and then the texts to and from the kidnapper.

'It was when the kidnapper called me "Granger" that I suspected who it was.'

After saying this, everything went quiet. The two policemen looked at each other and then back at me.

'Sorry,' Dave McKinley said, 'I think I might have missed something. Can I ask how the heck you could possibly know who this man was?'

It dawned on all three of us at the same time. Of course, these men would have no idea that we had come across Smith previously. Neither Kevin nor I had met these officers. Steve had spoken to the inspector a number of times about Jim's disappearance but, until today, he had had no knowledge of John Smith. I suddenly realized that, in his earlier call to the inspector, although Jim's text had been discussed, no one had mentioned John Smith. Up to now, there had also been no mention of our previous encounter with him.

So, for the next five minutes, Kevin and I gave them a quick, but comprehensive account of our dealings with Smith on the Congo trip. When we had finished our account, the two policemen looked a little more sympathetic.

'OK,' said Inspector McKinley, 'that puts a rather different slant on things. Smith might well be trying to get back at you for perceived injustices following that other expedition.'

'That's true,' I said, 'but he's also very interested in the work these guys are doing on ore deposits. He's asked me to provide him with information about it.'

Inevitably, they wanted to see the text messages and record some of the details. This included Jim's message to Kevin. They also wanted me to give them the number of Smith's mobile.

'Officer, I don't want this guy to find out I've been speaking to you,' I said, nervously.

'We understand your concerns,' Mike Zimmerman said calmly. 'You have our word that we'll be discrete.'

'Don't worry, Mr Granger, I'm not going to call his phone. I need the number so we can try to put a trace on it,' Inspector McKinley assured me.

I acknowledged this information with a relieved smile and a nod.

'Incidentally,' he continued, 'you don't happen to have a snap of this man from your previous trip, do you?'

'I haven't,' I said. I looked hopefully at Kevin who shook his head.

I suddenly remembered Andy Phillips. Inspector Andy Phillips had been the police officer with whom I had had many dealings following the previous expedition to the Congo. Although he had been the officer who had interrogated me over some false allegations, he had subsequently become something of a friend and I had met up with him on a number of occasions.

'The British police have got a mugshot of John Smith,' I said, 'and I think they also know his real name. If you can reach Inspector Phillips at Thames Valley Police, I think he might be able to send you a picture of this man.'

The inspector nodded. 'That would be very helpful.' He paused for a moment, writing down the details. 'By the way, next time Smith gets in touch, can I suggest you tell him that you won't be sending any information to him unless he provides you with conclusive proof that your brother is alive and well?'

I felt sick. 'Are you trying to tell me that you suspect Sam has come to some kind of harm?'

'Not at all. I just think it would be sensible to obtain some kind of evidence that he is OK. Apart from anything else, it also lets Smith know that if he does really want this information, he needs to ensure that your brother remains healthy.'

After saying this, Inspector McKinley spent another few seconds staring in the direction of the bedside lamp.

Eventually, he spoke up. 'OK, I think we've got all we need for the time being. We'll contact you if we need anything else.'

As the inspector finished, he rose to his feet. It seemed that the meeting was over. We all stood and shook hands. As the two policemen were heading for the door, my phone gave a ping.

We all froze. I retrieved my phone from my back pocket and looked at the display. It was a text from Dad. He said that he did not want to keep bothering me on my trip, but that he had still not been able to contact Sam. He wanted to know if I had an update. I shared his message with the others.

'What do I do about that?' I asked.

The inspector said, 'I'm afraid I'm going to leave that problem with you guys. We're going to concentrate on this Smith character. Needless to say, if any of you hear from him, I need you to contact us immediately. We need to get this guy in the slammer.'

We all heartily agreed with this assessment.

When the two policemen had left, the three of us spent some time considering what I should say to Dad.

Kevin had sauntered over to the window and was watching the two policemen leave in their car. He now turned to face me.

'Rob, I know it's tough, but I think you should be honest about this. I think you should tell your dad what's going on. Maybe you don't need to fill him in on every last little detail, but I do think you should let him know the basics.'

I put my head in my hands. 'Mum will be devastated,' I said.

Steve looked up from where he was sitting on the bed. 'This might sound harsh, but I'd let your dad worry about your mum. Your dad is over there with her and I'm sure he'll know the best thing to do.'

Wearily, I took their advice. After all, I had no better suggestion.

The next question was what to tell Smith. After a brief discussion between Kevin and Steve, it was suggested that Steve supply me with a full, written handout of the radiohalos' work and its significance with regard to the ore deposit benefits. This was great, because it overcame the problem of me needing to understand everything, and also explained why Smith would receive the information in detail from an expert.

That being decided and agreed, I sent the message saying that I would soon have the information and explained how I had cleverly managed to obtain this information. However, I ended the message by telling Smith that I would not be sending any information at all unless I received conclusive proof that Sam was alive and well. Off went the message, and the three of us sat and waited to see what the response would be. We did not have long to wait.

Smith responded: 'Granger, I'm not sure you are in a position to make any demands. It would only take one order from me for your brother to be history.'

This really annoyed me and I responded immediately.

'Sorry, my mistake. I thought that was why you had kidnapped Sam. To pressurize me into getting the information you want. If you can't prove that Sam is alive and well, you can whistle for your information on ore deposits.'

This time there was a longer period before a response came through. The foreboding began to grow heavy.

Ping. 'I don't like people messing me around, Granger. And when they do, I tend to remember it. However, as a display of good grace, I will see what I can do about obtaining the proof you say you require.'

On reading it, I snorted with derision.

Showing Kevin the text, I said, 'What does he know about good grace?'

Kevin laughed humourlessly. 'Not very much, I'd say.'

Kevin turned towards Steve. 'Apart from those of us in this room, Sue's the only member of our team who is currently aware of this issue. Are you happy for us to keep it like that for the time being?'

Steve nodded. 'That seems reasonable. Mind you, I'll want to put the others in the picture as soon as we reach the point where secrecy no longer serves any purpose.'

Chapter 13
A Horrifying Situation

The next morning, Tuesday, 13 August, had been set aside to learn more about the regrowth of vegetation within the Mount Saint Helens National Volcanic Monument. For half an hour, we had been studying an area where a number of trees had seeded themselves, when Kevin's mobile rang. The combination of Kevin having a fairly strident ringtone and the fact that he was standing right next to me startled me.

When he looked at the screen, he gave a short gasp. 'It's the mobile Jim called from,' he said to us. Then, tentatively, to the phone he said, 'Hello?'

He stood still, listening intently.

As we watched, a look of horror appeared on his face. I glanced at Sue who looked tense. We were all standing completely motionless. The wait was unbearable and seemed to go on for an eternity.

Eventually, with evident shock in his voice, Kevin said, 'Jim, you must stay calm. I'm just going to have a quick chat with Steve. Try to stay perfectly still.'

Kevin turned to Steve. 'Jim's kidnappers have left,' he said.

'So, what's the problem?' Steve asked.

'They've left him in the shack with a family of rattlesnakes and he's already received three bites. He doesn't sound great.'

Sue gasped and clamped a hand over her mouth. Most of us just stood staring at Kevin.

'Dear God,' Jenny said. 'Does he have any idea where he is?'

Steve got out his phone.

Kevin spoke into his phone again. 'Jim, can you give us any clue at all as to your whereabouts?'

We waited for a response.

Someone had obviously answered Steve's call, as he said, 'Can I speak to Inspector McKinley, please? It's Steve Collins.' There was a brief pause before Steve added, 'Sorry to interrupt, but this is a matter of life and death. I really do need to get in touch with the inspector.' After another pause, Steve said, 'Please ask him to ring me immediately on this number. It's an emergency!' He ended the call.

'OK Jim, hold on,' Kevin said to his phone. He turned to Steve, 'Jim still doesn't know where he's being held. He says there's some mottled sunlight coming through one of the windows, but it's obviously being filtered through trees. He can't hear any traffic noise. The only sound he can hear outside is from birds.'

I suddenly had a thought. 'Kevin, can I have a quick word?' and held out my hand.

He passed me his phone.

'Hello Jim, it's Rob here. When you were kidnapped, did they walk you to that shack, or did you get there in a vehicle?'

He sounded a little breathless and his voice was quiet. 'I was brought here in a car,' he said.

'Do you know how long it took to get there?' I asked.

'I think it was about thirty minutes.'

'You haven't got any idea which way you went?'

'No, they stuck a bag over my head so I couldn't see. I'm pretty sure we set off in the direction of the 504. I know we did make a number of turns. I tried to make a note of them, but I'm afraid I lost track. The first turn was definitely to the left.'

'OK Jim, thanks for that. I'll hand you back to Kevin.'

Not knowing anything about snake bites, I had not known what to expect but, to me, Jim sounded in a bad way. I was just passing Kevin his phone when Steve's mobile rang. There was a look of relief on his face as he answered.

'Hello Inspector?' After a few seconds silence, Steve said, 'We've got Jim on another phone.'

For the next minute or so, Steve filled the inspector in with all the information we had at that point, including the details I had just obtain from Jim. Then, there was an extended period where the only sound was of rustling leaves as Steve listened to the policeman.

Eventually, Steve said, 'Kevin, can you let me have the number Jim is calling from? The inspector wants to try to locate the phone through triangulation from local phone masts.'

Kevin read out the number and Steve repeated it to the inspector.

After a few moments, Steve spoke again. 'That's great. Let's hope you can find him pretty quick.' He ended the call.

Kevin passed on the news to Jim that the police were trying to locate him via the borrowed phone. Then Ben asked Kevin to find out how long it had been since Jim had been bitten.

After relaying the question to Jim, it went quiet for some time as Kevin listened to Jim's reply.

'OK Jim, hold on.'

Kevin had a worried look on his face. 'He's not sure how long ago he was bitten.'

Ben also looked concerned. 'Kevin, can I have your phone for a minute?'

Kevin handed it over, his hand shaking.

'Jim, can you give me a rough idea of when you received these bites?'

Once more it went quiet as Ben listened. These periods of silence became too much for Jenny.

'Can't you put him on speakerphone or something?' she asked.

'Jim, are you OK if I let the others hear your responses? They're concerned about you and want to be able to hear what you're telling me.' After a moment, Ben said, 'That's great,' and we were suddenly all able to hear Jim's voice.

'I should think I received the bites about three or four hours after I sent the text to Kevin,' he said weakly.

Ben's mouth fell open. He stared at Kevin. 'Hold on a second, Jim. I'll be back with you in a minute.'

Quietly to Kevin, Ben asked, 'When did you receive that text? I thought it was yesterday.'

'It was,' Kevin replied. He frowned, looked at his watch, trying to remember exactly when he had received it.

'It was about 10:15 am yesterday morning,' Sue offered.

Ben turned white. 'Unless he's completely confused, he's been in there with rattler venom in his system for nearly a day,' he whispered. 'We need to find him and we need to find him quickly.'

Then, in a normal and calm voice, Ben once more addressed the phone. 'Jim, how are you feeling at the moment?'

'Not great,' he said. 'I'm incredibly thirsty. I feel pretty weak and a bit lightheaded. It's difficult to describe how I feel. It's like a kind of numbness. I don't think it's particularly warm in here, but I'm sweating like a pig. My sight seems a bit hazy, and I'm having a struggle breathing. On top of that, I keep feeling like I want to throw up.'

As Jim went through the list of symptoms, Ben's expression became even more grave. 'Listen buddy, I need you to keep focused on talking to us. Can you explain to us how on earth you ended up with those rattlers in there?'

'It was horrible,' he said.

Jim told us that he had been positioned under one of the windows. He was still partially tied up. As the charming men had left, they had laughed as they opened the window above Jim and announced, 'We wouldn't want to leave you with no fresh air.' For a moment, Jim had felt relief as the men had left him. However, a few seconds after they had closed the door, he had heard a noise above him at the open window. He looked up to see a box.

'We thought you might like some company,' one of the men said, once more laughing.

The next thing Jim knew, there were around half a dozen rattlesnakes cascading down his legs and lower torso.

Jim's natural revulsion to snakes had caused him to move involuntarily to try to get away from the serpents. The result had been a couple of bites to his legs and one to his hip.

From that moment, Jim had attempted to stay as still as he possibly could. This had taken a tremendous effort, given his fear of snakes. Most of the reptiles had slithered off into darker corners of the shack. However, one had found a patch of mottled sunlight in the middle of the floor and seemed perfectly happy coiled up in a ball.

'I hope the cops find me soon,' he said. 'I'm beginning to feel a bit peculiar.'

'Hang in there, Jim,' Ben said. 'Can you tell us a bit more about your physical situation in that shack? When you sent the text to Kevin, you told him that you managed to partially free yourself to get hold of that phone. Is that still the case? Are you still partially free?'

'I am,' Jim said.

He told us that they had tied his hands behind his back with some cord. His feet had been fastened to a water pipe with a chain wrapped around his ankles and secured with a padlock. He had soon realized that there was little chance that he would be able to free his feet, but he thought there might be a chance of getting his hands loose.

'The trouble was that, although I could feel the knot with my fingertips, I knew there was no way I'd be able to untie it,' he told us. 'After a while, I found a nail sticking up from the floor of the shack. I used my fingertips to try to find out what kind of knot they had used to secure my hands. Then I spent ages attempting to hook the cord over the nail to try to start loosening the knot. It took for ever. I had to stop a couple of times when the men came back to check on me. Anyway, after a lot of frustrating failure, I managed to get my hands free. That's when I noticed the phone and sent a text to you.'

It was now Kevin that responded. 'That's great, Jim. In your text, you said you were going to erase all signs of your message and replace the phone. How did you manage to get hold of it again? Didn't they come back for it?'

For the first time there was a hint of amusement in Jim's voice as he said, 'Yes, they did. I did manage to delete all signs of the message and put the phone back, but then I changed my mind. I guessed that I might never get another opportunity to communicate with you guys, so I retrieved the mobile and hid it behind a small gas heater which was just in reach.

'When the men came back, the guy who was looking for his phone was cursing like mad. He obviously couldn't remember exactly where he'd left it and, after a brief search, he gave up. I think he assumed he must have left it somewhere else. Thankfully, they didn't check my wrists. Although I'd tried to make it look as if I was still tied up, it wouldn't have passed close inspection.'

Jim went quiet for a few seconds before continuing with a bit of a quiver in his voice. 'I didn't want to use the phone again until I knew it was safe. The trouble is that, when they left, I ended up with these vile creatures in here with me. When I did try to reach for the phone again, one of them started to rattle, it made me jump and I ended up pushing the phone just out of my reach. So then, I had to find something I could use to drag the phone towards me to retrieve it. I couldn't find anything.

'Next, I thought of the cord that had been used to tie my hands. I fashioned a loop in the cord that I thought might do the job. Two or three times I attempted to get the loop over the phone, but my movements would upset one of the snakes and I had to stop. After a while, I think I must have passed out.'

This was shocking. He must have been unconscious all night and still did not realize it.

'When I woke up, after checking that none of the snakes were in striking distance and after another couple of abortive attempts, I was eventually successful. By that time, to be honest, I was desperate to speak to someone.'

'I'm not surprised, Jim,' Ben said. 'How are you feeling now? Are you experiencing any pain in the areas where you've been bitten?'

'They're a bit sore,' he said. 'I'd describe it as a cross between soreness and burning.'

'OK, and are you still feeling about the same in yourself?'

'The sickness has gone off a bit, but I feel incredibly weak and my lower back is ...'

Jim suddenly broke off.

'Jim? Are you OK?' Ben asked.

All we could hear was Jim's breathing. It had become much faster as if he was feeling distressed. It was not long before we found out why.

'Jim!' Ben said sharply.

'One of the snakes is coming up my legs,' Jim whispered.

He sounded terrified.

Again, it was Ben that spoke. 'Jim, stay completely still. Try to control your breathing. You must do everything you can to stay calm.' After a short pause, Ben asked, 'What's it doing now?'

'It's still coming. It's reached my stomach.'

This was too much for Sue. She had begun to cry, and she now took herself off to a distance from where she could no longer hear what was happening in the shack. Jack and Briony went over to join her.

There was an extended period where no one spoke as we waited to see what would happen next. There was a feeling in our group of complete powerlessness. All we could hear was Jim's breathing as the snake slowly moved up his body. A whimper emanated from the phone. For some time, we had all been holding our collective breath.

Now, Ben asked, 'Jim, what's happening?'

You could hear the fear in Jim's voice as he whispered, 'It's curled up into a ball on the bottom of my chest. What am I going to do?'

'Jim, I know it's tough,' Ben said, 'but the instructions are the same. Stay still, try to control your breathing and keep calm. Nothing will happen as long as it doesn't feel threatened.'

It was at that point that Jenny said, 'We should bring this situation before the Lord.'

Kevin nodded. 'I agree.' He turned towards Ben and me. 'You guys keep talking to Jim, and we'll go and have a time of prayer.'

All the others left and walked over to where Sue was standing with Jack and Briony.

Left alone with Ben, I was grateful to hear that Jim's breathing had become a little more relaxed.

Once more, Ben leant forward to speak into the phone. 'Jim, you're doing well. As I'm sure you're aware, snakes are cold-blooded. Your new-found buddy has probably been attracted by your body heat and has decided to take advantage of the free source of warmth. The bad news is that he could be there for some time. The good news is that he won't cause you any problems as long as he doesn't feel threatened.'

As Jim would already have a quantity of rattlesnake venom circulating in his bloodstream, this was another good reason to stay as motionless as he possibly could. The less he moved, the slower his heart would beat. The only problem was that the snake on his torso was likely to be causing a significant release of adrenalin, and hence, a faster heartbeat.

This whole episode was beginning to have an effect on me too.

As I tried to imagine what it must be like to be in Jim's situation, I felt physically sick. My brother had more of an aversion to snakes than I did, as had been demonstrated by an incident during our Congo trip. Nevertheless, I did not think I would appreciate having a rattlesnake sitting on my chest for any length of time.

Jim whispered from the phone again. 'Guys, I don't think I can take much more of this.'

Ben's eyes locked onto mine. 'Jim,' he said, 'you're doing really well. Please stay calm. The cops are trying to locate that phone. We need you to keep talking to us, and, above all, don't upset that rattler.'

Ben thought of something else. 'Jim, can you see how much charge you've got left on your phone?'

There was silence for a moment, then Jim said, 'twenty-one per cent.'

Ben shot me a concerned look. However, when he spoke, he sounded completely relaxed. 'That's great, Jim. I'm sure that will give the cops plenty of time to locate you.'

Ben's mind seemed to be racing, the fingers of his free hand drumming against his thigh. 'Rob, keep talking to Jim. I want to have a quick chat with Steve.' He headed in that direction and I could see Steve listening to Ben.

That left me in a quandary; I could not think of anything to say. Ben seemed to be saying all the right things to him; he was so calm. But I could not think straight, and I was not confident I could sound as reassuring as Ben.

'Jim, have you noticed any significant change in your condition recently?' I could only think to echo the questions previously asked, and hoped I sounded more composed than I felt inside.

Jim whispered his response, presumably so as not to spook the snake on his chest. 'I'm beginning to feel really rough. I think I'm going to require medical attention fairly soon.'

With relief, I noticed Steve give a short nod and Ben turn away to head in my direction.

When he arrived back, he whispered in my ear: 'I was just suggesting that Steve contact the cops who are looking for Jim to make sure they're careful when they look into the shacks. The last thing we want is for them to go barging in and spook the snakes.'

'Good thinking,' I said.

I looked back over at Steve and could see him on his phone again. Hopefully, he had managed to get the inspector.

At that very moment, a different sound came from the phone. I frowned, concentrating on the noise. 'That sounds like a car,' I said to Ben.

'It does,' he agreed. 'Wait here.' He dashed back over to Steve and I could see him urgently speaking to him.

Over the phone, I could now hear some footsteps which seemed to be getting louder. I noticed my hands getting sweaty and wondered how I would be coping if I were in Jim's position.

As Ben once more headed in my direction, all of a sudden, everything seemed to happen at once. I heard the loud click of a door latch over the phone, followed by a squeak of hinges. There were two heavy footsteps and then a sound that made my blood run like ice through my veins. It was a steady menacing rattle, and it sounded as if it was in very close proximity to the phone. This rattle was immediately followed by a terrified shriek. Apparently, Jim's nerve had finally gone. There was a right commotion coming from the phone: the warning sound from the tails of multiple rattlesnakes; men shouting; and shockingly, Jim saying over and over again, 'He got me again! He got me again!'

There were then two deafening shots.

Ben was horrified. 'This is terrible,' he said. 'They're just making matters worse.'

'Sir, don't move.' More shots rang out through the phone. 'Do you know how many rattlers are in here?'

Worryingly, there was no response from Jim.

I could still hear one rattle which seemed to be a fair distance from the phone. That was good, at least. A few seconds later, and another couple of shots were heard. The final rattle had stopped and I suddenly learned how to breathe again.

My horror over the events being played out at the other end of the phone must have absorbed me totally, as I suddenly noticed that all the others had joined us. There were a lot of concerned, dismayed faces around.

From Kevin's phone, we heard an officer on his radio saying, 'We need a medical team up here fast. Also, we could do with a trained herpetologist. There are a number of dead rattlers in here and it will probably help to know exactly which species they are.'

Kevin became very business-like. 'I think we should all head back to base.'

Steve nodded. 'Yes. Apart from anything else, I suspect the cops will want to speak to us pretty soon.'

With that, we all headed for the Land Rovers and set off for the hotel.

As we were sitting in the meeting room at the hotel and drinking coffee, low chatter ebbed and flowed. With all thoughts of our intended focus for the day far from our minds, we tried to make sense of what had happened. Steve had been on the phone to the police a number of times. When he hung up from his latest conversation, he told us that they would be paying us a visit within the next couple of hours.

Sue was overcome by the situation and was sitting next to me having a little weep.

'Have the cops given you any further information on Jim's condition?' Jenny asked.

'No,' Steve said. 'Most of what they told me related to how they found him. They also told me roughly the location of the shack where he was being held, but they didn't give me any news about his condition. Also, they said that they currently have no information on the whereabouts of the kidnappers.'

We had continued to discuss Jim and his situation for another half an hour when Steve's mobile rang again. As he glanced at his phone, a look of mild surprise came over his face. 'It's Terry,' he announced, seemingly talking to himself. 'Hello, Terry. Everything OK?'

Jenny quietly explained to us that Terry Newman was another geologist working for the Genesis Foundation.

There was a long pause as Steve listened to his colleague. At one point his eyes flicked in Jenny's direction briefly.

'OK Terry, thanks for that. I'll pass it on to the others. Please let me know immediately if anything changes.'

After ending the call and placing his phone on the table, he looked up at us with a steady gaze. 'It might be a good thing that we've managed to complete most of our trips to the volcano.'

'Why? What's happened?' Jenny asked.

'There have been a number of readings coming from Mount Saint Helens which indicate that she might be beginning to come to life again. They're similar to the readings from March 1980 when some of those steam and ash events occurred.'

'Does that mean we won't be able to see the volcano again?' Sue asked.

Steve briefly looked at his phone before looking back up at Sue. 'It's a bit frustrating, Sue,' he said. 'If there's going to be another major eruption, I suspect that it won't happen for another month or two. However, we can't risk taking you guys back to the volcano.'

Sue interrupted him. 'Oh, come on, Steve. You must let us go back once. Even if it's just to see it from a distance.'

'I'm afraid I can't do that, Sue.'

Jack now joined the discussion. 'Steve, that would be terrible. I'd be gutted if we couldn't go back just once more.'

'Sorry Jack, it's not going to happen.'

For me, I had mixed feelings about it. I certainly did not relish the idea of being anywhere near Mount Saint Helens if she blew her top, but I could see why the others might want to take one last look. I decided to contribute.

'Steve, if some of us really want to go, couldn't we sign some kind of disclaimer? Would that be possible?'

There was a lengthy silence as Steve considered my proposal. Then, after a big sigh, lifting a weary hand, he conceded. 'Look guys, I probably shouldn't even be considering this, but I'll discuss it with my colleagues. However, don't build your hopes up.'

After that, the subject was dropped.

It was around 2:15 pm when the police turned up. We were still sitting in the meeting room when Inspector McKinley and Sergeant Zimmerman were brought in by a member of the hotel staff. They grabbed a couple of chairs from one of the unoccupied tables and swung them round to face us, placing them close to where Steve and Kevin were sitting.

Steve took a moment to introduce the members of our group to the policemen.

'Afternoon, folks,' Dave McKinley said, a grave expression on his face. 'Some of you have already met us, but we're from the local police department and we're looking into the kidnap, imprisonment and attempted murder of Dr Jim Redfern. I'm not sure how much you know, but he's in quite a bad way. We need to find out why this has happened to him.'

'What can you tell us about Jim's condition?' Jenny asked.

Dave McKinley looked sympathetic. 'Not very much at the moment, I'm afraid. When the medics got to the shack, he was drifting in and out of consciousness. Understandably, they just wanted to get him to the hospital as soon as they could. If we hear anything about Dr Redfern's situation, we'll let you know.'

Steve thanked the inspector and asked him how we could help.

'Before the medics turned up, one of our officers managed to ask Dr Redfern a few questions. He told them that there had been three men who had been holding him. Only two of those men had been with him most of the time.'

Kevin nodded. 'That matches the details Jim gave me in his text.'

'That's right,' said the inspector. 'The two men who were left with him were Americans, but there was also a British man who seemed to be their boss and who I think some of you know. Incidentally, the British police have furnished us with a mugshot of this man.'

A murmur went round the group along with some puzzled glances.

Steve looked around our party. 'Some of you won't be aware of this yet, but the man that Inspector McKinley is referring to disrupted one of Kevin's previous research trips.'

The murmuring increased in volume.

Ben looked particularly irritated as he said, 'Hold on a minute, Steve. I take it that some of you have already met up with these two officers. How come you didn't think that was worth sharing with the rest of us?'

Steph did not look exactly thrilled either. Jenny, on the other hand, just looked upset.

Steve sighed. 'Ben, I understand why you might feel slightly aggrieved, but there's a good reason why we kept things quiet. I'll explain more when we've given these guys the information they need.'

Ben was not happy but decided not to push the matter further.

Inspector McKinley picked up where he had left off. 'We performed a thorough search of the shack, but there wasn't much to discover. We retrieved the phone Dr Redfern used to text you and I suspect that'll be helpful in identifying one or two of the people involved. We're obviously very keen to learn all we can about Dr Redfern's relationship with this Smith character. So, anything any of you can tell us would be very much appreciated.'

At this point, Kevin was able to give the policemen some limited information, but no one else was able to provide any other helpful details.

The policemen left us, repeating their promise to contact us with any news about Jim.

As soon as they had gone, Ben demanded to know why he had been kept in the dark about Jim and his kidnapping. After checking with me, Steve explained the situation to the rest of the group. On receiving the information, they completely understood why I had been keen to keep things quiet. I got the distinct impression that Ben felt a little embarrassed about getting upset. In any case, they all expressed their deep regret over Sam's situation.

At 4:30 that afternoon, Steve received another call from Inspector McKinley. He had been permitted to see Jim at the hospital and had a few valuable minutes with him. The doctors told the inspector that Jim's situation had been made worse because of the number of bites received, and the length of time between being bitten and the commencement of his treatment. On top of that, he had unfortunately had an unusual reaction to the antivenom. The doctors insisted that the inspector would only be able to see Jim briefly. Although he was very weak, Dave McKinley had long enough with him to ask a few crucial questions. He discovered a few more details regarding Jim's period of imprisonment. However, they were concerned that some of Jim's recollections might have been a bit jumbled up due to his physical and mental condition.

Sitting in the bar, discussing serious matters, was becoming an unwelcome habit. Kevin was tired and was starting to look a bit older than his years. Jim was the subject of our conversation and, as Kevin was talking, a vague memory arrived unbidden in my brain.

'Kevin, I've just remembered something that Jim said in your office before we came out here!'

'What's that?'

'He said something about Smith contacting him and asking him for some kind of specialist information.'

Kevin's brow furrowed. 'I don't remember anything about that.'

I noticed Sue walking towards our table, so I stood and pulled out a chair for her.

'Well, I'm pretty sure I haven't just dreamt it up,' I said, retaking my seat.

'And you say that was in my office?'

'Yes, I'm sure it was.' As Sue joined us, I turned to her and explained what we were discussing. 'Do you remember?' I asked.

'Yes,' she said, 'there was something. I don't think Jim told us what the subject was, but whatever it was, I think he said that he was unable to help Smith with it.'

Kevin looked baffled. 'I've got no recollection of that at all.'

'I don't think you were there, Kevin,' Sue said. 'I think you'd gone to find the itinerary for our trip.'

Kevin looked relieved. I knew he felt responsible for the safety of the people here on this expedition.

'Do you think Smith might have seen the article in your magazine?' I asked. 'You said that you'd announced this trip a couple of months before you came to see us.'

'It's possible,' Kevin retorted.

My phone suddenly indicated the arrival of a new message. Talk of the devil, it was from Smith himself. All it said was: 'Granger, here's the proof you wanted. Now, send me the information.'

My heart skipped a beat. Was I about to hear from Sam? There was a link attached to the message which I now clicked on. It was a video clip. I almost did not recognize him. Sam had never been one for facial hair, but there he sat with a moustache and beard. It would seem that he had not got access to shaving equipment. I wondered how he was being treated.

As I studied Sam a bit more closely on the small screen, it looked as if there might be some discolouration around Sam's left eye. I also thought I could see a small nick just above the same eye. Wherever he was, I fervently hoped that he was not being badly mistreated, although he had clearly been in a physical altercation. However, even with these concerns, just to see him gave me incredible relief.

As I watched, he picked up a newspaper and held it up in clear sight of the camera. 'This is the front of the *Daily Mail* for Tuesday 13 August,' he said.

That was today, I realized. This was fantastic news.

Sam both looked and sounded rather annoyed. He went on: 'I've been told to tell you that I'm fine and being treated well.'

After saying this, his eyes shifted to a point slightly to the left, presumably to look at the person operating the camera. There was a look of dislike in his eyes and, a split second before the screen went blank, I noticed what I took to be a defiant smile appear on his lips.

I had such a feeling of relief mingled with pain at seeing Sam in his personal prison, but this brief video clip, albeit of only about fifteen seconds, did give me a few reasons for optimism. Although it would appear that Sam may well come out of this ordeal looking like a hippy, he did seem physically fit, with the exception of his black eye. In addition, while he seemed a bit low, there were also signs that he was not about to let his circumstances crush his spirit. That was reassuring, and the faint smile at the end of the video suggested to me that he had defied his captors' instructions in some way. As I replayed the clip, I noticed the phrase, 'I've been told to tell you ...', and suspected that this had been inserted by Sam to convey the fact that he was being forced to make the statement. It might seem a small point, but I knew Sam. I thought that in his current circumstances, any small act of defiance would be likely to give him a bit of a lift.

I turned to Kevin. 'Can we get a message off to Smith this evening?'

'I'm sure we can,' he said. 'Wait here.'

He got to his feet and strolled over to where Steve and Jenny were in conversation over a laptop. I saw Steve give a brief nod and glance in my direction before Kevin returned to us.

'When Steve's finished with Jenny, he'll be over,' he said. 'I don't think it should take long to fire something off to Smith.'

As we waited for Steve, I took the opportunity to send my dad a very brief update, explaining that we had received conclusive proof Sam was still in good health.

When Steve joined us, a discussion started as to how Smith thought he would possibly be able to profit from obtaining this information. Steve was halfway through saying something about the technical problems involved in identifying different radiohalos when he screwed up his face.

A frown, and deep concentration marred his features as he tried to recall something.

'Do you remember a couple of days ago, Jenny was explaining that we had been approached by some companies who had expressed an interest in our work on ore deposits?'

We all nodded.

'Well, one of those companies is a relatively new player in the business. That's not a problem in and of itself, but both Jenny and I felt uneasy about them.'

He paused for a moment as if reflecting. 'They were the only company to actually send people out to us. All the others got in touch via email.'

'What was it that caused your feelings of unease?' Kevin asked.

'I'm not entirely sure,' Steve said. 'There were two guys who came out to see us. One of them was friendly enough, but there was something about the other one that concerned us. Neither of us could really put our finger on it. Nevertheless, we both experienced the same discomfort and we decided that we would not be sharing our findings with them. In any case, we felt the other companies were more professional and ...'

Suddenly, Steve broke off what he was saying and an expression of dawning revelation appeared on his face. There was a pause before he said slowly, 'That's who it was.'

We waited to be enlightened.

He turned to look at me. 'Rob, you remember last Wednesday afternoon when it was throwing it down with rain? We'd just had our session in the bar and you were going to go back to your room. Do you remember me telling you that I'd just seen someone I recognized?'

'Yes,' I said. 'You said you couldn't think where you knew him from.'

'That's right. Well, I do now. That's who it was. He was the guy that Jen and I didn't take to.'

'Are you sure it was him?' Kevin asked.

'Absolutely certain.'

'And is their company based in this area?' Kevin continued to probe.

Steve looked as if he were trying to remember. 'No, I don't think so. They were from somewhere down in Texas.'

Kevin voiced my own thoughts as he surmised, 'So it would be a bit of a coincidence if he were to turn up in our hotel here?'

'It would certainly be surprising,' Steve agreed.

'I'm not a big fan of coincidences,' Kevin said. 'I think we need to let the inspector know about this.'

We all agreed.

As Steve had been talking, a deep feeling of unease came over me.

'Do you remember much about this guy?' I asked.

'Not much, really. The guy who did most of the talking sounded as if he was a Texan and, to be honest, he was pleasant enough, as I said. It was the other guy. There was just something about him, and both Jenny and I had this unease in our spirits.'

'What can you remember about him?'

Steve thought for a moment. 'I couldn't place the accent,' he said. 'I suspect he might have been from somewhere in your neck of the woods.'

'Can you describe him to us?'

'Oh, I don't know. I would say he was slightly shorter than average, maybe 5 feet, 8 or 9 inches. He was quite muscular and had very short dark hair.'

Kevin and I locked eyes.

Steve noticed. 'What's up?'

After another glance at Kevin who gave a nod of agreement, I said, 'Steve, it's possible that the man you've described may be this John Smith. I suspect he's managed to get connected to this company in some way. It would certainly explain why he wants me to send the information on ore deposits.'

'I'm sure that's right,' Kevin agreed. 'Steve, we'll get this information off to Smith, but then I think we need to give the inspector a ring.'

As Kevin and Steve began crafting their message, I thought back to the previous Wednesday when Steve said he had seen the person we now suspected was Smith himself. I remembered going out to retrieve Sue's notebook from one of the Land Rovers. On my way out, I had called at the hotel reception to borrow an umbrella from a member of staff. However, the girl on reception had already been talking to someone else. I also remembered that that individual had beat a fairly hasty retreat, apparently requiring an urgent visit to the little boys' room. I frowned as I thought back to the incident, trying to picture the back of the person in my mind's eye. It certainly could have been Smith. I obviously would not be expecting to bump into him in Washington State. I supposed it was irrelevant whether it had been him or not. It seemed clear that he was in the area and intent on causing more mischief.

When the message to Smith was completed and had been sent, Steve shook his head and gave a little chuckle. 'Nearly all this information is already in the public domain. We're not really telling Smith anything that we haven't already published.'

As for me, I began to hope that we might get Sam back from his captivity completely unharmed.

Jenny was still at the table where Steve had been talking with her before joining us.

'Have you got a moment, Jenny?' Steve said.

She smiled and came over to our table. 'What's up?' she asked.

'Remember those guys who came up to see us from Texas? The ones asking about our mineral work?'

'Yes, sure,' she said.

'Well, that guy that we didn't take to, can you remember anything about him?'

Her eyebrows shot up. 'Yes, I do,' she said. 'I'd forgotten all about them. But it's funny you should bring him up now, because when I escorted them off the premises, he asked me if I knew Kevin.'

Once more, Kevin and I glanced at each other.

'Well, that would appear to remove any doubt,' Kevin said. Jenny did not need to be a genius to realize there was a problem. 'What's the matter?'

Kevin ignored her question. 'What did you tell him, Jenny?'

'I told him that I didn't know you particularly well, but that we had met on a couple of occasions.'

'And what was his reaction?'

'It was strange. He was still looking at me, but it was more as if he were staring straight through me. It made me feel a bit creeped out,' she said with a shiver. 'It only lasted for a split second. Then he smiled pleasantly and said what a good man you were.'

Kevin laughed. 'Yes, I bet he did.'

Jenny briefly looked at me, and then at Steve. ‘Sorry, would someone like to tell me what’s going on?’

Kevin put her in the picture, then, addressing Steve, suggested, ‘I think we had better give the inspector that call now.’

Chapter 14
Vengeance

The following morning, we learned that Steve had received an update from the hospital on Cecil's condition. Apparently, although his burns were still significant, it seemed that they were not quite as serious as first believed. We were all relieved to hear this and asked Steve to send our best wishes to him.

Having received this relatively good report, we were now hoping to be able to take our last look at Mount Saint Helens. The weather was currently clear, but rain had been forecast for later in the day. Thinking back to Wednesday's torrential downpour, I decided to run up to my room to collect a coat; I did not want to be looking like a drowned rat again. As I picked up my coat, the phone rang. Looking at the display, I froze. It was Smith. I was not sure whether to ignore the call or whether to take it in the hope that it would provide some important information. I did not know what to do. I hesitated right up to the point where I knew the answerphone message was just about to kick in. I held my breath and accepted the call but did not speak.

'Granger? Are you there?'

I put the phone on loudspeaker, gently placed it on the bed and stood listening, gazing into the mirror. I continued to say nothing.

After a few seconds of silence, Smith spoke up. 'I know you're listening, Granger.' Realizing I was not going to speak, he went on:

'How's Redfern? Has he croaked yet? He got what was coming to him. You need to know that I haven't finished. I won't rest until all of you who were involved in the Congo expedition have paid for your actions. My vengeance will be terrifying. Just as it was for Redfern. You'll all be looking over your shoulders for the rest of your lives waiting for your own personal axe to fall.'

There was one more pause, before he put in his final words: 'You may have seen the last of me for now, but you can be sure I'll be back in the future. Enjoy the wait.' There was an evil laugh, then the line went dead.

When I got down to reception, Steph was just coming in through the front doors.

'Hi Rob,' she said, 'I'm just going up to my room; I forgot my phone. Most of the others are already outside. They're waiting to see if we get permission to go for one last look. I'll be with you in a couple of minutes.'

I nodded in acknowledgement and went out to join the others.

Spotting Kevin standing on his own studying a map, I walked over to him.

'I've just had a call from Smith,' I said.

His head jerked up. 'What did he say?'

‘I might as well tell everyone at the same time,’ I said, and looked around. They all appeared to be there except Steph.

As soon as she was back with us, I filled them all in about the details of Smith’s call. I explained about his obsession for vengeance, and his prediction that the members of the Congo expedition would all be looking over their shoulders for the rest of their lives.

Kevin laughed humourlessly. ‘“Vengeance is mine, I will repay, sayeth the Lord”.’

Steve immediately called Inspector McKinley to inform him of Smith’s contact. As soon as he had hung up, his mobile rang again. I assumed it would be the inspector calling back for further information, but it was not.

‘It’s Terry,’ Steve announced. He answered the call and listened.

‘OK, thanks Terry. As before, please let me know if anything changes.’

After hanging up, he relayed the message. ‘There were only a few minimal readings from Mount Saint Helens last night. That’s good. Terry has emailed over a disclaimer. Anyone who wants to go and take a last look at the volcano can do that, but only if you read and sign the disclaimer.’

A little cheer went up from the group. I glanced across at Sue. All I could see in her face was excitement and anticipation. I was thankful to get the opportunity to visit the site again, but the thrill Sue was experiencing was unrivalled. I must admit to being a little surprised by her apparent lack of concern, especially following Cecil’s unfortunate accident. As relieved as I was that we could go back once more, there was a degree of nervousness that I could not quite shift.

As copies of the disclaimer were printed off and signed, I chatted to Steve about other volcanic events that he had witnessed. He was a mine of information and knowledge and, as the discussion rumbled on, his enthusiasm for Mount Saint Helens rubbed off on me. The knot of fear I had was displaced by a feeling of exhilaration at visiting the site one more time. Steve had convinced me there was very little chance that any major volcanic event would occur in the next couple of weeks. So, it was with a group-wide feeling of excitement that we got into our vehicles and headed for the volcano for one last time.

I was keen to take some more snaps on my phone, as well as wanting to leave with a clear mental image of Mount Saint Helens before any future eruption, which might drastically alter the profile of the volcano. As the track rose towards the ridge from which we would be taking our last look at her, I found my excitement rising in anticipation.

Kevin swung the Land Rover around so we would already be facing in the right direction when it came time to leave. I could not wait to get out and crest the ridge to have a final look at this amazing volcano. I was fascinated by my own emotions. We had been studying various aspects of the geological aftermath of the earlier eruptions for about a week and a half, but it was only now that I was about to leave, that I truly caught the excitement that Sue had presumably been experiencing from day one. Part of this excitement was almost certainly down to the knowledge that the volcano was beginning to rumble again. The site had also had a deep impact on me that I could not explain.

My hand was already poised to open the passenger door before Kevin had applied the handbrake. As I jumped out, I noticed two other vehicles coming up the track towards us. The contrast was stark. One looked like a brand-new Chevrolet which came right up to where we had parked, but the other was a battered old jeep which stopped on a piece of ground about 50 yards further down the track. The prospect of taking a look at Mount Saint Helens before she blew her top appeared to have attracted all sorts of different people to the area. More interested observers: if only they knew about the information that we had been privy to this week, I thought to myself as I turned to follow Kevin up the incline.

At the top of the ridge there was a huge boulder. It was about 15 feet by 10 feet and about 8 feet high. Kevin and I walked past the massive rock, another reminder about how extraordinary this place was, and we joined the others about 20 yards further on. They were all standing in silence, staring across at the volcano. I grabbed my phone from my back pocket and started to take snaps of the area; others began to do the same.

We had been there for around three quarters of an hour, relishing our last look at Mount Saint Helens when I heard a low, distant rumble. We were all looking round at each other when the sound came again. I also thought I could sense a very slight tremble in the ground beneath my feet.

'That sounds ominous,' Steve said with concern. 'I think we'd better make tracks.'

His mobile sprang to life. He answered. 'Hi Terry.' There was a pause, then he said, 'I know; we heard it. We're just about to leave.'

Everyone was taking last-minute snaps on their phones and I decided to do the same. It was bizarre. I had felt an element of reservation about this last trip to Mount Saint Helens, even when I had been told that the chance of an imminent eruption was highly unlikely. Now that we had been instructed by the same geologist that it was definitely time to go, I found myself strangely reluctant to leave.

Some of our group began hurrying towards the Land Rovers. I was standing facing Kevin and could see the volcano over his left shoulder. As I watched, the top of the mountain exploded. Material shot skywards immediately followed by a pillar of thick smoke.

'We need to get out of here!' Steve shouted. 'Everyone, get in the vehicles.'

Kevin had spun around to stare at the spectacle. We were both transfixed.

Three of our Land Rovers started to roll. Steve hung out of the window of his vehicle and barked at us, 'Kevin, Rob, move it!'

We were shaken out of our brief trance-like state and ran for our own vehicle which was just over the ridge. The others disappeared in a cloud of dust and roared away from us.

Although Kevin was a couple of decades older than me, he could certainly shift when he needed to. He was ahead of me as he drew alongside the boulder at the top of the ridge. As I followed, with horror, I saw a leg shoot out from behind the rock. Kevin's right foot hit the outstretched leg and he crashed heavily to the ground. A familiar figure rose from behind the rock and moved towards Kevin's prostrate form. I adjusted the direction of my sprint and crashed into the side of John Smith's chest with my right shoulder. With some satisfaction, I heard a woosh of breath as it was expelled from his lungs. I landed heavily on top of him and realized with alarm that he was grasping a revolver. Clutching at the hand with the gun, I desperately tried to prize it from his grasp.

Although I had badly winded him, Smith had a vice-like grasp of the gun. I gasped with pain as his other fist slammed into my ribs. He tore his gun-hand free and I thought that was going to be it.

Kevin had picked himself off the ground to join the fracas. Grabbing Smith's gun-hand, he smashed it into the ground. Smith's hand fell open and he dropped the gun. Then came the left hook, crashing into Kevin's jaw. Kevin crumpled to the floor while Smith and I raced for the gun. As Smith bent to grab it, I swung my right foot at it. Making good contact, the revolver went spinning high into the air and a fair distance into the adjacent valley. With relief, I saw Smith charge off to retrieve it. 'Time to get out of here,' I thought.

However, turning back to Kevin, with horror I noticed he was still crumpled in a heap on the ground. Rushing over to him and giving him a shake, panic rose. He was out cold. I dragged him up and shook him but his head just rolled from side to side. I slapped him across the cheek with the palm of my hand.

‘Come on!’ I shouted. I shook him again. ‘Kevin!’ I screamed, starting to drag him towards the Land Rover.

He groaned and grasped my shoulder.

‘Kevin, Come on! We need to get away!’

It was all taking far too long. I dragged him round to the passenger side of the vehicle and bundled him in, slamming the door. Running round to the driver’s side, I was reaching for the door when I heard a gruff voice boom in the air: ‘Granger!’

I stopped and closed my eyes. Rumblings and volcanic explosions from Mount Saint Helens continued as the primary sensory input to my consciousness.

I opened my eyes and slowly turned to see Smith standing next to the boulder at the top of the ridge, the gun in his hand.

From where I was standing at a lower elevation, I was having to look up at Smith. I could still see Mount Saint Helens belching smoke and ash into the air about thirty degrees to the left of him.

Smith, a maniacal grin on his face, was triumphant. ‘Thought you’d managed to get away, didn’t you?’

He had to raise his voice to make himself heard above the eruption which was growing in intensity.

Smith began to raise his gun. So, this was it. This was what it felt like to know you were just about to die. I had a feeling of déjà vu as old memories began to flash through my mind. I was transferred back to a river in the Congo: my brother Sam looking back at me, and then a startled look appearing on his face, turning to see Smith hobbling along the riverbank and levelling his gun to shoot at us; Sam and I frantically paddling to get our canoe away from the bullets; then the agonized cry from Sam as one of those bullets smashed into his leg. Remembering all this, suddenly I felt incredibly tired. What was the point of struggling? Smith was only a matter of yards away. He was not going to miss from there; this was it.

Then something strange happened. Although only the very top of Mount Saint Helens was visible above the ridge, suddenly, it disappeared altogether. Some kind of veil appeared to have completely obscured it. In spite of my position being hopeless, I was transfixed by the spectacle.

Smith noticed my fascination, and following my gaze. He looked back over his right shoulder and a look of horror appeared on his face. A piercing scream rent the air a split second before he disappeared in a ball of flame.

I ducked, expecting the same fate to overtake me a moment later, but it did not happen. The heat was incredible, but I was still alive. I jumped into the driver's seat of the Land Rover, slammed it into gear and took off. Thankfully, the track was downhill all the way, and the Land Rover tore away from the ridge at a great rate of knots.

Abruptly, I felt intense heat at the back of my head. I reached behind my neck and patted at the back of my head. Most of my hair at the back seemed to have been badly singed, and a chunk of it came away at my touch. The top of my jacket also appeared to be smouldering. As I considered Smith's demise, it appeared to have been the extreme righthand edge of what was presumably a pyroclastic flow that had caught him.

The cloud of smoke, steam, ash and other volcanic gases was travelling much faster than we were. Looking through the windscreen, I could see that the cloud was now far in front of us, and we were indeed under the far-righthand edge of that cloud. Thankfully for us, the road swung to the right in about half a mile's time. If we could reach that point before being engulfed by the volcanic cloud, there was a reasonable chance that we might escape.

The cloud was getting lower and lower, looking menacing. We were about 30 yards from the bend in the road when the canvas roof of the Land Rover burst into flame behind us. With my foot to the floor, the flames were all blown backwards away from Kevin and me. A split second later we were at the bend. Jerking the steering wheel to the right, I very nearly flipped the Land Rover over. We teetered on two wheels for what seemed like an eternity, before the righthand side of the vehicle slammed back down on the track, bounced once, and then we were racing away from the killer cloud of volcanic material.

All this time, Kevin had been thrown around all over the place. I had had no time to put his seatbelt on when I had bundled him into the Land Rover, and he had been too dazed to fasten himself in. As we had torn away from the volcano, we had bumped, bounced and lurched our way down the track. Kevin had ended up slumped forward with his head against the dashboard. I slowed the vehicle and attempted to pull him upright but could not manage it.

Glancing to my left, I tried to locate the exact position of the volcanic cloud. With relief, I realized that we were gradually getting further away from the deadly mixture of gas, steam and ash. I chanced a brief look back over my left shoulder to make sure that no new flow of volcanic material was chasing after us. With the canvas having been totally burned up from the top of our Land Rover, it allowed me a clear view behind. 'Handy,' I thought sardonically.

Seeing no additional danger, I brought the Land Rover to a stop. I grabbed Kevin's shoulders and pulled him into an upright position. That was when I noticed the blood. There was a nasty gash on his forehead just above his right eye. Ignoring this fact for a moment, I reached across his chest, pulled the seatbelt in front of him and secured it.

Once again, I looked back to check that there was no immediate threat from Mount Saint Helens. Reassuring myself of that, I took out a bottle of water, splashed some of the contents over Kevin's head and gave him a gentle shake.

He groaned and half opened unfocused eyes, lifting his hand to the right side of his jaw.

I poured a little water on a clean, folded handkerchief.

'Kevin,' I said, 'hold this on your forehead and put some pressure on it.'

He took the proffered handkerchief and lightly dabbed at the wound before checking it to see how bad it was.

'You'll be fine,' I said. 'Just press firmly on the cut.'

He did so, and we set off again.

As well as the pyroclastic flow that Mount Saint Helens had fired almost directly at us back at the ridge, there was a sizeable mushroom cloud that was forming over the summit of the volcano. This was getting larger by the second. The daylight was gradually being replaced by an eerie yellowish haze, and there was a sickly sulphurous stench that grabbed at the back of the throat.

Eventually arriving back at the hotel, we had a welcoming party as everyone was gathered around, eagerly watching for our return. As I opened the driver's door and got out, Sue came running over, tears running down her face.

She flung her arms around my neck. 'Thank God,' she sobbed. 'I thought you were dead.'

She took a half pace back and looked into my eyes. Suddenly, her focus shifted. It was at that moment she noticed the charred struts at the back of the Land Rover where the canvas cover had once been. A look of horror appeared on her face and she turned white. The tears started again and, once again, she threw her arms around me and held me very tight. While it was certainly gratifying to experience her concern and affection, her embrace resulted in a stab of pain to my neck. It was only then that I became aware of the soreness. Until that moment, my body had been pumped so full of adrenaline, I had not noticed it as we had attempted to escape first Smith, and then the volcano.

After a few seconds, I loosened her grip on my neck and eased myself away from her. 'I'm fine,' I said, giving her what I hoped was a reassuring smile. 'Sue, I need to see how Kevin is.'

However, there was another shock in store for Sue. As she withdrew her arms from around my neck, she stared at her forearm. I followed her gaze and noticed the grey smear that had caught her attention. I could also see burnt hair.

'Turn around,' she said.

'Sue, I'm all right. I need to go ...'

'Turn around,' she repeated.

Reluctantly, I did as I had been told. I felt her hands investigating the collar of my jacket and then the back of my head.

'You're not all right,' she said. 'You've got a nasty burn on the back of your neck.'

The rest of our team were on the other side of the vehicle attending to Kevin. Sue grabbed my arm and led me around the front of the Land Rover to where Ben was cleaning the gash over Kevin's eye. The rest of the team were looking on with concern.

'Steph!' Sue called.

As with the rest of the group, Steph looked shell shocked by the recent events. She turned her head in our direction. Seeing Sue's concern, she snapped out of her dazed state of disbelief and came over to us.

'Rob's got a nasty burn on his neck,' Sue told her.

Steph, who was even shorter than Sue, led me to a bench and sat me down so she could get a better look at my neck. I heard her suck in her breath as she examined the burn.

'That's nasty,' she said. 'Come inside and I'll sort you out.'

Steph made a brief detour to her Land Rover to retrieve her own medical bag, and then the three of us entered the front of the hotel.

'Come up to my room,' she said. 'I need to bathe that before I dress it.'

As we went up in the lift to our floor, Steph asked me what had happened back at the ridge after they had left in their vehicles. I began to tell them about Smith and his intervention. They were both horrified.

'What happened?' Sue asked.

I considered whether to leave out the details about Smith's revolver but then decided that, given his fate, it did not really matter now.

I had just reached the point at which I had kicked the gun into the next valley when we reached Steph's room. She inserted her cardkey and the three of us entered.

'Sit here,' she said, patting the corner of her bed.

Dutifully, I sat down as Steph disappeared into the bathroom and began running water into the basin.

'Take off your jacket and shirt,' she called from the bathroom.

This was a task I did not relish much. The more time I had had to think about my injury, the sorer it had become. I stood and began to gingerly shrug off my jacket. Sue could see I was rather uncomfortable and helped me to ease the jacket off my shoulders. Then came the bit I really was not looking forward to. I sat back down on the bed and began to lift the bottom of my T-shirt, trying my best not to move it at the top.

Again, Sue came to my aid: 'Leave it, Rob. I'll do it.'

As I raised my arms, she gently lifted the T-shirt over my head.

'Thanks,' I said, giving her a sheepish smile.

Sue still looked visibly upset. She held out my T-shirt so I could see its condition. The area that had been at the back of my neck was very badly scorched. Looking at it, all of a sudden it began to dawn on me what a close shave we had had and a wave of nausea swept over me.

Steph came back into the bedroom with a plastic bowl of warm water and wads of gauze. In spite of my medical circumstances, I was feeling a wave of awkwardness, suddenly self-conscious about my uncovered torso. I told myself that was ridiculous and waited for my treatment, which I suspected might be rather uncomfortable.

I could see Sue out of the corner of my eye studying my neck with a degree of concern on her face.

Steph perched on the bed immediately behind me. As she began to bathe my neck, I winced. I have never been the bravest of patients, but I had always found burns to be one of the most painful injuries. Sue came to sit next to me and grabbed my hand. Every cloud has a silver lining, I thought, and managed an inward grin.

After about five minutes Steph smeared some cream on the burn and stood up.

'Rob, that's a really nasty burn you've got there. I think it'll be fine, but I'd rather they checked it out at the local hospital.'

My heart sank. The last thing I wanted was more people prodding and poking at my neck. 'I'm sure I'll be fine,' I said.

'You probably will, but I'd still rather you got checked out.'

Apparently, I was not going to have any say in the matter.

Ten minutes later, Steph, Kevin and I were back in a Land Rover and heading for the hospital where Cecil had been taken. Ben was adamant that Kevin also be checked out suspecting that he was suffering from severe concussion following Smith's left hook. As we headed for the hospital, Kevin was understandably curious to know how the events on the ridge had developed. Although he had actually been there, he had absolutely no recollection of any of it. However, at that moment, I just did not feel able to go into it all. Kevin looked over at me.

'Rob, I can imagine how traumatic all this has been for you. Obviously, it doesn't matter now, but, at some point, I really need to know what happened out there.'

I glanced at him briefly and gave a curt nod. 'Sure,' I said. 'In your position I suspect I'd feel the same.'

Kevin stared into my eyes. 'Rob, thanks mate. I don't yet know how you did it, but thanks for getting me out of there.'

When Steph and I returned about five hours later, we found the rest of the team in the meeting room, concerned for Kevin's and my health. As we walked in, everyone jumped up to greet me and they all started speaking at once. I held up my hand and the tumult subsided.

I smiled, flattered at the attention. 'Firstly, they have decided to keep Kevin in overnight for observation. They think he'll be OK, but they don't want to take any chances. As far as I'm concerned, I'm fine. It'll take more than a volcanic eruption to keep me down.'

They all had a laugh, and it was heartening to see the delight in their faces at my return. Then all the questions started. Sue had already filled them in regarding the details I had given her earlier, but there was still much they did not know. So, I picked up the account from the point where I had kicked Smith's gun into the next valley. They were completely silent as I told them of my efforts to try to get Kevin into the Land Rover.

It was almost comical to watch their faces as I arrived at the moment when Smith had caught me about to get into the vehicle. I explained how I had turned to face him, how I had spotted the gun in his hand, my experience of time standing still, recollections of the events in the Congo, and how I had seen the top of Mount Saint Helens disappear from my sight.

Up to this point, to be honest, I had quite enjoyed telling the story, but I was about to have a rather unexpected reaction. I arrived at the point where Smith had turned to see the cloud of volcanic material racing straight towards him, but I found myself temporarily unable to speak. Up until that moment, I had not given Smith a second thought. The events had happened so quickly; everything that happened felt like I was on auto pilot, responding moment by moment, not having time to pause for thought. Now, I could not get him out of my mind. All I could see, over and over again, was an image of his look of terror and his piercing scream as he turned into a ball of flame. I just stood there, gazing sightlessly across the meeting room.

It was some time before I became aware that they were all asking me if I was OK. Sue knelt beside me and touched my arm. It was that physical touch that eventually broke through and released me from that perpetual replay of Smith's horrific death.

I suddenly noticed their concerned faces and realized that I must have been totally absorbed by that hideous event. I lifted my hand to my forehead and spent a few moments composing myself.

'Sorry,' I said. 'I don't know what just happened. I'm afraid I'm going to have to finish the story later. I need a drink.'

'I'll come with you,' Sue said and we headed for the bar together.

When we sat down, I had a stiff whisky in front of me and Sue had a coffee.

'How are you feeling, Rob?' Sue asked, with deep concern in her eyes.

I had a sip from my glass and allowed the peaty flavour to run over every part of my mouth. 'A little better now. I felt a bit overwhelmed in there with all the others.' I stopped and gazed across the bar, my mind once more returning to the events on the ridge.

'You've got that look in your eyes again,' she said. 'The look you had when you stopped speaking in the meeting room.'

I screwed my eyes shut and tried to banish the terrible images assailing my brain. For a while I could not respond. Finding words at last, I confided, 'Sue, it was something straight out of a nightmare. I couldn't face talking about it to all those guys in there.'

'Can you talk about it to me?'

I considered that question. 'I think so,' I answered. 'To be honest, Sue, I think it will help in the long run. Don't get me wrong, I don't really want to talk about it. It was horrible.'

Sue stretched out a hand and rested it lightly on my arm. 'If it gets too difficult just stop,' she said. 'But I think you're right. I do think it will help you to talk about it.'

I breathed deeply, contemplating putting it into words; I looked down at my whisky, as if it might help. I really did not fancy talking about Smith's death, but felt it was the best way to deal with my current mental state. I picked up my glass and took a healthy swig.

'I think I broke off at the point where Mount Saint Helens had just disappeared?'

Sue nodded.

'It was fascinating. One second, I could see the top of the volcano; the next, it was gone. I guess Smith noticed my expression. He turned to look back over his right shoulder and'...'

Once again, I had to stop. I could see his face in my mind's eye as if I was actually watching the moment all over again. His face had expressed horror and fear in equal measure—an expression that I had never seen before and never wanted to see again. When I rediscovered how to speak, I tried to describe the scene to Sue, but felt my attempt was completely inadequate.

I rolled the whisky around the bottom of the glass as I attempted to find the words to describe the next bit.

In the end, I just blurted out: 'Sue, he just went up in a ball of flames.' I closed my eyes and felt Sue lay her hand on my arm again.

For some time, neither of us spoke. Eventually, Sue prompted softly, 'What happened next?'

'It's all a bit of a blur, really. I jumped into the Land Rover and we took off.'

Once I had got the bit about Smith out of the way, the words flowed easily. I described as much as I could remember about our flight away from the ridge. I told her about the canvas cover going up in flames just before we reached the bend in the track. I told her about almost flipping the vehicle over and then pulling up to see to Kevin. All this time Sue sat there wide-eyed and with an astonished look on her face.

'Apart from that, the journey was pretty uneventful,' I said, giving her an ironic smile.

Sue shook her head slowly. 'It must have been terrible. No wonder you're traumatised.'

'It wasn't great,' I admitted. 'Anyway, there's nothing I can do about it. I need to put it out of my mind I guess.'

I looked down at her coffee cup. 'So, now you've become a Christian, is alcohol off the table?'

'Actually, I'm not sure,' she said. 'I just fancied a coffee.'

It was not until after we had had our evening meal that I met up again with the others. Unsurprisingly, they were still very curious as to what had happened back at the ridge. So, once again, I began to relate the events from earlier in the day.

This time, I was able to get my story out. Steve explained to me how it was almost certainly the contours of the terrain at the ridge that had saved our lives. From my description, he guessed that the ridge had deflected the pyroclastic flow up and over the top of Kevin and me. It was also amazing that it had been the very far right of the volcanic cloud that had caught Smith. If that flow had been just 10 feet further to the left, Smith would have survived and I was certain that I would have taken a bullet from his revolver. On the other hand, if it had been 10 feet further to the right, I do not think Kevin and I would have made it out alive.

The following day, the activity at Mount Saint Helens had reduced dramatically. Steve, Jenny and three other local geologists were to accompany representatives from the state police to attempt to get back to the ridge where we had been when the volcano went up. From Steve's and Jenny's point of view, their main motivation was professional. They both wanted to see what effect the pyroclastic flow had had on the landscape. However, the authorities also wanted to retrieve and hopefully attempt to identify John Smith's remains. All those making the journey would have to wear special protective boots as the ash lying on the ground would still be extremely hot.

I suddenly had a thought and ran to catch Steve before they left. He had just been getting into his Land Rover when I shouted to him. Turning, he came over to me.

'Steve,' I said, 'do you know the policemen who are going with you?'

He looked slightly puzzled. 'No. Why?'

'Look, I know it's pretty likely that anything on his body will have been totally destroyed, but can you ask them if they'll look for any surviving names and phone numbers Smith might have been carrying? I wouldn't expect them to share the information with me, but it might be important in helping the British police to find my brother.'

I saw the dawning comprehension in Steve's eyes. 'Of course,' he said. 'Leave it with me. But Rob, don't build your hopes up. I'm guessing everything will have been completely incinerated.'

I nodded gloomily. 'I know. I just thought it would be worth a try.'

Steve turned away and I watched him get into the vehicle before I walked back towards the hotel entrance.

It was approaching midday when Kevin arrived back at the hotel from his overnight stay at the hospital. The doctors were happy with his condition but had told him to get back in touch with them if he developed any headaches, nausea or problems with his vision. It was then that I filled him in with the details he was so keen to hear. When I told him how unlikely it was that we had survived while Smith had died, he reminded me of the words he had uttered yesterday: 'Vengeance is mine, I will repay, sayeth the Lord.'

I had not even considered the possibility of divine intervention. However, reflecting on the precise set of circumstances that had resulted in Smith's death and Kevin's and my own escape, I had to admit, the odds against both those things happening at the same time were astronomical.

When Steve and Jenny returned, having been gone for around two and a half hours later, Steve immediately came looking for me. 'We found him,' he said. 'Or perhaps I should say, a lump of charred carbon which used to be him.'

The hope that had fleetingly risen at his first words was immediately dashed by the others.

'Never mind,' I said. 'It was always going to be a long shot.'

'Well, let's wait and see. You never know; something might have survived.'

'I wouldn't hold my breath,' I thought.

It was so frustrating. Just the day before, we had sent Smith most of the information he wanted on the mineral work, and I had hoped that would mean we would be close to being able to negotiate Sam's release. Smith's death had changed all that. I was struggling to see how we would be able to locate Sam now. I did not currently have an answer for that, but I knew I would have to try to do something.

'Steve,' I said, 'I'm afraid I'm going to have to cut this trip short. I need to go back to Britain to try and find out what's happened to my brother.'

Steve nodded. 'I quite understand, Rob.' He laid a hand on my shoulder. 'I'll be in touch with you. Please let me know when you have any news.'

'I will,' I said, and smiled with genuine affection. 'At some point in the future, I'm going to want to understand more about this whole subject. When that time comes, I'd like us to get together so you can continue my education.'

He smiled. 'I'd love that, Rob. I'll look forward to that day.'

Chapter 15
The Search Begins

On the flight to Heathrow two days later, my mind was spinning from the recent traumatic events, but my determination was firmly set on the task of finding my brother. Sitting on a plane for hours was not helping my stress levels, and the mood was gloomy. Sue and Kevin were also taking the flight home and, despite Sue's efforts to make conversation, I was too weary and too distracted to engage. We passed much of the long journey in silence.

Gliding eastwards above the clouds, horrific scenarios took turns in tormenting my mind. Because I knew so little about Sam's position, all I had was speculation. I knew nothing about his location, nothing about the conditions in which he was being held, no idea how he was being treated, I did not even know if he was still alive! The impossibility of the situation was dragging me into a mire of despair.

We arrived back in London soon after midday on Sunday 18 August. Our flight had included a significantly shortened night due to our direction of travel. Remarkably, I had managed to get a little nap which was unusual for me on a flight but, being so exhausted as a result of worrying about Sam, I had succumbed. Nevertheless, as we disembarked and retrieved our luggage, I could hardly keep my eyes open. Kevin had decided to get a train back up to Manchester while Sue and I were to share a taxi back to our respective homes.

Home was a welcome sight. Falling into an armchair, I pulled out my phone. Although I had had no success in messaging Sam, I reasoned that I would not lose anything by trying to call his number. It rang the usual seven times before the answerphone message kicked in. I waited for the tone and then left a message: 'Hi Sam, it's Rob. If you pick this up, give me a ring. We're all worried and need to hear from you.'

My next course of action was to try to contact Inspector Phillips. He had been the policeman with whom I had had many dealings following the previous expedition to the Congo. Although he had been the officer who had interrogated me over some false allegations, we had become friends and I had met up with him on a number of occasions since then. It felt like a long shot, but I wondered if he might be prepared to look into the situation and see if he could shed any light on proceedings.

To my surprise, not to say, relief, he answered. He was delighted to hear from me and keen to learn what I had been doing over the last year. I explained that I did not really want to go into the subject over the phone, but I asked him if it would be possible to meet up with him briefly. He said it would and we arranged to meet up at 7:30 pm that evening.

With little else I could do now, I began unpacking my bags and chucked some clothes in the washing machine. After around thirty minutes, restlessness prompted me to try Sam's phone again. However, this time, I hung up as soon as the answerphone message began. Even though I knew it was futile, I tried at least another five or six times over the next three hours.

Glancing at the clock, I wondered whether I should make myself a meal. I had not got much food in, and I was not really that hungry anyway. I looked down at my mobile. As I tentatively picked it up, I decided to call just once more before leaving it for the day. Once again, it began to ring. I was so certain that it would not be answered, that when it was, I was taken completely by surprise.

A hesitant female voice on the other end that I did not recognize said, 'Hello?'

'Hi,' I said, in shock. 'Can I ask who I'm speaking to?'

'I'm a member of staff at the Roadchef service station on the M6.'

'Do you know how you came to have this phone?' I asked.

'I'm not sure.' The voice was still hesitant and, in fact, almost nervous. 'I'm in the lost property office,' she went on. 'The ring tone wasn't on, but I heard it vibrating. I'm guessing the phone was left by a motorist and was handed in to us.'

'Would it be possible to speak to your manager?' I asked.

Heart hammering in my chest, I was up on my feet. This was fantastic—a spark of hope struck. With any luck this would be a lead that the police could follow up on. Finally, another voice came on the line.

'Hello, my name is Rob Granger,' I said. 'I've just been told that you have my brother's mobile phone there. Would it be possible for me to come up and collect it at some point?'

There was a lengthy pause. Then the voice said, 'Well, yes, but we'll obviously need some way of identifying that it is your brother's phone.'

After a brief discussion, I made a tentative arrangement to drive up the next day to pick it up.

At 7:30 pm that evening, I pulled into the car park of the Fox and Hounds pub. On entering the pub, I saw Andy Phillips sitting at a corner table with a pint of bitter in front of him. He jumped up and came across to greet me.

'Hi Rob, great to see you.'

I explained that I had been on another trip with Kevin Robinson and that, as with last time, I was having to endure some real issues.

Initially, Andy's reaction was one of amusement, but very quickly he detected that the issues to which I had referred were significant and serious. All light-heartedness left his voice as he asked about the problem.

'The problem isn't me, it's Sam.'

'Not again.'

'I'm afraid so. Let me grab a drink and I'll tell you all about it.'

When I returned to the table a minute later with a pint, Andy asked, 'So what's happened to Sam?'

'He's been kidnapped.'

'You're joking. When did that happen?'

So, I went back to the start of the adventure and explained to him everything that had occurred. When I had finished, Andy frowned. 'That doesn't sound good,' he said. 'So you've had no contact with Sam for over a week and a half?'

'That's right.'

'Did he say anything about the people that he thought were watching his house?'

'Not really,' I said. 'He just referred to them as freaks.' Then I stopped. 'Actually, he did say something about their vehicle. He said they had a white van parked across the road from his house. Let me show you.'

I got my mobile out and began scrolling through my messages. 'Here we go,' I said, passing the phone to Andy. He took it and began reading. He quietly read and then reread some of Sam's messages.

'This information about the white van could be helpful. It may well be the vehicle in which Sam was abducted.'

'I've got some more news,' I said. 'Before I left home to come and meet up with you, I found out where Sam's phone is.'

Andy's eyebrows shot up. 'And where's that?'

'The Roadchef services,' I said. 'They're just north of Stafford.'

Andy nodded. 'Yes, I know where they are. It sounds like they were heading for Manchester or Liverpool.'

Before we parted company that evening, Andy said he would like to borrow my key to Sam's flat. He wanted permission to send a couple of colleagues in to see if they could find anything that might help them to locate Sam.

On the evening of the following day, Andy and I walked into the Roadchef service station and asked for lost property.

We were greeted by a young lad in his early twenties. 'Can I help you?' he asked.

'Yes,' Andy said. 'We've come to pick up a mobile phone that was handed in here, but we'd also like to speak to your manager if that's possible.'

'Sure,' he said. 'I'll just get her.' And he disappeared into the back.

I turned to Andy. 'Do you think we'll be able to find out much?'

He gave a shrug. 'Very difficult to say. Sometimes this kind of discovery yields absolutely nothing, but on other occasions it can be the key breakthrough we're looking for.'

'Hello, gents, can I help you?'

These words came from a smartly dressed woman—the manager—who I guessed was in her early forties.

Andy produced his identification and passed it to her. 'Inspector Andrew Phillips, Thames Valley Police,' he said. 'Officially, I'm off duty at the moment, but would it be possible to go somewhere where we can have a little chat?'

The woman glanced at the identification and handed it back. 'Of course, Officer. Is there a problem?'

'Nothing you need to be concerned about,' he said, 'but we're investigating a potentially serious crime and we believe there's a chance you might have some information which may be able to help us.'

'We'll certainly do our best,' she said, and led us through the back and into a small office.

Andy put his hand on my shoulder as he introduced me. 'This is a member of the public, Robert Granger. We believe you have his brother's mobile phone in your lost property. We want to pick that up, but we also want to know when it was found, where it was found, and any other information you might be able to give us. At some point, it may also be necessary to ask you to hand over to the Staffordshire constabulary any CCTV footage you have of vehicles entering and leaving your service station on the relevant day.'

The woman looked rather concerned. 'This sounds serious,' she said. 'I hope nothing terrible has happened?'

'So do we, Miss?'

'Sorry, Inspector. My name is Maureen Carter. I'm the manager of this service station. And it's Mrs, not Miss.'

'Thank you, Mrs Carter. Well, first of all, do you think we can retrieve Mr Granger's brother's phone?'

'Of course,' she said. 'By the way, how did you find out that it was here?'

I ran through the story of ringing Sam's phone and eventually speaking to a member of her staff. I also explained that that employee had promised to put the phone in an envelope with Sam's name on it.

Mrs Carter left the room and was back in a moment carrying an envelope which she handed to me.

'Is that the one?' she asked.

In spite of my all-consuming concern for Sam's safety, I very nearly burst out laughing. Unless someone else called Sam Granger had just happened to call here on the relevant day, and had also just happened to leave his mobile phone, and had also just happened to have that phone put in an envelope with his name on it, I thought that there was a pretty good chance that it was indeed the one.

I took it from her and thanked her. However, no sooner was it in my possession than I lost it again.

'You had better give that to us for the time being. We'll leave it in the envelope until we've passed it to forensics to check it for prints, and then we'll try to find out if there are any numbers on there that might lead to some interesting individuals.'

That made sense. I was grateful to have Andy with me.

Mrs Carter sat down at her desk. 'OK, Inspector, what would you like to know?'

'I'd like to speak to the member of staff who found the phone. Would that be possible?'

Mrs Carter rose from her seat again and once more headed for the door. 'It might take me a few minutes to discover who found it. I'll be back as soon as I can.'

In less than five minutes, she returned with a young girl, probably in her late teens. 'This is Mandy Deacon,' she said to me. 'It was her who was given your brother's mobile.'

Then she turned to Miss Deacon and said, 'This man is a police inspector, Mandy.' She gestured in Andy's direction. 'These gentlemen are here to find out about the mobile phone you were given the other week.'

The girl nodded.

'Have a seat, Miss Deacon,' Andy said. 'We're very keen to find out when you were handed this mobile phone. Can you remember exactly when that was?'

She thought for a moment. 'Yes, it was a week ago last Wednesday. I was on my way to get a mop and bucket to clean up a spillage in the restaurant. I was stopped by a member of the public and handed the phone. They said they'd found it in the carpark. I just took it to lost property.'

I recognized that was the first day I'd failed to get a response from Sam to one of my messages.

'Can you remember what time that was?' Andy asked.

Mandy thought for a moment but then shook her head. 'Not really. I'd say early afternoon, but I'm not certain about that.'

Andy gave Mandy a warm smile. 'Well, thank you very much, Miss Deacon. That information might turn out to be very helpful indeed.' He paused briefly and then he continued: 'I suppose you can't remember any of the customers who you saw that afternoon? You didn't notice anyone acting at all suspiciously?'

Once more, Mandy attempted to remember, but again, shook her head. 'No, I'm afraid not.'

Andy smiled again. 'Never mind, you've been very helpful. Thanks very much, Miss Deacon.'

The following morning, Andy called to let me know that the police had been round to Sam's flat and found nothing to help the investigation. This was disappointing, but Andy did say that it had been a bit of a long shot. However, he was much more positive about managing to retrieve Sam's mobile. He told me that there are many thousands of CCTV cameras dotted around our country these days. A good number of those are on our motorway system. In addition, most of the service stations on those motorways are also well equipped with cameras. To my relief, the Roadchef services was one of these. Andy seemed fairly confident that these cameras would have picked up the vehicle in which Sam had probably been transported.

On ending the call, I sent Dad a fairly upbeat message explaining that the police were now involved and that we had already managed to locate Sam's mobile.

At 4:30 pm that afternoon, I received another update from Andy. He had been in touch with DCI James Beckford of Staffordshire police. Andy told me that the Staffordshire force had promised to keep him up to speed with any progress they made on Sam's case. He explained that the Staffordshire force currently had an officer searching through all the CCTV footage from the service station, particularly looking for white vans. He said that they would let me know as soon as they had anything significant to pass on. Unfortunately, the police were going to have to study all the vehicles entering and leaving the site during the whole day of August 7. I thanked Andy for his update and ended the call.

Nothing yet was definite, but that an investigation was in progress and under way, comforted me. Andy was going to keep me in the loop, so all I could do now was wait.

True to his word, Andy rang the following morning. Staffordshire police had found five sets of fingerprints on Sam's phone. The presence of three of these had already been explained. One set was that of Sam himself, one was from Mandy Deacon, and one from the member of staff to which Mandy had handed in the phone. One of the remaining two prints presumably, belonged to the member of the public who had found the phone. The other unmatched set almost certainly belonged to one of the gang responsible for kidnapping Sam.

However, this was only one small part of the investigation. Both the Thames Valley and Staffordshire forces were working from the very reasonable assumption that the discarding of Sam's mobile at the Roadchef services indicated the direction in which he was being taken. In turn, this strongly suggested that Sam was being held captive somewhere in the northwest of England. The police were currently engaged in attempting to identify the most likely areas to search.

As I ended the call, I had an inspiration. Getting out my mobile, I started to scroll through Sam's messages as I had done so many times. I had just remembered a comment he had made. At the time, I'd not given it much thought, but thinking about it now, I wondered if it might be significant. I began reading through them carefully, until I stopped at one particular message. I grabbed my car keys, flew out of the house, jumped into my car and headed for Sam's place.

On my arrival, I let myself into his flat and started having a look round.

Sam hated anyone to keep anything from him, as had been amply demonstrated by the events which had taken place before our Congo adventure. However, in his own life, he had a tendency to be quite secretive. He had rarely told people any more than they absolutely needed to know about him. He did not trust anyone with any information, especially if that information was about him. When we were kids, he had even gone to the extreme of communicating with me in various codes so no one would overhear what we were saying. There were times when I felt this behaviour bordered on paranoia.

This had gone through my mind at the start of my American trip when Sam and I had been swapping messages. It was unlike Sam to mention something like the people outside his house if he genuinely thought there was nothing to worry about. But, as usual, he had not given me more than the minimum possible amount of information about those involved. However, what he had said was that he was 'keeping a record of everything'. If Sam really had been freaked by these people, it was very likely that he would have hidden any comments he had jotted down about them. Knowing him as I did, he wouldn't want them breaking into his flat and coming across those remarks.

I began to look through some of Sam's drawers in the hope of finding the record that he told me he had made. It felt odd to be snooping around his flat, but I knew he would not mind under the circumstances. I found nothing. Deflated, I decided to make myself a coffee. Taking the hot mug in his lounge, I sat in an armchair and bleakly looked around the room. I had been stupid!

So far, I had looked in exactly those places that anyone would have looked in, had they been trying to find something significant. But the whole point of this exercise was that Sam would not have put his notes in an obvious place.

I took a fresh look around Sam's lounge. My eyes were drawn to an ornamental house sitting on the windowsill. I smiled to myself. That's more like it, I thought. I stood and crossed to the window, picking up the house. It was about seven inches across, four inches from front to back, and about four inches high. I picked it up and returned to the armchair.

One of the quirky aspects of Sam's nature is that he loves working out puzzles. Over the years, he had had hundreds of different kinds of puzzles to solve. One of the things that fascinated him was items which looked ornamental, but which had hidden compartments that you had to work out how to access. This was exactly the kind of place I would expect Sam to hide something he did not want people to find.

I held the house with my right hand holding the base, and my left holding the roof. I tried to slide the top of the house to the right and then to the left but, in both cases, there was absolutely no movement. I gently exerted a little pressure in a circular direction; there was no movement at all. I tried in the opposite direction; again, there was no movement. I began to wonder if I was wrong. Perhaps this was just an ornament after all.

I had a closer look at the house. I could see no join, no slight crack indicating the existence of a secret compartment. All the same, something convinced me I was right. I examined the ornamental house in minute detail, feeling all the way around the house, putting a tiny bit of pressure on each small section in turn. Nothing.

I turned my attention to the two chimneys. There was one at either end of the roof. I put small amounts of pressure on each of these in turn. Nothing! Then I tried again, but exerting pressure to both chimneys at the same time. The result was the same.

I put it down on the coffee table, frustrated, picking up my coffee and taking a sip. If this really was one of Sam's devious trick items complete with secret chamber, it was one of the best I had seen. I picked up the house again, turning it over and over. There were some ridges over the roof, and I wondered if one of them had a very fine gap adjacent to it. I looked at the windows at the front and back of the house which were immediately below this ridge, but they looked exactly like the others. Nevertheless, I persevered trying to get them to move in some way, with a total lack of success. All the same, it gave me the idea of pressing in each pair of windows at the front and back of the house. I had almost reached the other end of the house when I heard a very soft click. I smiled with satisfaction. Bingo! I looked at the house. The windows below the ones I had pressed in were protruding slightly, and the chimney above those windows had disappeared into the roof.

Feeling extremely pleased with myself, I slid the main section of roof over and immediately saw the little diary that appeared to have been specifically designed to fit into the cavity. I carefully lifted the little book from its hiding place and put the house to one side.

Opening the first page, I noticed that it was a real diary. Sam appeared to have been using this throughout the year. Not wanting to pry into his private thoughts, I flipped to the back of the book. Working my way backwards through the blank sheets, eventually, I got to his last few entries. Just a few more pages and I found the point where Sam had recorded the fact that I had flown out to the States. I read forward a day at a time. Then I saw it. Sam had written: 'Who are the cretins staring at my flat?' There were a few other entries of no real consequence, then another that was relevant: 'The freaks are back. What can they possibly be doing?' Finally, I arrived at the page which promised to be extremely valuable. It said, 'The freaks are sitting in a white Transit van. I think I'll note the registration.' Below these words was the registration 'DV05 MHL'.

I closed my eyes, rested my head on the back of the armchair. It was amazing. I could not believe I had actually managed to obtain the make and registration of the van which very possibly had been used to abduct Sam. I made a note of the details and got my mobile out to call Andy.

He answered after four long rings. 'Hello Rob. Any news?'

'Yes,' I said, ecstatically. 'I think I've found out the make and registration of the van.'

'You're joking,' he said. 'How did you manage that?'

'It's a long story. I'll fill you in some time. The point is, do you want the details or do you want me to contact Staffordshire Police?'

Andy became business-like, professionalism taking over. 'Give them to me,' he said. 'I'll pass them on to Staffordshire. I'll have to call you back to find out how you obtained the information.'

'No problem,' I said, and gave him the details.

While I was waiting for Andy to call back, I thought I'd better put the diary back in its hiding place. Having placed the book back in the little secret chamber, I slid the roof back into position. As I pressed the two lower floor windows back into place, the chimney shot back up out of the roof and everything looked as it should.

I finished my coffee, washed up the mug and put it back in the cupboard. I had just closed Sam's front door and was heading for my car when my mobile rang. I answered the call as I got back into my car. 'Hi Andy,' I said. 'Have you spoken to Staffordshire?'

'Yes,' he said. 'They're pretty impressed. By the way, before we go into that, I should tell you that they've finished going through the CCTV footage of the vehicles entering their services on the relevant day. They've identified fifty-three white vans that they want to follow up on, but they are focusing on those that entered the services before 2:00 pm. That's because we think the phone was handed in to Miss Deacon in the early afternoon. However, I suspect your information might significantly reduce the time they need to spend searching for those vans.'

'I hope so,' I said. 'But it's possible that Sam wasn't transferred in that vehicle.'

Andy agreed. 'That's true, of course, but I think there's a very good chance that he was. Anyway, I told them I'd let them know how you got hold of the information. So, fire away.'

I sat in the car, relaying what had happened, then drove home feeling more positive than I had in days.

The investigation was making progress, which was gratefully confirmed by another call from Andy shortly afterwards. He let me know that he would stay in regular touch with his colleagues in Staffordshire and continue to keep me informed of any progress. He asked if I was happy with that; of course I was!

'Rob, I'll pass on everything to you that I get through from Stafford, but you mustn't share this information with anyone.'

'That's fine, Andy,' I agreed. 'Apart from anything else, I'm guessing it might put Sam in more danger.'

'Yes,' he said seriously, 'you're probably right about that.'

'Andy? What about my friend, Sue? She's bound to ask me how the search for Sam is going. Can I tell her anything?'

'Is she your partner?'

I hesitated as I attempted to identify what really was the status of our relationship. 'Not officially, but let's just say that we're pretty close.'

'Well, use your head, Rob. Don't give her any operational details at all. However, if you want to give her general updates about how the search is going, that's fine. But Rob, don't let me down on this. You must not give her any information which is at all sensitive.'

I assured him that I would not.

At 2:15 pm, Sue turned up at my front door. As I let her in, predictably her first words were, 'Any news?'

I told her about the events of the morning and gave her limited information from the updates I had received from Andy. She was delighted.

'Rob, that's fantastic. You must be feeling very good about that.'

I smiled wearily. 'I was pretty chuffed at the time,' I admitted, 'but Sam's situation has prevented me from feeling too pleased with myself.'

I did tell her that there may be certain details I was given by Andy that I would be unable to pass on to her. I had been uncertain how she would receive this news, but she understood why that might be necessary.

We continued to discuss the situation as I made us a coffee. Scrambling at the bottom of the jar for the last few granules, I made a mental note to make a trip to the corner shop; I was going to need plenty of coffee to get me through the days.

As we settled ourselves in the lounge, Sue switched the conversation. 'Did you ever get around to looking at those Bible verses I suggested you read?'

I had not; it had been the last thing on my mind. Saved by the bell from having to make that admission, the song, 'Message in a Bottle', began chiming from my phone.

'That's Andy,' I said, looking around for my phone and grabbing hold of it.

Andy had some interesting news. The first was that the white Transit which had been outside Sam's flat had been stolen from a house in Birmingham two weeks previously. That was not great news, but his other news was more positive. This same van was one of the vans that had been spotted pulling into the service station on 7 August. Another potential piece of evidence was that a grainy CCTV image had been obtained of a man who might possibly have been one of the occupants of the white van. This was far from definite, but the man had entered the building soon after the van had arrived and parked up.

They had calculated that the vehicle had been in the services for a total of thirty-eight minutes, but then it had been seen leaving the site and continuing to head north on the M6. After this, the police had temporarily lost track of the van. It seemed to completely disappear at Junction 15—the junction for Stoke South. It had not continued north; neither did it appear to have used the various exits. They eventually realized that the van had done a 180 degree turn and was heading back down south on the M6.

This had concerned the police, as they suspected that there might possibly have been some kind of transfer to another vehicle at the services. However, the van was then seen to exit the motorway at junction 14, which was the Stafford North junction.

This was truly welcome news. It really did feel as if we were getting closer to locating Sam.

When I ended the call, Sue said, 'How did you know it was Andy?'

'"Message in a Bottle"', I said with a grin.

She looked perplexed.

'By the band, "The Police"?'

The penny dropped and she groaned and rolled her eyes. 'I might have known,' she said.

Within half an hour, my catchy ring tone sang out again. Andy informed me that Stafford had been in touch. They had reported that, within an hour of the target van leaving the motorway at junction 14, it had been spotted re-joining the motorway again at the same junction and heading back down south. As a result of this news, the police were fairly confident that Sam was being held somewhere within a relatively short radius of that junction. This was great news and I began to allow myself to hope that Sam would be found very soon.

Chapter 16
Breakthrough

After the positive steps made the day before, I had woken up early, feeling hopeful, and considered this might be the day that would provide the information needed to lead the police to Sam's location.

It was fortunate I had been up early because at 9:15 am, Sue knocked at my front door.

'Any more news?' she asked, as I let her in.

She seemed as concerned for Sam's safety as I was myself.

'I've not heard anything yet,' I said. 'I'm sure Andy will be in touch as soon as he has any news.'

It was just after 10:00 am when Andy called. It turned out that images of the white Transit van had been caught on various cameras in Stone, a small town between Stafford and Stoke-on-Trent. This was good news but, unfortunately, the point where the vehicle had stopped and the occupants disembarked had not been captured. This was disappointing, but there were a number of clues from the images which did exist.

The target vehicle had been identified leaving Stone on the

A520 leading to Meir Heath but had not been spotted by a camera a mile and a half further down that road. The implication was that the van had either turned off or had visited a property somewhere along that stretch of road. Hence, the police had been led to focus on a relatively small area just outside Stone. The main part of the investigation would obviously now be centred on the outskirts of this town.

However, the police were also keen to track the white Transit to its ultimate destination. This work had largely been completed. After re-joining the M6, it had continued to travel south all the way to the Oxford area, via the M42 and M40. This had brought the van back into the jurisdiction of the Thames Valley Force. Andy ended the call having promised to let me know as soon as he heard any more. I relayed the update to Sue.

'That sounds pretty positive,' she said.

It did. I tried to not let the new surge of hope overtake me. They still had to find him, and there was no guarantee he was still wherever he was a week ago.

Waiting is always tough, and it was 1:15 pm when the phone rang again. Full of anticipation, I hurried to answer, but this time, the news was not so encouraging.

'The guys at Stafford are puzzled,' Andy revealed. 'They've visited all the properties along the Stone to Meir Heath road under the pretext of looking for a runaway horse. They've asked to see all the occupants of each house to ask them if they've seen anything. As the horse query is entirely bogus, it's not surprising that no one has seen anything, but the problem is that they found nothing at all suspicious at any of the addresses.'

The officers doing the door-to-door investigations all had a photo of Sam as well as a copy of the grainy image from the Roadchef Services. No one resembling either person had been found.

Deflated, I sat on the arm of the chair. 'And what about turnings off that main road?' I asked. 'Maybe Sam's being held somewhere off the main route.'

'I think they'll have thought of that, Rob. Don't worry; they will be thorough.'

'Sorry, Andy,' I said. 'Of course they will be.'

It was two hours before I heard anything else. When I did, it was an update I could have done without.

'I'm afraid the latest report is rather frustrating. The officers up there are convinced that there's nothing to find in that area. They're beginning to suspect that some kind of transfer took place.'

'Great,' I said in exasperation. 'So, what happens now?'

'They're having a look at some more CCTV footage. There are a couple of fairly quiet lay-bys along that road, and one or two tracks where someone could be transferred from one vehicle to another without anyone noticing.'

I said nothing.

Sensing my frustration, Andy said, 'Rob, I know this is a blow, but it's not the end of the world. The boys up there are a good bunch. They're currently studying the other traffic that used that road at the same time. That involves a lot of vehicles. However, they're looking for specific patterns of behaviour, and there's a fairly short window of time within which any such transfer could have taken place. They've already identified all the vehicles which could have possibly been involved and, at least to some degree, some vehicles are much more likely to have been used than others.'

'What do you mean?' I asked.

'Well, for example, they think it's much more likely that another van was involved. We don't think that the kidnappers would want to use a car and risk Sam being able to signal to someone through a window.'

I sighed heavily. I knew I was being impatient, but all this waiting around when Sam was imprisoned somewhere with no idea of what was happening was taking its toll on me.

'I know it's tough, Rob,' he said, 'but you're going to have to let them get on with it.'

I had woken up full of hope but, as the day wore on, that hope was ebbing away, and I was getting tetchy. It felt like hours, but within another hour and a half, I received another update.

'They think they've identified the other vehicle,' Andy said matter-of-factly, without any customary 'Hello's.

The relief these words sent through me was almost inexpressible. I had been wound up like a spring, and could hardly take Andy's words in.

'Thank you, God.' The words were out of my mouth before I realized what I was saying.

I looked at Sue who smiled and gave a tiny nod.

'What happened?' I asked.

'They were right,' he said. 'They spotted a van coming from the direction of Meir Heath. As with the white Transit, this vehicle arrived heading in one direction and it left going in the other. Now, we can't be absolutely sure that this van met up with the white Transit, but if it didn't, it's a massive coincidence.'

I agreed. 'So, have they got any idea where this other van has gone?'

'Not yet,' Andy said. 'They'll have to repeat the process they carried out with the Transit. Unfortunately, it's not as straightforward as when you've got a vehicle on the motorway. We're not always sure where there are cameras. Also, there are intersections with other roads. Whenever the target vehicle arrives at a junction, there will be multiple directions it can take. However, they do have a partial registration for the van. Any of the police cars fitted with our automated numberplate recognition system will be on the lookout for this van.'

'It could take days to find them,' I said in exasperation. 'They might still have had 50 miles to go before they reached their destination.'

'I don't think so,' Andy responded. 'If they had much further to go, I think they'd have come off the motorway at a different exit. There are a limited number of places to which they're likely to be heading.'

I guessed this was logical. 'Do you think the police will have locations they believe are more likely than others as an ultimate destination?' I asked.

'Probably,' he said. 'It's difficult to say. There's a lot of countryside up there and plenty of properties that are a bit off the beaten track. I know it's not what you want to hear, but there are many secluded places where they might have taken Sam.'

After another couple of comments, we ended the call.

I spent a few minutes filling Sue in with some of these details. She was very attentive and seemed encouraged that they had managed to identify the other van.

Suddenly, her expression changed. 'By the way, where did that come from?' she asked.

Her question threw me for a few seconds, but then, having spotted the twinkle in her eye, I realized what she meant. I felt slightly embarrassed.

'You mean the "God" bit?'

She nodded and smiled.

'Don't know,' I said. 'I suppose it's because I've heard you say it a few times. I guess it seemed appropriate at the time.'

'At the time?' she repeated. 'And what about now?'

Once again, I felt a tinge of mild embarrassment. 'Sue, I don't know. I don't know what to think. All the stuff I've learned from Kevin and Steve and Jenny is amazing and it's all very convincing, but the idea of believing in a God is so alien to me. Seriously, Sue, I'd love to believe in Him. Apart from anything else, I can see what an affect it's had on you. But I can't say I believe in God just to please you.'

Sue smiled sadly. 'Rob, I wouldn't want you to. That would be terrible. You must be honest about it. Honest with me, honest with yourself, and also honest with God.'

An awkward silence set in. I could sense how much Sue wanted me to share her faith but, in spite of all the evidence that had been presented to me, an all-knowing, all-loving, eternal God just was not believable to me. I tried, as gently as I could, to explain all this to Sue. Her head dropped and I feared she was going to get upset. However, when she looked up, although there was sadness etched on her face, there was no sign of tears.

'Rob, as you know, I'm very new to this. I'm only just beginning to understand what my new-found faith means for me. But one thing I think I have grasped is that this isn't really about science. As you know, science, and especially geology, is very important to me. But I'm not a Christian because the science convinced me that the Bible is true, I'm a Christian because I came to realize my own need for a Saviour. It's not the science you need to be convinced about; it's the significance of the cross of Christ that needs to become real to you. Jesus died on that cross for the forgiveness of our sins so we can have a loving relationship with our Heavenly Father."

The words hung in the air. I surmised that she was giving me time to consider her last comments. I did consider them, as I had assumed the science had been the catalyst to her conversion, and that Steve's and Kevin's presentation of physical evidence had produced her faith. What she was saying was that it was a more personal, spiritual encounter she had had, rather than scientific and logical, as I had presumed.

'If what you say is true, why are they spending so much time trying to convince us all that the physical evidence supports what the Bible says?'

'Because we're constantly told that the evidence contradicts the Bible. And this is used to convince people that the Bible is not trustworthy. And if the Bible is not trustworthy, then neither is the message of Jesus. Kevin and the others want us to recognize that the whole Bible is completely true in everything it says. But to do that, they have to refute the claims of the secular scientific world. The evidence they've shown us at Mount Saint Helens is compelling evidence which, potentially, completely overturns the claims of the atheist camp. That's why it's so important.'

Sue got to her feet. 'Is it OK if I go and make us some coffee?'

'Oh, for goodness's sake!' I said in frustration. 'I'm sorry Sue, I'm all out of coffee. I meant to go and get some first thing, but with all this stress over Sam I completely forgot.'

'Don't worry,' she said. 'I'll nip down to the shop and get some. Is there anything else you need?'

I got to my feet. 'No, I don't think so. Anyway, I'll come with you.'

'Don't worry about it,' she said. 'You wait here in case the police call.'

Sue went to the shop and left me considering our little chat. While she was gone, I did review our conversation, but not only the one we had just had, but also those we had had over the last few weeks. I recalled our chat when she told me about her grandmother and their trips to the chapel. Then I remembered the way Sue had looked and behaved when she had suddenly realized that the Bible was true—or, at least, when she had believed that that was the case.

In turn, these memories reminded me of some of the conversations I had had with Kevin on the previous expedition.

Both Kevin and Sue appeared to think that what you did or did not believe about the Bible was hugely significant. At the end of the previous trip, I had made a promise to myself to look into the subject. While I had kept that promise to some degree, I had not gone into it in the depth I had intended. Having had this conversation with Sue, I felt that this might be a good opportunity to start seriously investigating.

These thoughts were running through my mind when I suddenly remembered another incident. I recalled waking up in the middle of the night in the hotel. This prompted another memory. Jumping to my feet, I opened a drawer in the wall unit. I was certain that was where I had put the notebook.

On lifting a sheet of paper containing travel details, I spotted it immediately: the notebook I had used to record the details we had obtained from Steve and Jenny. I grabbed it and went to sit on the settee. Flicking through the pages, I eventually found what I wanted. In my own handwriting were the following words:

> Woke at 1:56 am. Bizarre. Just dreaming about logs in the lake. Had an amazing sense that what I'm learning here at MSH is going to change my life. I'm certain I'll be getting involved with this work in some way. No idea why, and no idea where this feeling has come from. Wait and see what happens.

I sat staring at the pages, not entirely sure why this incident had come to mind at that moment. All the upset over Sam had put this episode right out of my mind. However, as I read through the notes that I had scribbled down in my hotel room, I relived that instant of bewilderment. True, I had only just woken from sleep when I had jotted down these comments, but I had been wide awake, and I could still recall the confusion I had felt at the time.

I flipped to the back of the notebook where I had laid out a brief summary of its contents. Scanning through the sub-headings, I started to recall some of the more memorable facts we had received. There were headings such as rock layers, fossilized trees, canyons, the lava dome, coal and others. As I read each heading, some of the details I had learned flashed through my mind. I surprised myself at how many of the facts I could remember. One after the other, the various arguments we had been given supporting a young earth and a global Flood raced through my brain. Again, I marvelled at how completely one-sided the information was that was presented to the public.

Sitting on my settee, letting the notebook flop onto my lap, the events at Mount Saint Helens continued to flash through my mind. An image of finely layered strata. Then, I was in a boat, looking at logs floating in a lake. Next, I was standing on the bottom of the lake attempting to move a tree which had been deposited in an upright position. The subsequent image was from a chopper flying along a canyon which had been carved through sedimentary layers in a single day. I had recalled and considered these things before, but the revelation of what they implied had never had the effect they were having on me now. They were just facts beforehand—fascinating facts, I will admit, but nothing more. Yet, Sue also mentioned that it had not been the information which had caused her heart to change, but rather the personal revelation of the need for a Saviour. All this sounded intimate and meaningful rather than being distant and aloof.

The next moment, I was experiencing feelings that were almost impossible to describe. They were a combination of fear, awe and excitement, with other jumbled emotions in there as well. At the same time, I knew something that could not possibly be true, *was* true. There could not possibly have been a Flood that covered the whole earth, including all the high hills and mountains, but the evidence appeared to be heavily in favour of that scenario. I was struggling to make sense of it. Something, or someone, appeared to be messing with my brain.

I turned back to my notebook. Again, I read through the rough notes I had jotted down when I had woken in the middle of the night. I could still remember the dream: the logs in the lake and the sense that what I was learning would change my life for ever.

Another recollection forced its way into my mind. Kevin had spoken about Noah's Ark. He had said something about the Ark being like Jesus Christ. It had something to do with the fact that the only way to escape the Flood had been to enter the Ark through the door. That was the only possible way that anyone could be saved from the judgement of the Flood.

Then, Kevin had said that the only way to escape the final judgement would be to accept Jesus as Lord and Saviour. He had mentioned that Jesus had likened Himself to a door, and that those who entered through that door would be saved. I thought of Sue's comments about the cross of Christ and recognizing my own need for forgiveness—understanding that I could be forgiven for all the wrong things I had ever done if I would only humble myself and acknowledge that I was a sinner in need of a Saviour.

It was at that precise moment that a folded piece of paper slipped from between the pages of my notebook. As I unfolded it, I recognized Sue's small, neat handwriting. It was a list of Bible references along with their corresponding quotes. The first was Romans 3:23. It said:

All have sinned and fall short of the glory of God.

I remembered Sue telling me that we had all done things that were wrong. We had all fallen short of God's perfect standards.

The second reference was Romans 6:23. This one said:

For the wages of sin is death, but the gift of God is eternal life in Christ Jesus our Lord.

I remembered Sue saying something about our sins deserving death.

The third verse was Romans 5:8 which read:

But God demonstrates His own love toward us, in that while we were still sinners, Christ died for us.

Each of these verses reminded me of comments Sue had made to me over the past week. She had explained that 2,000 years ago, God had sent His Son, Jesus, into the world to die on a cross to pay the penalty for anything I would ever do wrong in my life. God had made the provision thousands of years before I was even a twinkle in my dad's eye. I smiled as I recalled when she had said that to me.

The fourth and final reference was Romans 10:9. It said:

If you confess with your mouth the Lord Jesus and believe in your heart that God has raised Him from the dead, you will be saved.

This was the one verse that Sue had quoted which had already made a bit of an impression on me. She had said that, if I would accept Jesus as my Lord and Saviour and truly believe in my heart that God had raised Him from the dead, I would be saved. Although I had not come to a firm conclusion that God even existed, there was something about this verse which attracted me—something that had caused me to question my hitherto sceptical outlook.

I sat considering these verses, as a series of episodes and situations from my past began filing their way through my mind. Although I had not been guilty of some of the misdemeanours that some of my friends had, I was suddenly conscious of a state of personal defilement which I had never recognised before. That was when it happened. It was almost as if there was a benevolent presence in the room. With this presence came an overwhelming sense of love and peacefulness. The next thing I knew, I was on the floor on my knees, curled up in a ball with my forehead on the carpet. I was blubbing like a baby and repeating, 'Father, forgive me, forgive me.'

I have no idea how long this went on. All I know is that, after a while, I became aware of a gentle arm across my back, and Sue's voice saying, 'Rob, are you OK?'

The calmness in Sue's voice had the effect of penetrating the raw emotion which was shaking my body. As my consciousness began to return to my physical surroundings, I tried to sort out in my head what exactly had just happened to me. There was no doubt in my mind that it had been spiritual. I started to pick myself up off the floor. Normally, I would have felt like a complete fool if someone had come in and found me blubbering away on the floor. However, for some reason, there was no embarrassment, no self-consciousness—no negative feelings at all.

Sue grabbed me by the hand and led me back to the settee, where we both sat and, for a while, neither of us spoke. I did not feel the need to speak. There was a comfortable silence, and I was happy to sit in the bubble of peace I felt I was inhabiting. I was having difficulty understanding what exactly had just occurred. There was a sense of forgiveness and a realization that all my past misdemeanours had been completely blotted out.

Although I was not looking directly at Sue, I was aware of the expression on her face. The look in her eyes suggested that there were a number of thoughts in there just waiting to be loosed. I got the feeling that she was bursting to ask me what I had just experienced but also wanted to give me the opportunity to open up when I felt able. Knowing how keen she must be to ask her questions, she showed a tremendous amount of self-control. Eventually, I took pity on her.

'Well, that was different,' I said.

She gave a little laugh. 'So, are you going to tell me what happened?'

'If I'm honest, Sue, I'm not quite sure. But I think I've just become a Christian.'

'You think?'

For the first time, I noticed the new jar of coffee sitting on the table in front of me.

'Well, all those things you told me that I should do, I believe I have done.'

I explained to her what had happened after she had left to go to the shop. Sue had never heard about my dream at the hotel and the comments I had jotted in my notebook. She looked as if she were about to ask me about it, but decided to let me continue with my account. It was almost impossible to describe to her how I had felt as I had the revelation that the Flood had actually happened, as laid out in the Bible and the combined feelings of fear, awe and excitement that had come over me after receiving that realization.

Sue looked thoughtful. 'From the discussions I've had with Kevin and Jenny, I'm not sure that the fear part of your experience will have come from God.'

'Well, actually, I'm not sure the way I've described it to you is accurate,' I said. 'It was one feeling, but at the same time, a combination of feelings. I don't really have the words to describe it. I suppose if I had to use a single word it would be 'awe'. I suddenly had this overwhelming conviction that the Flood was true. The problem is that I still couldn't see how that was possible. In my mind it appeared totally paradoxical.'

'So, what happened next?'

I told her about the sense I had had of someone playing with my mind and noticed a knowing smile appear fleetingly on her lips.

'I think you're probably right,' she said.

As I continued, when I told her about the conversation with Kevin in which he had likened Jesus to the Ark, Sue stopped me. 'I hadn't heard that,' she said. 'That's really interesting.'

I paused as I thought back to the conversation. 'Well, it kind of made sense to me. If the Ark was the only hope of salvation in Noah's day, I could understand that Jesus is the only way of salvation today.'

Sue nodded thoughtfully.

'Anyway,' I went on, 'it was then that I found the Bible verses you had written down for me. The next thing I knew, there was all this stuff from my past being laid out in front of me.'

I looked at Sue. 'You know you said that I had to acknowledge that I was a sinner who needed a Saviour? Well, at that moment, I did.'

I noticed a couple of tears begin traveling down Sue's face, one either side of her nose.

'I felt this loving presence right here in the room with me. That's when I lost it.'

I had to stop for a moment as the recollection of the moment threatened to overwhelm me again. My expectation was that, after a moment to compose myself, I would be fine. However, the sense of love and forgiveness was too much for me and, after another attempt to get a grip, I just had to let it out. They were not tears of sadness, but tears of joy. The next moment, Sue and I had our arms around each other and we were crying and laughing at the same time. We stayed like that a while until Sue gave me a kiss on the cheek and said happily, 'Welcome to the land of the saved.'

This joyous moment was interrupted by my mobile. It was Andy.

'Rob, they're getting closer. The van has been spotted

in a market town called Leek, up in the northeast corner of Staffordshire. It took a turning heading towards Ashbourne in Derbyshire.'

I groaned. 'Will that mean another police force has to get involved?'

'Don't think so. As I said before, I don't think they have far to go now.'

I very much hoped he was right.

Half an hour later he was on the phone again.

'OK, Rob. There are cameras at certain points along the A523 which is the Leek to Ashbourne road, and those cameras have not seen our target vehicle. The guys at Stafford believe the van turned off somewhere before a village called Waterhouses. Now, that doesn't mean that they're on the point of identifying where Sam is being held, but they do think they're pretty close geographically to that point. There are a number of small villages in that area and the police are busy trying to discretely identify businesses which have CCTV cameras.'

I had been trying not to raise my hopes too much, fearful that I might be unable to endure another crushing disappointment. However, this news did sound like it was potentially a real breakthrough. In spite of myself, I began to hope again.

Chapter 17
Surveillance

Sue and I drove up to Leek the following morning and booked a holiday suite above the Blue Mugge—a family-run pub on the outskirts of the town. It was ideal. Not only did it have three separate bedrooms, but it meant that there would be room for Sam if we were successful in freeing him from his captivity.

The drive to Leek had been a bit of a spur-of-the-moment decision. After a long discussion about what we should do, we had come to the conclusion that it would be better for my own peace of mind if we travelled to the area where Sam was almost certainly being held captive.

Sue and I walked into Leek's local police station on Fountain Street where we were due to meet up with DCI James Beckford. Although the use of Leek's police station had been scaled back in recent years, the police had set up an incident room at the Leek facility which was to remain operational until the current situation with Sam had been successfully resolved. We had only been there about five minutes when DCI Beckford came out to see us.

'Mr Granger, nice to meet you,' he said.

We shook hands and I introduced him to Sue.

'What's the latest position regarding my brother's situation?' I asked.

'Well, we're confident that we're very close to locating the property where your brother is being held. Just this morning, we've received CCTV footage from a pub in a village called Butterton. The images weren't particularly clear, but we're sure it's the right vehicle.'

I decided to mention something which had started to concern me. 'If the people who are holding my brother are anything like the man that I think they were working for, then they'll be ruthless men. Please don't do anything that might result in them harming him.'

DCI Beckford smiled. 'Mr Granger, Inspector Phillips has informed us about the man you've come up against on a couple of occasions, and you're right, he is ruthless. However, if we're going to get your brother out, it won't be possible to do it totally risk free. I'm afraid it's about minimising the risk, not eliminating it. We'll do everything in our power to ensure no harm comes to him, but to be honest, if we weren't prepared to take any risk, we'd have to leave him in there.'

I did not particularly like his bluntness, but I saw his point.

'OK,' I said. 'So, what happens next?'

'We've currently got a number of our personnel in Butterton on an information gathering exercise.'

'What happens when you identify the property where Sam's being held?'

'That will depend on the circumstances. If it's possible to observe the target property from another building, we may well do that. The problem is that there are a number of fairly isolated properties in these parts. It wouldn't surprise me at all if these people are holed up in one of those.'

'If that's the case, what happens then?'

'Again, it very much depends on the circumstances. There are any number of possibilities. I'm afraid we'll just have to wait until we have more definite information.'

We were just about to leave when the policeman called out, 'Oh, by the way, I know Andy Phillips has been updating you with our progress. I told him that I was happy to keep you informed. Is that OK with you?'

'Of course,' I said. 'That's really kind of you.'

Sue and I decided to return to the Blue Mugge for lunch while we were waiting for another update. We were halfway through a game of pool and I was just about to attempt to double a red into a centre pocket when 'Message in a Bottle' started to ring out from the back of my jeans. Getting up off the shot, I rested my cue against the wall and slipped my mobile from my pocket.

'Hello.'

'It's good news, Mr Granger. We think we've identified the property where your brother is being held.'

I blew out my cheeks. 'Thank goodness for that,' I said with relief. 'Where is it?'

'It's about half a mile outside the village of Butterton.'

I shot a glance at Sue who was looking expectantly at me. 'That's fantastic news. How difficult will it be to get him out?'

'Unfortunately, we currently have no clear plan as to how we're going to release him. As you already know, the man you knew as John Smith had a history of extreme violence. This also goes for those with whom he worked. We have no reason to believe that these people will be any different. We'd normally break our way in and attempt to take them by surprise, but our problem in this case is that the target property is so far from other houses. If we were to just drive up to the property, even if we use an unmarked van, they'd probably be highly suspicious. So, we need to devise some kind of plan to get close to the property without raising their concerns. That might be easier said than done. One thing we do have in our favour is that, as far as we know, they'll have no idea we've located their base. I'd like to keep it like that. Anyway, our first task is to try to get some intelligence on your brother's situation.'

'Great, so how will you do that?' I asked.

'We'll have to try to identify which room he's being held in. If he's in a room on his own, things might be a little easier. However, at present, we don't have that information.'

I was curious. 'How do you know it's the right place?' I asked.

'We don't actually know,' he said, 'but we're 99% sure. The van we believe they used to transfer your brother is parked outside.'

'That's great news. So, what happens now?'

'We're trying to identify the people who own the property and, depending on what we find, take it from there.'

Probably sensing my nervousness, he continued, 'As I said before, we'll do all we can to minimise the risks. We have an experienced team of people up there and they'll be watching the place like hawks.'

An hour and a half passed but, when the next call came, the news from the DCI was mixed.

'It's going to be a bit tricky,' he explained. 'As I mentioned, the house is very isolated. As a result, it's not the easiest place in the world to keep under surveillance. However, we have a good team there and they'll do everything they can to observe the comings and goings and, if possible, get photographs of all the occupants.'

Although still very concerned for Sam's safety, I felt as positive as I had since I first found out about his kidnapping. That being said, I was incredibly impatient to get another update. Thankfully, I did not have too long to wait. It was 2:50 pm when I got another call.

'Mr Granger, we're now as certain as we can be that your brother is being held at the property I mentioned earlier.'

'Fantastic,' I said with feeling. 'How did you find out?'

'Our team in Butterton has found a relative of the couple who own the property under surveillance. He's the cousin of the woman who lives in the house and has been asked to keep an eye on the place while they're away.'

'Who are the owners?' I asked.

James Beckford explained that they were a local couple who had lived in the area all their lives. It was felt very unlikely that these two people had anything to do with Sam's kidnapping. They were currently in Australia visiting their daughter and were not expected back for another six weeks.

'If this cousin is supposed to be keeping an eye on the property for them, how on earth can someone be using it to imprison Sam?'

'That's where things get interesting,' he said. 'It seems that a couple of weeks before the owners went to Australia, they were contacted by a friend and asked if they would consider letting their house for part of the time they were away. They were told that a couple from Gloucester was looking for somewhere in this neck of the woods during August as they were keen walkers and wanted to visit this part of the Peak District. They were hoping to come to some kind of financial agreement with someone in the area who would be happy to rent out their property.'

'Did the Barkers do any checks on these people?' I asked.

'The cousin believes they had a chat with them on the phone but has no idea about the details of that call.'

'Has the cousin met them?'

James nodded. 'Yes, they go into the village quite frequently.'

Optimism began to filter its way into my mood. 'Couldn't your men pick them up next time they come into the village?' I helpfully enquired.

'We've considered that Mr Granger. Our problem is that we have no idea how many people they have up there. If there are some thugs looking after your brother and the couple don't turn up back at the house when expected, things could get a bit awkward.' There was a tone to his voice which reminded me that he was the expert, and I was just Joe Bloggs. I considered that it might be better if I kept my thoughts to myself. These guys were professionals and did not need assistance from me to do their job.

'This couple have been in the house for about four weeks. That fits in perfectly with what we know about the plans to kidnap your brother. They would have wanted somewhere which was ready to take him.'

'Do you know how they knew that the house would be empty?'

'No. That's something we're going to have to look into, but at the moment, that's not our priority. We now need to come up with a plan to get your brother out.'

I ended the call and sent Dad a message letting him know that the police were confident they had found Sam's location.

The temptation to sit and stare at the phone, waiting for it to stir to life was overwhelming. I could not keep my eyes off it, willing it to ring. Yet, at 4:20 pm, when it rang out on the table beside me, it made me jump.

'We've managed to track down the owners of the house,' James informed me. 'They're at a hotel in Melbourne'

'That's great,' I said.

My insides began to whirl in anticipation. It felt as if we were really getting somewhere. Apparently, the daughter they were visiting lived on the outskirts of the city. They had obtained her address from the husband's sister who lived in Butterton. Although they had not managed to speak to the owners yet, they wanted the couple to give them a detailed layout of their property. James explained that they were keeping the property under constant surveillance. He said that the gang were apparently performing regular patrols of the grounds, but that there appeared to be no set time for those checks. He finished by telling me it was unlikely that I would hear from him again until the morning.

I thanked him and ended the call.

The urge to check my mobile had subsided after this latest call and I accepted that, once again, it was a waiting game. It was 11:45 that evening and I had been in bed for a quarter of an hour when 'Message in a Bottle' began playing on the bedside table. My stomach lurched. Getting a call from the police at this time of night did not fill me with optimism. I fumbled for my mobile and eventually managed to grasp hold of it.

'Hello?' I said and held my breath.

'Mr Granger, don't worry, nothing has happened to your brother. However, we might need your help.' It was James Beckford. 'Sorry about the lateness of the hour, but a situation has arisen and we think you may be able to help us out.'

Relief flooded over me. Sitting up, I perched on the side of the bed. 'Of course. What do you need from me?'

'You don't happen to know Morse code, do you?'

I frowned in the darkness. 'Morse code? Yes, I do as it happens. Why?'

'Thought so,' he said. 'I'm sending a car to pick you up. I'll explain when you get here. For now, get ready and wait on Osbourne Street. By the way, if you have dark clothes with you, please put them on.'

He rang off. I was impatient to know the details but did as I was told. I found a black pair of jeans and was pleased to notice that I had thrown a black sweatshirt in my bag. My trainers were black with prominent white flashes on them. They probably would not be appropriate, but I did have a black pair of shoes that would have to do. After throwing my clothes on, I knocked softly on Sue's door. Receiving no reply, I went as quickly and quietly as possible out of the suite and waited outside for my lift. I sent Sue a quick text telling her not to worry and explaining that the police had contacted me. I promised to give her an update as soon as I could.

As I stepped out onto the pavement, the headlights of a car briefly blinded me as it approached from my right. It came to a stop right in front of me and I opened the passenger door.

'Mr Granger?' the driver enquired.

I nodded and hopped in. 'Do you know what's going on?' I asked.

As we pulled off, he explained, 'We're going to drive out to a place just beyond the village of Butterton. A couple of my colleagues are waiting for us there. By the way, my name's Alan.'

'Nice to meet you, Alan. I'm Rob. Do you know what this is all about?'

He kept his eyes on the road ahead. 'I understand you know Morse code,' he said. 'Is that right?'

'I'm pretty rusty, but I used to know it quite well.'

'Great. Well, the good news is that we're confident we've located the room your brother is being held in. While we were watching the back of the property, we noticed a flashing light in one of the upstairs windows. Someone was sending the famous 'S' 'O' 'S' signal. Unfortunately, apart from that sequence, none of us are familiar with Morse code, so all we could do was to send a single couple of flashes to let him know we'd seen him. After that, a more complicated message came from the window, but we hadn't got a clue what it said. We didn't have any officers who were immediately available who know Morse code. Hence, the call to you. It was decided that we needed to get someone up there as soon as we could.'

While Alan had been speaking, I was trying to recall the Morse code signals. I had had a good knowledge of the code about twenty years ago but I had not used it since.

'What am I going to signal with?' I asked.

'We'll show you when we meet up with the others.'

As Alan drove, he gave me a running commentary as to where we were going. 'This is the main Leek to Ashbourne road,' he said.

This matched what Andy Phillips had told me when they had been tracking the van into which they believed Sam had been transferred.

'In about 4 miles, we'll be turning left at Bottomhouse crossroads. That takes us onto the B5053 towards the village of Onecote.'

'Is that near our final destination?' I asked.

'Pretty close,' he said. 'After we go through Onecote, we'll be turning right onto Butterton Moor Bank, which takes us onto Lime Kiln Road. The property we're interested in is just the other side of Butterton. We'll probably be there in another ten to fifteen minutes.'

He was right. We had just left the village of Butterton and were driving down a country lane when Alan announced, 'In about 100 yards you'll see a track on your left. If we were to turn down there, the house where your brother is being held is about 200 yards on the righthand side.'

Alan began to reduce his speed. I noticed the track as we passed by and felt a wave of emotion over being in such close proximity to Sam. About 250 yards beyond the track, Alan brought the car to a halt behind another vehicle in a small lay-by on the left.

We both got out of the car and were greeted by DCI James Beckford and a woman who I had not met before.

James held out his hand. 'Hello, Mr Granger, this is DS Janice Elliott.'

'Hi,' I said. 'Nice to meet you.' Turning back to James, I said, 'By the way, I'd rather you called me "Rob".'

'OK, Rob. Will do.'

James produced a strange looking object and held it out. It was black, cylindrical in shape, and about 3 feet long, one end slightly thinner than the other.

I frowned. 'What on earth is that?'

He chuckled. 'That, Rob, is the latest in high-tech police kit.'

It turned out to be a fairly powerful black torch, some black card which had been rolled into a tube three to four inches in diameter, and the two attached to each other with black masking tape.

I was puzzled. 'What's with the black card?' I asked.

'We need to make sure only your brother sees the flashes,' he said. 'The black card will hopefully ensure that the beam of the torch is only seen from a very limited area of your brother's window.'

That made sense. 'Ingenious', I thought as my pulse was racing.

James continued. 'We've also rigged up a little contraption which will fix the torch in position. When you're signalling your brother, we don't want the torch to move at all. If it did, with that card on there, he might miss part of the message.'

'OK, yes, I see that,' I acknowledged.

Alan chipped in. 'As soon as we arrive at the surveillance point, we'll attach the torch to the platform and we'll have to spend a few minutes adjusting the angle of the torch. Once that's done, you can try to get your brother's attention.'

Janice, who, to this point, had not said very much, spoke up. "Rob, it would probably be worth you having a little play with the torch while we're still here. There's nothing complex about it, but it'll probably help if you know how much pressure's required to turn on the beam.'

I thought this was a little unnecessary but dutifully took the torch from James and tested the button. I immediately recognized that it required more pressure than I had anticipated. I mentally apologized to Janice for unfairly judging her suggestion and pointed the torch and its attachment towards the ground. I spent a few minutes sending meaningless messages to the ditch which ran along the roadside.

Satisfied, I said, 'OK, that's fine.' I handed the torch back to James.

'Right,' he said quietly. 'Everyone make sure your phones are either off or on silent. We don't want any sound at all when we're in position.'

I checked my own mobile, but I knew I had already turned it off.

We set off back down the lane along which we had just driven. After about 50 yards, we came to a public footpath on the right which ran along one side of a field. There was no street lighting along the lane so it was difficult to recognize that there was a path at all. James and Janice turned on to the path with Alan and me following along behind.

As we walked through the field, Alan leant towards me. 'The other side of this field is a wood,' he said quietly. 'This path continues on through the wood for about a mile until it intersects an old disused railway track, now used as a path for ramblers and cyclists.'

I nodded; probably a useless gesture given the darkness, but I was afraid to make any noise.

Alan continued. 'Around 50 yards into the wood, we'll be turning left onto a smaller and less-well-used path that'll lead us to a position which is directly behind the house where your brother is being held'

I was nervous, excited and fearful all at the same time. It was amazing to be so close geographically to Sam after the last couple of weeks. But, in some respects, it seemed as if we were as far away from him as ever. While we might know where he was physically, we were still a long way from knowing how we were going to bring his current trial to an end.

As Alan had predicted, around 50 yards after entering the wood, we found the path going off to the left. This being narrower, Alan dropped back slightly but continued to speak quietly.

'In about 20 yards, there's a small, wooden bridge over a stream.

We're still some way from the target property but try to make as little noise as possible.'

'OK,' I whispered.

We continued on our way until Alan tapped me on the arm. 'The bridge is coming up any moment.'

We all stepped lightly across the bridge. As soon as we were across, Alan spoke again.

'We've only got another 50 yards or so.' He was now communicating in whispers.

As we drew nearer the property, James and Janice slowed their pace to reduce further any sound we might be making. After another 10 yards, we came to a halt and I peered past James and Janice to try to get a first glimpse of Sam's prison.

Over the last few minutes, my eyes had started to adjust to the darkness and I could see that we were about a dozen feet from the end of the path. There seemed to be a fairly sizeable metal gate at this point which gave access to an open area of scrubby ground about 20 yards across. Beyond this again, was what looked as if it were a wooden gate into the back garden of the house. The garden itself was only about 10 yards from the building to the back fence.

From our position, on the righthand side, there appeared to be a shed and a small greenhouse but, in the dark, I could not pick out much more detail. However, I could tell that the garden was significantly wider than the house and ran down both sides of the property.

Then, there was the house itself. It did not appear to be a particularly large property, but it was difficult to be certain from our position. I could see four windows facing us. On the ground floor, there was a back door roughly in the middle of the house. To the left of this was a window, which I imagined might be the kitchen window. To the right was a fairly small bay window which looked as if it might be at the end of a lounge. Above these, on the left, was a larger window that I suspected might be the room Sam was in. On the right was a much smaller window that I surmised was a toilet or bathroom.

As I studied the scene in front of me, James, Janice and Alan busied themselves with the task of setting up our improvised signalling device. James had brushed leaves and twigs from the ground where the base of the contraption was to be positioned. Once this was in place, Alan took the torch from Janice and spent some time fixing it to the base. When this had been achieved, I shifted out of James's way as he stood back to check the angle at which the torch was pointing at the house. He made a minuscule adjustment and then stood back again and rechecked it. Happy, he lay on the ground and checked the elevation. As he did this, Alan came over to where I was standing.

'Rob,' he whispered, 'James is making sure that the torch is higher than your brother's room. We're going to switch on the torch and adjust it downwards until we're projecting its beam on to the top portion of his window. Obviously, the last thing we want to do is accidentally flash the beam at one of the other windows.

I agreed.

A point of light appeared suddenly at the very top of the roof of the house. As I watched, that point of light began to slowly track its way down the roof, and then onto the guttering.

Alan whispered in my ear. 'OK, Rob, get ready.'

A thrill of nervous excitement ran through me, heart hammering heavily in my chest. In a few seconds, I might well be communicating with Sam. The point of light tracked its way onto the top of Sam's window. When it had reached about halfway down, James got up and indicated that I should take his place.

I cautiously moved forward and gently felt for the torch. Kneeling on the ground behind it, I just sent the word, 'Sam', and waited.

All four of us were staring at the window. To help with this, James had a pair of night glasses and was keeping them trained on Sam's room.

There was no response to my message. I left it for a couple of minutes, then sent the same message. Again, nothing.

James spoke softly in my left ear. 'It's approaching 1:00 am,' he said. 'He's probably asleep. Keep trying.'

I sent the same message every two minutes for the next half an hour. It seemed as if we were not going to be able to contact him that night.

I turned round to my left. 'What do you want to do, James?' I asked.

'We'll give it till 2:00 am and then have a rethink. It might be that we leave it and come back a bit earlier tomorrow night.'

I resumed sending the message. Elation at the expectation of communicating with Sam had deflated like a popped balloon.

I had been full of hope when we had arrived at the location, thinking that Sam's ordeal might nearly be at an end. But, having clicked out the same message to his window multiple times, I was thoroughly disheartened.

I glanced at my watch after sending yet another signal—1:53 am. Just another three times and we might have to leave.

As I looked back up at the house, I could hardly believe my eyes. Bang in the middle of Sam's window was a blinking light. Joy flooded my heart.

At exactly the same time as I saw the light, James whispered excitedly, 'Great. He's seen us.'

I knelt there transfixed. It was a couple of seconds before I remembered that I was supposed to be translating the message for the others.

'What's he saying, Rob?' Alan prompted.

'He wants to know if we can get him out of there. What do you want me to tell him?'

As I asked the question, I sent another message which said, 'Hi Sam, it's Rob here.'

I got the immediate response: 'What kept you, Bruv?'

At least he had not lost his sense of humour, I thought to myself.

James was next to me, having noticed our private conversation. 'Rob, stop the chatter. We need some information from your brother and we need to get it fairly quickly.'

I started to send again. 'Sam. Stop signalling. With police. Have some questions. Keep answers brief.'

Sam's light went off and stayed off.

James leaned over and spoke quietly in my ear. 'Tell your brother that if you send two very quick flashes, it means there's some kind of danger. If that happens, he should immediately retreat from the window.'

That made a lot of sense, and I sent the message.

Sam signalled his understanding.

James kept the instructions coming. 'Ask him if he knows how many people are in there with him.'

I sent it and got the response: 'Usually three, sometimes four.'

James wanted to know if they were all male. The reply was: 'Usually two men and a woman. Sometimes another man.'

I then sent: 'Are they armed?'

Sam responded: 'Yes. At least one handgun. Also, a couple of knives.'

After this communication there was a hushed discussion between James, Janice and Alan. I did not hear much of what was said, but it was clear that there was not total agreement between them.

After a couple of minutes deliberation, they wanted to know if Sam was kept locked in his room. I sent the message.

The response that came back was: 'Yes most of the time.'

The next question I had to send was: 'Do you have any way of barricading yourself in your room?'

After this query there was a lengthy pause. I could imagine Sam looking round his room and trying to come up with a way of achieving this result.

Eventually, the reply came back: 'Think so. It depends how long for. Why do you ask?'

'He wants to know why you want to know,' I relayed.

'Just in case we decide to bust our way in. It would be helpful if we knew that Sam couldn't be reached by the other occupants.'

'Do you want me to send that?' I asked.

James shook his head. 'No. Just tell him that it might have a bearing on our decision-making at some point'

I sent the message.

There was a hushed conversation between the others. I very much hoped they were beginning to formulate a strategy to get Sam out.

After a few moments, James had another question. 'Ask Sam if he's able to open the window to his room.'

Once again, I sent the message.

His reply was: 'Only about an inch.'

There was another short discussion between the police.

My next message was sent as directed: 'Can you give us some idea of their routine? Do you know if there are certain times of the day that some of them go out? Are there any other patterns of behaviour you can tell us about?'

We received: 'No. The guy with the dog goes out every couple of hours or so. There doesn't appear to be any set times for these patrols. I haven't noticed any patterns to when people leave the house. They probably go out at times and I'm not even aware of it.'

Once more there was a discussion. This was longer than before.

Suddenly, light poured out from the house as the back door was opened. A man stepped into the back garden accompanied by a massive dog.

I flashed the short 'danger' signal to Sam as agreed.

James raised his night glasses and confirmed that Sam had immediately withdrawn from the window.

The light from the house vanished as the door closed behind the man with the dog. I could not see or hear either the man or the dog. For over a minute nothing seemed to happen at all. Then, suddenly, a torch sprang into life. It slowly began traversing its way around the back garden and, for the first time, I could see that there were herbaceous borders on the lefthand side. There was a significant area of grass before the torch light confirmed the structures of the greenhouse and shed. There was at least one small window in the shed, and the torch remained on the window for a few moments before continuing its sweep around the garden. The circuit complete, the beam moved back in a clockwise direction until it reached the shed. The torch, presumably accompanied by the man and dog, moved towards the shed. Apart from a faint glow from the window, the beam of the torch disappeared from our sight as the man inspected the interior of the shed. This checked, the man and his dog then went down the righthand side of the property towards the front of the building.

James used his night glasses to check Sam's window, but there was no sign of him. This was good. We all stayed perfectly still. After a period of about five minutes, the torch reappeared on the left of the property as the man began what we assumed would be the final leg of his inspection. However, when he had checked the lefthand side of the grounds, instead of going back inside the house, he headed straight towards the wooden gate leading to the area of scrubby ground behind the property.

'Is he going to check out here as well?' I whispered.

James did not answer the question but just whispered, 'Don't move.'

The man leaned right over the gate and swept the beam of the torch over the area of rough ground. Then, starting from the lefthand end, he played the beam over the edge of the wood. As the beam approached, Alan put his hand at the back of my head and gently but firmly forced my face down to the ground. The light passed, and as we heard no cry of alarm, I assume that the man had seen nothing to concern him. After another minute in which no one stirred, Alan removed his hand from the back of my head. I looked up to see man and dog returning to the house.

After he had gone inside, Janice said, 'That was a near thing.'

'Do you want me to send Sam another message?' I asked.

'Yes,' James said, 'but leave it for a minute or two. Just in case anyone is still near the back of the property.'

We waited for two minutes but, just before I was about to send the message, the light started blinking from Sam's room. It said, 'Are you still there?'

I passed this on to the police.

'Tell him that we'll be going in a few minutes,' James said. 'But let him know that we'll be back again tomorrow night. Let him know that we'll try to get here a bit earlier tomorrow.'

I sent the messages and received an immediate

acknowledgement from Sam. But then James said something that I was not so happy about.

'By the way, Rob, don't expect to be coming with us tomorrow. You've been very helpful tonight and we're very grateful, but we wouldn't normally include members of the public in our operations; particularly when we believe we're dealing with violent men. The only reason we contacted you is because we needed someone as soon as possible who knew Morse code. Sam's obvious familiarity with the code caused me to suspect you may also know it. There wasn't time to go through the normal channels, so I decided to step out on a limb and give you a call. However, now, I need to go down the correct channels and obtain the services of someone within the force who has expertise in this area.'

I interrupted. 'But I want to be here. Apart from anything else, I believe it'll help Sam to know I'm around.'

'Rob, it's not going to happen. I can't risk it.'

I protested a bit longer, as best as one can in hushed whispers, but then had to face defeat.

When Alan dropped me back at the Blue Mugge, he tried to reassure me. 'Someone will contact you in the morning to let you know how we'll be proceeding.'

I thanked him, bid him goodnight and watched the lights disappear around the corner at the end of the street.

Chapter 18
The Rescue Attempt

Although the suite of rooms at the Blue Mugge had their own cooking facilities, Sue and I decided to stroll into town to get some breakfast. Unsurprisingly, she was full of questions. As we munched our way through our full English breakfast, I started to explain how I had received the late-night call and all the subsequent events. She sat transfixed, amazed over my adventure in the early hours. It was as we were sitting having a final leisurely cup of coffee that James Beckford called.

'Morning Rob,' he said. 'I've just got off the phone after speaking to Andy Phillips. I was bringing him up to speed with our progress to date. While I was on the phone, I told him what had gone on last night and mentioned your desire to continue as our Morse code expert. I know he's become a friend of yours and he speaks very highly of you, but even he thinks it would be tremendously risky to continue to involve you.'

I started to object, but he cut across me. 'Let me finish,' he said. 'I also mentioned to Andy your point that having you there may well help Sam psychologically.'

‘And what did he say?’

‘He’s still not comfortable about it, but he does understand the point. Basically, he’s left the decision up to me.’

‘And what’s your decision?’

Hearing a heavy sigh in my ear, I braced myself. ‘Rob, you were extremely useful to us last night, and we’re very grateful for that. However, that fact alone isn’t enough to justify me continuing to use you.’

I was gutted and not a little annoyed. Sue could not hear the other end of the conversation, but she saw my expression and reached out, laying her hand on my forearm.

I was just about to remonstrate with James when he continued:

‘If your expertise regarding Morse code was the only consideration, I would have to say “no”. However, I’ve had another think about your point, and I tend to agree with your assessment. It’s my judgement that your presence there may well be a significant advantage with regard to your brother’s state of mind. As a result, I’ve decided to request special dispensation to have you conscripted to our team for the duration of this operation, or for as long as I deem it necessary.’

I looked at Sue and smiled. ‘That’s great,’ I said down the phone.

‘Well, hold on a minute,’ he said. ‘There are one or two conditions I will require you to agree to before we proceed.’

I was not at all concerned. I would have agreed to just about anything to ensure that I would be included in the team.

‘And what are they?’ I asked.

‘If you’re to come along with us, you must, at all times, obey any instruction given by us. Whatever situation arises, if you catch sight of Sam, you must never, never call out to him. You must leave all aspects of the rescue to us. Remember Rob, it's not just your brother's life that is in danger here, but also the lives of my officers.'

I told him I understood that, and that I agree to all his conditions.

'Good,' he said. 'In that case, welcome to the team.'

I was relieved that that was settled. 'OK, so what happens now?'

'I'll call you later to tell you when we'll pick you up.'

I thanked him and assumed that that was the end of our conversation. However, he had another message.

'I just thought I should let you know that Andy Phillips told me to take good care of you. I think he holds you in pretty high regard. So that's another reason to stick to our rules. Andy will be after my guts if I let anything happen to you.'

'That's nice to know,' I smiled, as I hung up.

Later that day, DCI Beckford was back on the phone again. 'We have an officer who is going through the details supplied to us by the American police,' he said. 'One of the numbers obtained from the mobile in John Smith's hotel room is very interesting to us.'

'Go on,' I said, in anticipation.

'It's a number in a place called Kedleston on the outskirts of Derby.'

'And why the interest?' I asked.

'Does the name "Charles Thompson" mean anything to you?'

My stunned silence presumably told him all he needed to know.

'I assume it does,' he said. 'Would you like to tell me what you know of this man?'

'Did Andy Phillips mention anything to you about our previous dealings with John Smith?'

'I know you had some problems on a foreign expedition,' he said. 'Unfortunately, I don't know any details.'

'Charles Thompson was the man who organized the expedition that interfered with our work. What has he got to do with all this?'

'Currently, we're not sure. However, it's interesting that John Smith had been calling his number. And it also seems rather curious that Kedleston is only about 25 miles from the property where your brother is being held. Of course, it may just be a coincidence, but I find it difficult to believe that.'

The phrase, 'impossible to believe', seemed more appropriate in this case. I gazed sightlessly across the room. A surge of bitterness flooded through me. Some of that bitterness was directed at the person of Charles Thompson himself. However, at least as much again was reserved for those who had let him get off scot-free for his part in that previous expedition. He had hired John Smith who had intimidated and used violence against our team, ultimately resulting in Sam losing his leg. If Charles Thompson was involved in our current problems, I promised myself that I would do everything in my power to make sure he did not get away with it again.

It was around 11:30 pm that night, that I was picked up to go back to the village of Butterton. As on the previous evening, James and Alan set up and adjusted the torch. As soon as the beam found the top of Sam's window, he sent a signal to us.

'Where have you been? I need to get out of this dump.'

Although Sam was a habitual joker, I got the distinct impression that this message was a serious one. I wondered about his state of mind. I could imagine, having been cooped up in there for two and a half weeks, he would be on the verge of tearing his hair out. I also suspected that the fact he knew we were there, would be increasing his impatience to be released.

James noticed the signal. 'What's he saying, Rob?'

'He's pretty keen to get out of there,' I said. 'I think it's getting to him.'

James nodded. 'I'm not surprised. We'll get him out as soon as we can, Rob.'

James thought for a moment, then said, 'Tell him we're working on a plan to get him out. For now, he just needs to be patient. Tell him to be looking for a signal from us on Monday morning from about 6am.'

This was the first time anyone had mentioned any kind of timescale. A thrill of excitement ran through me as I passed the information on to Sam.

After a brief pause, Sam's light began blinking again. 'What day is it today?'

This took me by surprise. Maybe it should not have, because I knew Sam never wore a watch, and he obviously had not had his phone for over two and a half weeks. After that length of time, I probably would not have a clue what the date was either. I checked the time. It was 12:15 am on Sunday 25 August. While I passed this information on to Sam, I explained the situation to James and the others.

As on the previous evening, there were a number of exchanges between Sam and the police. Most of these were requests for information from Sam, along with the answers. Sam was halfway through one of these responses when the back door of the house was opened. I flashed the danger signal as before, but Sam obviously missed it. The man had stepped into the back garden accompanied by his dog. If he turned round, he could not possibly fail to notice the blinking light from Sam's room.

Again, I sent the danger signal and hoped that the black card attached to the end of my torch would do its job. To my relief, this time the blinking light stopped.

James used his night glasses to improve his view of the man. He had been watching for about two minutes when he let out an expletive.

'What's up?' Janice enquired.

'The dog,' said James. 'It's looking straight at us. I've just realized that the breeze has changed direction. We're almost directly up-wind from the house. I think it's picked up our scent.'

No sooner were the words out of his mouth than we all heard a low, menacing growl from the direction of the back garden. I heard the rasp of a metal chain as the dog strained at its leash.

'We need to get out of here,' Alan whispered.

Making as little movement and noise as possible, Alan detached the torch from the base and passed it to Janice. He grabbed up the base and we prepared to retreat along the path back through the wood. James was still studying the events in the garden. Understandably, the dog handler wanted to check out what it was that had interested his pooch and moved towards the gate.

'Get going,' James whispered.

Alan, Janice and I started to head back through the wood, although I noticed that James did not move straight away.

I heard the latch of the gate click as the man left the back garden of the property and headed in our direction.

We were making very little noise apart from the pounding of my heart which was thumping in my ears. The police had traversed this path through the wood in the dark a number of times before, so they were familiar with it. Unfortunately, this being only my second visit to the site, I did not have the same familiarity and was finding it a challenge to keep up with Alan, who was immediately in front of me. It was almost pitch black and I was relying nearly as much on my hearing as my sight in order to follow him.

The growls from behind were continuous, but they did not seem to be getting any closer.

Suddenly, a voice from behind shouted, 'Who's there?'

James, who was behind me, realized I was experiencing some difficulty keeping up with Alan. He brushed passed me, grabbing hold of my forearm and began guiding me. As we increased our pace, I noticed that we were making a bit more noise, but I was certain the man behind us would not have been able to hear over the snarling of his dog. I was fairly sure he would not be able to see us either because of the blackness in the wood.

No sooner had I thought that when things changed. Suddenly, I noticed a small patch of shrubbery light up about 15 feet away to our right. It slowly began sweeping towards us. I was just wondering what would happen as the torch caught us in its beam when James dropped to the ground dragging me with him. The others in front did likewise. We all stayed perfectly still. It seemed that the man with the dog had also stopped as he scanned the wood with his torch.

Faintly, in the distance, I heard him say, 'Tyson, be quiet.'

After another couple of growls, the man said, slightly more forcefully, 'Tyson! Shut up!'

There was silence for some time. I wondered what would happen if the man decided to check the wood out more thoroughly. There were distant sounds of movement, but then all went quiet again. Next to me, James began very slowly to shift his position, attempting to glance back over his left shoulder.

'Don't move,' he whispered.

There was no movement at all from those ahead of us on the track. We just lay there and waited.

I am guessing that we lay there for about five minutes with no one moving a muscle. Suddenly, there were a couple of deep-throated rumblings from the dog. The beam of the torch once more sprang into life. Three or four times it swept back and forth above the place where we were laying.

As the woodland path had a few twists and turns in it, I was hopeful we would be hidden from the sight of our torch-wielding pursuer.

There was another deep growl, followed by a couple of menacing barks which sent a shiver through me.

Immediately, the voice from behind us spoke again: 'Show yourself, or I'll let the dog loose!'

My stomach flipped at the thought of having a 120-pound German Shepherd charging along the track behind us. Once again, we all continued to lay perfectly still.

Thankfully, the threat of releasing the dog did not materialize. The torch danced across the foliage another few times but then disappeared. I thought I briefly heard the sound of someone moving in the distance, but then, again, all went quiet. Still, none of us moved. We must have lain there for another fifteen minutes before James felt it was safe to move.

Five minutes later we were in the car and heading back to Leek.

After two eventful, very late nights, I did not get up quite as early as normal. It was just after 9:30 am when Sue and I left to go and get some breakfast. Naturally, she was anxious to hear what had happened during the night.

'It was a bit dodgy,' I said, and began going through the sequence of events. Even after our food arrived, she sat with a shocked look on her face. This continued for so long that I had to remind her to eat her breakfast.

I did not hear from the police again until after lunch. When I did, it was James.

'As you know, we want to go in and get your brother out early tomorrow morning. Especially after last night's events, we think it's possible the folk in the house might be getting a bit twitchy.

We've come up with an idea of how we might be able to get into the property without too much fuss.'

'What will you require from me?' I asked.

James told me that I would be picked up at about 5:45 in the morning and I was to make sure I was dressed in clothes suitable for a country walk. I assured him that I would.

'By the way, we've managed to contact the owners of the house. They're furious about how their property has been used in their absence. They've also provided us with a detailed layout of the house. This information could prove to be invaluable when we attempt to get Sam out.'

As I filled Sue in with the details of the call, I could see her becoming more and more excited. She interrupted me: 'We should get that other bed made up in your room for Sam for tomorrow night,' she said.

This brought me up short; I had not even considered that. 'He may want to get straight back home,' I said.

'But surely the police will want to speak to him?'

I considered that was almost certainly true. However, as far as Sam's release was concerned, I did not want to count any chickens before they were hatched. 'Let's wait and see how it goes in the morning,' I suggested.

But Sue was adamant. 'No! We've prayed that Sam will get out safely. I'm convinced that everything's going to work out fine. Let's have the extra bed prepared in an act of faith.'

I stared at Sue. 'You're serious, aren't you.'

'Of course. What's the point in praying if you don't believe those prayers will ever be answered?'

The next morning, as the minibus pulled up and parked outside the Blue Mugge, I noticed a couple of bicycles strapped to the top. I wondered if they were just there for show or if they would actually be used in the operation. Sue had come out to see me off. I gave her a hug and a quick kiss on the cheek.

'See you later. I hope I won't be too long. And I hope I'll have some company.'

'Take care,' she said. 'I'll be praying for you.'

As I clambered aboard, I was surprised to see how many there were crammed in the minibus. A quick scan round the seats revealed eleven of us. James, Janice and Alan were there as before, but there were seven others dressed in a variety of kit. Only four of them were dressed in police uniform. Two—a man and a woman—were dressed in full cycling garb: helmets, lycra shorts, t-shirts and shoes suitable for the activity; that, at least, explained the bikes on the roof. It all looked very convincing. The rest of us were clad in various forms of hiking gear including walking boots, rucksacks and energy drinks. I must admit to being reassured by the relaxed attitude of the others on the minibus. From their demeanour, and with the exception of the guys in uniform, one could have been forgiven for thinking that they were a genuine walking group just going out for a decent walk on a sunny, summer morning. I sat in one of the available seats, which happened to be next to Alan.

'What's the plan, Alan?' I asked.

He glanced sideways. 'We're going to stop in Onecote,' he said.

'A couple of the team are going to cycle to the property from there. The rest of us will stay on the minibus until we get a bit closer.

'I take it my presence here means you'll require me to signal to Sam again,' I said.

Alan nodded. 'James will explain everyone's role when we stop in a few minutes.'

Approximately fifteen minutes later, we pulled up at the entrance to a pub carpark. Mandy and Jerry, who I now discovered were the designated cycling enthusiasts, got out and removed the bikes from the top of the minibus.

The rest of us followed them off the bus for a team talk from James.

'OK guys,' he said. 'Let's get down to business. Some of you will already know this, but the folk in the target property have started to get a bit twitchy. We've noticed some changes in their surveillance habits over the last twenty-four hours. We think it's probably related to the events the night before last. Although they didn't spot us, we're guessing the dog handler was still suspicious over his dog's reaction. They're probably only being extra cautious, but it's made things a little more difficult for us.'

This prompted a query from Jerry: 'What changes have they made, Sir?'

'One difference is that they now leave that German Shepherd out there all the time. It's been chained to the large waste pipe coming down from the bathroom. Janice and Alan were approaching the rear of the property yesterday afternoon and the dog either heard or smelt them coming. That does make things slightly trickier for us. That's why Phil's come along. We decided it would be a good idea if we could knock the pooch out before we go in. Unfortunately, not only do those dogs have a much more acute sense of smell than us, but it's the same with their hearing.

'Anyway, down to the operation. The timing here is key. We'll be splitting into two teams: one to approach from the front of the property, the others from the rear.'

James turned to me. 'Rob, as before, you'll be coming with us and approaching the target property through the wood. We need you to signal to your brother to barricade his door. He also needs to find a spot in the room which is out of the line of fire from the door. If the gang realize they can't get in, it's possible they may shoot through the door. I don't expect that to happen, but I'd rather we covered all the bases. Once he's ready, we just need a signal from him to let us know.'

James turned to Phil. 'That's when I need you to get that dog tranquilized. As soon as that's achieved, we go in.

'Mandy and Jerry, as soon as the dog's been taken out of the equation, I'll call you to start your approach. When you've simulated your blowout, you can knock on the door as discussed. I'll be listening in.

'Raj and Karen, you need to be approaching and going over to Mandy to offer help. Help her to get to the front door.

'Mandy, lay it on a bit thick. Make sure they know you're in pain and ask if you can use their bathroom to clean up. The rest of you, keep out of sight until you know you can get in.'

Alan asked, 'What if Sam hasn't managed to barricade the door well enough? If they're able to get in to him, things could go south in a hurry.'

James nodded. 'That's true, Alan, but we're just going to have to trust that he manages it.'

I had a little inward grin to myself, knowing how Sam's mind worked. I remembered sending him the message the night before last. There had been a delay before he had responded. I knew for certain that he would have scanned round the room, making calculations and assessing how difficult it would be to move the various objects. His eye for spatial awareness was brilliant, and I was certain he would have been able to mentally make the relevant calculations in a few seconds. I raised my hand.

James spotted me. 'Yes, Rob?'

'If Sam says he can do it, I don't think we need to worry about that. I reckon he'll have come up with a way of wedging that door so firmly shut that it would take a tank to get in.'

James nodded. 'Thanks, Rob. Let's hope so.'

After a few more questions it was time to go. Mandy and Jerry mounted their bikes and pedalled off down the road. The rest of us boarded the minibus again and headed for the village of Butterton.

We parked in the same place that we had stopped on the other occasions. When we were in situ, once more, James handed the torch to me. All I had to do, initially, was to make sure Sam was at the window ready to receive the message to barricade his door. This message was sent and a response from Sam was received confirming that he was ready to go.

James laid a hand on my shoulder. 'Rob, when we go in, you'll have to stay here. Hopefully, you realize we can't include you in this part of the operation.'

I nodded.

'I need you to stay concealed,' he said, looking around. His gaze fell on a clump of bushes about 20 feet from the end of the path. 'Stay behind these,' he said. 'Whatever happens, don't come out. When all this is over, one of us will come and fetch you.'

Once again, I nodded my understanding.

'Right,' he said. 'Let's get this show on the road'

He took out his radio and called the other members of the team to make sure they were all in place. They were. He gave the order for the other units to begin their approach towards the house.

'OK, Rob,' he said, 'I'm hoping this will be the last message you need to send to your brother. Tell him to barricade himself in and to let us know when it's done.'

I sent the message and held my breath.

A few seconds later, James spoke softly into his radio.

'Jerry, are you ready to go?' Then there was a pause as he listened to the reply. 'Good.'

James whispered, 'OK, Phil, take the dog out.'

Phil raised his tranquiliser rifle and after a short pause, squeezed the trigger.

The dog jumped up and there was a short yelp which was noticeable even from the distance we were from the house. We all held our breath, wondering if anyone would come out to see what had upset the dog. No one did. Before long, the German Shepherd was sleeping peacefully on the grass.

James looked at me, waving a hand back down the track and I took up my position behind the bushes.

He briefly spoke into his radio. Finally, he gave a quick short nod, and he, Janice, Alan and Phil swiftly and quietly moved forward to the metal gate at the end of the path. They waited for a few moments, James with his ear to his radio. Suddenly, James motioned with his hand and the four of them raced across the 20 yards of scrubby ground between the wood and the garden. One by one I saw them vault the small wooden gate and sprint across the grass, past the nose of the sleeping German Shepherd and up to the back door of the house. I heard shouting coming from the front of the property and, at the same time, noticed James try the handle of the back door. It opened. The next moment, they were all inside.

No sooner had they disappeared than I noticed a window open on the righthand side of the house. A leg appeared, and this was swiftly followed by another, and then the rest of the body. The person, who looked at that distance like a man in his forties, ducked down and shot into the garden shed. Then all was still.

My eyes stayed glued to the shed. I was aware that there was very little noise coming from the house. This, I told myself, had to be good news. Presumably there would be quite a commotion if any significant resistance had been encountered. All the same, I was very much hoping that one of our team would emerge from the back door so I could direct them to the escapee. Unfortunately, this did not appear to be about to happen.

Two, three, then four minutes went by without any noticeable change to the scene in front of me. I did not even see any movement through any of the windows visible to me from my position.

I guessed the man was wondering what he should do. Should he sit tight and hope that no one checked the shed, or should he make a bolt for it and hope no one spotted him? In a second the question was answered.

All of a sudden, he burst from the shed and began sprinting towards the gate at the back of the garden. Just as the members of our team had done a few minutes before, he vaulted the gate. Watching his flight, I recognized that he was a slight man, although he did look reasonably athletic. He came straight towards me across the scrubby ground and I wondered what I should do. I had promised not to break cover, but here was a situation that I suspected no one had anticipated.

As the man reached the metal gate, over his shoulder I noticed a figure come out of the back of the house. I could not immediately tell who it was. A split second later, I realized it was Alan. At exactly the same time, Alan noticed the fleeing man and shouted. As the man negotiated the gate, he looked back over his shoulder and spotted Alan who was now breaking into a run. The man, gate now behind him, charged in my direction. There was no time to prevaricate. I remembered a boulder on a ridge in Washington State; as the man was about to pass my position, instinctively, I thrust out a leg and was greatly satisfied when I felt the contact. As I rose to follow his direction of travel, there was a certain sense of gratification as the man hit the ground with some force and bounced once with arms and legs flailing.

All of a sudden, all the worry, all the upset, all the stress of Sam's kidnapping and the subsequent search for him got the better of me. Anger rose up in me. I flung myself on top of the sprawling figure. The impact appeared to have severely winded the man as he did not put up much of a fight. I grabbed his right wrist and thrust it up between his shoulder blades.

'Imprison my brother, would you?' I growled in his ear. 'We'll see how much you enjoy prison now, matey.'

Having caught the man, I was dumbfounded by my physical state. Although I am reasonably fit, I had never considered myself to be particularly strong. Nevertheless, there was not a chance that the individual beneath me was going to get away. I suspect he sensed this too, as there was barely a twitch from him.

I suddenly became conscious of pounding footsteps behind us rapidly getting closer.

'Leave him, Mr Granger!'

It was Alan. I did not move from the man's back until Alan was right with us. Even when I did get off him, I made sure I retained a firm grip on the man's right wrist.

'Don't move!' Alan shouted. 'Spread your arms and legs!'

He complied.

'Have you got anything on you that you shouldn't have? Any weapons? Anything sharp?'

'No,' the man said, quietly.

Alan proceeded to frisk the man for nefarious items. Finding none, he handcuffed the man's hands behind his back and dragged him to his feet.

Looking at him close up, I guessed the man was a little younger than I had first estimated. I suspected he was not much over thirty-five. He now looked very sorry for himself. As Alan grabbed him by the top of his right arm, we began walking back towards the house.

I asked the only question that really mattered to me. 'How's Sam?'

'I haven't seen him yet,' Alan said. 'We didn't come up against much resistance.'

Our conversation was briefly interrupted while the three of us made our way across the scrubby ground. As we entered the back garden, Alan went on: 'All the suspects have been apprehended and are now wearing fetching bracelets. Some of our team went upstairs, but there was no indication of any problem from up there. As all the excitement appeared to be over, James asked me to come out and fetch you.'

He turned to me and grinned. 'We didn't anticipate you having such a dramatic part to play.'

I laughed. 'Can't say I expected it myself,' I said. 'Never mind. It was good to be able to contribute in some small way.'

Walking across the grass in the back garden, I glanced up at the bedroom window where Sam had been held. Suddenly, Sam's bearded face appeared behind the glass looking down at the three of us. I grinned, waved and gave him a double thumbs up.

As we went through the back door into the house, James was just entering the kitchen. His eyebrows shot up as he saw we had another prisoner.

For the moment, he ignored that and said to me, 'Rob, we could do with you upstairs. Sam won't come out of his room until he hears your voice.'

I chuckled. 'He probably doesn't trust that you're the police.'

James led me to the bottom of the stairs, and I went up. When I got to the top, I noticed Janice standing with the male cyclist.

'Your brother's in here,' Janice said, indicating a door. We've just heard some movement, so I think he's already removing the barricade.'

On the door, in Morse code, I tapped out, 'Hi Sam, it is your Bruv here.'

His response was not repeatable, but I think it is fair to say that he was pretty pleased his ordeal was over.

Bumping and scraping was coming from behind the bedroom door as I turned to Janice.

'Would you guys mind going downstairs for a couple of minutes?'

Janice briefly looked at the door and then back at me. She gave a smile of understanding and a slight nod, and she and Jerry descended the stairs.

After another thirty seconds, the door opened. Sam stood there, one empty jean's leg hanging down from his left thigh. We stood there staring at each other for some seconds with neither of us speaking. Suddenly, I noticed Sam's eyes begin to moisten. I stepped forward and grasped him in a massive bearhug.

'How are you doing, Sam?' I asked with difficulty, struggling to contain the mix of emotions that had caught in my throat.

For some time, there was no verbal response from Sam. I felt him trembling against me and suspected he was having trouble controlling his own emotions. Minutes passed as we hugged.

Eventually, the trembling ceased. Finally, Sam spoke. 'Where are the bunch who have been holding me?'

I released my grip on him and stood back half a pace. 'I think they're downstairs.'

'I don't want to see them, Bruv.' He hopped over to his bed and sat on the edge.

The bed appeared to be in a very unnatural position in the room, and I guessed that Sam had used it as part of the barricading of the door.

As I got my first really good look at him, I couldn't see any sign of a black eye. However, there did seem to be a tiny scar at the place where I thought I'd noticed a small cut.

Sam leaned forward, his forearms resting on his thighs. 'I suppose you've not heard anything about my phone, have you?'

'Funnily enough, I have,' I said. 'It's in my room back at my digs. I'll let you have it as soon as we get back. Incidentally, what have they done with your leg?'

'No idea, Bruv. I guess they thought if they took it off me, I wouldn't be able to do a runner.'

'I'll go and ask the police to have a look for it,' I said. 'Presumably, they'll be able to ask the thugs what they've done with it. Back in a minute, Sam.'

I ran downstairs.

Janice and Jerry were standing at the bottom.

'Are the gang that have been holding my brother still here?' I asked.

'They're just being loaded into a police van.' This came from Jerry.

'I don't know if you're all aware of this,' I said, 'but my brother only has one leg. These *delightful* people have taken Sam's prosthetic leg from him. Would you mind going and asking them what they've done with it?'

Janice looked disgusted. 'Are there any depths people won't stoop to? Hang on here, Rob, I'll go and ask.'

While I was waiting for her to return, I passed the time with Jerry. His role in the exercise had been to cycle past the house with Mandy and fake a blowout on her bike. They had also had some stage makeup which allowed them to quickly mock up a bleeding graze on her left knee. Four passing walkers, also undercover colleagues, helped the stricken cyclist to hobble to the door of the house to ask if they could briefly use their bathroom to clean her up.

Unsurprisingly, when the woman, calling herself Michelle Boyde, had answered the door, she had been nervous about agreeing to the request. She had suggested she bring out a bowl of hot soapy water so the clean-up could be carried out outside. When one of the walkers who had stopped to give a hand heard this, he feigned a degree of indignation, not believing that such a request would be turned down. After Mrs Boyde had called one of the male occupants of the house and had a brief conflab, Mandy had been allowed in the property with Jerry, but no one else had been admitted.

It had been at about this time that James, Janice, Alan and Phil had entered the property from the rear. At the same time, the rest of the team had entered the front. Jerry explained that everything had gone smoothly and virtually no attempt had been made to resist.

I had just started to explain what had happened round the back when Janice returned carrying Sam's missing appendage.

'Thanks,' I said, taking it from her. 'We'll be down in a couple of minutes.'

I ran upstairs and handed Sam his leg.

As promised, moments later we were both downstairs and Sam started going round the police thanking them for getting him out. I noticed Phil, our tranquilizer expert, heading in the direction of the back of the house. He was carrying an empty lead and I guessed he was going to attend to the beautiful animal he had earlier sent to sleep. I caught his eye, smiled and gave him a thumbs-up.

As this was going on, Alan and James were in deep conversation. Every now and again, James would shoot a glance in my direction. After a while, I saw James give a quick, short nod and he came over to me. He did not look desperately happy.

'Mr Granger, I thought you promised to abide by any directions I gave you,' he said sternly. 'I warned you to stay behind those bushes no matter what happened. I now find that you completely ignored those instructions.'

I sighed, looked down at the ground and then back up at him again. I was just about to apologize when the mask of disapproval vanished from his face and was replaced by a broad grin.

'Thankfully, you didn't take any notice,' he said, heartily slapping me on the back.

We both began to laugh.

Chapter 19
Many Questions Answered

Due to his lengthy captivity, the police strongly advised Sam to be checked over by a medical professional, so this was our first port of call. When we were eventually dropped back off at the Blue Mugge, Sue gleefully greeted us.

After introducing her to Sam, I said, 'I'm starving. Shall we grab some breakfast?'

'Sounds good to me,' Sue said. 'Are we going to our usual café?'

I wondered if Sam would prefer to have something in the privacy of our holiday suite, but he was only too happy to go out for a full English.

'Before we go, I reckon there are a couple of people who would like to hear your voice.' I called Dad and handed Sam the phone.

When we were settled with our food, Sue said, 'Come on then guys, tell me what happened.'

Sam and I took it in turns to give an account of the morning's events from our own position. Sam would speak while I shovelled food into my mouth. Then I would take up the story as Sam attacked his own breakfast.

Sam began with a commentary on his thoughts as he anticipated the rescue attempt. That was good, because one of the things I had been so concerned about was how he would be coping psychologically. It turned out that this had not been much of a problem for him on that particular morning. His mind had been occupied by watching out for our initial signal and then waiting for the instruction to barricade his door. This was another detail I was very interested to hear about.

Sam had calculated the length of his bed, matched this against the gap between the bedroom door and the opposite wall, and then judged which other items available to him would neatly fill the remaining space. It turned out that two small bookcases were ideal for this purpose. When these were in place, Sam was adamant that no one would have been able to force the door open.

'It might have moved about a quarter of an inch,' he said, 'but certainly no more.'

I laughed. 'Did that get put to the test?'

He grinned at me. 'No. Mind you, after shoving the second of the two bookcases into place, they did ask me what I thought I was playing at. I was just sending the message to let you know I was ready. Anyway, no one tried to come in.'

Sue had a puzzled look on her face. 'How on earth did you ...' she started, and then stopped, looking a little embarrassed.

Sam grinned at her, guessing what was on her mind. 'You mean, how did I manage to shift all that furniture with one leg?'

She flushed slightly.

'Where there's a will, there's a way,' he said. 'You'd be surprised what's possible when you really put your mind to it. If I need to shift something a bit bulky at home, I've found that the easiest way to do that is to kneel down. Because my left leg was removed just above the knee, if I have my left leg pointing straight down with my right leg slightly out to the right, I can cope quite well. Yes, of course, it's still a little awkward, but it's certainly manageable.'

He had a quick sip of coffee before continuing. He glanced at me. 'When you asked me if I could barricade myself in, I spent a few moments assessing the situation. The bed was a single bed and it was on some pretty good casters, so it wasn't particularly difficult to move. As I say, I was pretty sure that the bookcases would fill the remaining space, but when I tried to shift them, I couldn't move them at all. However, although I didn't check at the time, I was pretty confident that I'd be able to move them when I'd removed all the books.'

Then it was my turn again. As I told them about the beginning of the operation to release Sam, Sam interjected.

'I was watching when the police came out of the wood. I had heard the front doorbell chime and the woman go to answer it. After a moment, she shouted something to someone else in the house, but I didn't catch what it was. Seconds later, all hell broke loose. Your friends came through the back door, and the guys at the front started shouting "Armed police!" That's when I really allowed myself to begin to believe that I was going to get out of there.'

Sam's greatest display of emotion was when I told him about

the kidnapper who had attempted to escape from the back of the property.

'I saw him!' he said. 'I'd left the window for a moment to listen to what was kicking off downstairs, but when I returned, I saw that guy come out of the shed and hurdle the back gate. What happened?'

So, I told him.

He was delighted when I described my part in the operation. 'Good on ya, Bruv,' he said. 'I wish I'd been there to see it.'

Knowing what had occurred that morning was certainly interesting, but what I really wanted to know was what had happened before that. So, I asked him.

'OK, come on, Sam, tell us what happened from the start?'

Sam stared across the café for a few seconds before giving me a sideways glance.

'It was the day after we last swapped messages,' he said. 'I didn't get up until about 9:30. I guess I was just feeling a bit lethargic. Anyway, I took a peep through the curtains to see if their van was there. It wasn't. After having a bit of breakfast, I took a leisurely shower and got dressed. It was our recycling day and, as I put the bins out, I noticed that there was still no sign of the white van. I began to think that they'd decided watching my flat wasn't the most exciting thing they'd ever done and had taken themselves off to bother someone else.'

Sam paused and gazed across the café again. Sue and I just sat and waited.

'It was about half an hour later that they turned up,' he said.

There was another pause, slightly longer this time. I got the distinct impression that he was not enjoying reliving the episode much. This was interesting in itself. Sam was not someone who liked to display any kind of weakness.

'There were two of them that came for me,' Sam went on. 'As soon as I opened the door, they barged it open. The door smacked me in the chest, I lost my balance and ended up on the floor.'

Sue looked disgusted.

'Did it do any damage?' I asked.

Sam shook his head. 'Not really. I discovered later that I'd got a slight graze on my stump, but I didn't notice anything at the time. I think I was too outraged to notice any injury.'

'What happened then?' Sue asked.

'They told me I was going on a long trip with them. They said I should get a few things in a bag unless I wanted to be sitting in the same clothes for a significant length of time. I asked how long I would be away for, but they didn't answer. So, I just did as I'd been told.'

Sam stopped to take a sip of coffee. 'They were both big blokes,' he continued. 'I wouldn't have fancied messing with either of them normally, but they both made sure that I noticed that they were carrying knives. Anyway, one of the thugs came into the bedroom with me to make sure I didn't try anything. I chucked a few things in a sports bag and we left.'

I was curious. 'We know they transported you in their white van, but how did they deal with actually getting you into it? As you've said on many occasions, you live in a cul-de-sac where half the neighbours are nosy old busybodies. With that van being there for some time, I bet the curtains had been twitching for days.'

Sam shrugged. 'I don't think they really cared. Before we left the flat, they made it clear that if I made a fuss or tried to signal to anyone, I'd get a blade in me. Not fancying that, I decided to comply with all their instructions.'

I couldn't blame him for that, I thought.

'Anyway, they bundled me into the back of the van and got in with me. Until that moment, I hadn't realized that there was a third man in the driver's seat of the van.'

As they set off, they had gagged and blindfolded him, tied his hands behind his back and sat him with his back against the side of the van.

I frowned. 'Why did they do that?'

Sam shrugged. 'Don't know. I guess they didn't want me trying to call for help, and didn't want me to see which direction we were going in.'

Sam then went on to give us a few details of the journey, but there was not too much of great interest until they arrived at the Roadchef Services on the M6. At the time, Sam obviously had no idea of their location, but it was clear that that was where they were.

I interrupted Sam's account. 'Is that when they took your mobile from you?' I asked.

'No. They took my phone as soon as we got in the van. One of them put it in his jacket pocket. When they'd come for me, there was a bit of a chill in the air, but as the day warmed up, he must have taken his jacket off and chucked it on the floor of the van. Anyway, when we stopped at the services, the driver disappeared for about a quarter of an hour. The rest of us just sat there till he returned. The other two were speaking to each other, but didn't say a word to me.

When the driver returned, he came to sit in the back with me while the other two disappeared. But before he got in, he paused to have a hushed conversation with the other two just outside the back of the van. While they were out there, I tried to shift my blindfold with the top of my shoulder. This wasn't tremendously successful, but it did allow me a tiny amount of vision at the extreme righthand side of the blindfold. Anyway, after their little chat, the driver got in the back with me.'

'Was he any more talkative than the other two?'

'No. However, it was while the other two were gone that I got a bit of a break. I think they'd parked the van in the most remote part of the carpark. As I was sitting with my back to the righthand side of the van, I could only see a small amount out of the front of the van. Most of the other vehicles seemed to be parked some distance from our own. But, as I watched, I noticed a Ford Cougar pass in front of the van and it looked as if it was swinging round to park close to us. This was confirmed when I heard two doors bang shut fairly nearby.

'Unbelievably, the next moment there was a light tap on the side of the van. The driver told me that if I made a sound, I'd end up with a knife in me. He then moved to the back of the vehicle and got out to see what the problem was. While I was on my own,

I moved my head around to see if I could learn anything useful. That's when I noticed the jacket. I took a chance, moved to the other side of the van and felt over the jacket with my tied hands. When I found the phone, after a bit of a struggle, I managed to retrieve it and tried to replace the jacket roughly where it had originally been. Returning to my position on the righthand side of the van, I tried to work out what I should do.

'As I thought about it, I guessed it was almost inevitable that the phone would be missed, that I'd be searched, the phone found and once more confiscated. In addition, I suspected I'd get a bit of a kicking for my troubles. That was when I decided to try to leave my phone somewhere where it might be found and handed in. The driver hadn't yet returned, and I could still hear voices coming from outside. The back door of the van had been left open a crack, so I moved towards it. That's when I realized that their conversation was coming to an end. I heard the driver say, "OK, thanks guys, I really appreciate that. I'll get it fixed."'

I had to make a split-second decision. I barged the back door of the van wide open, intentionally falling to the ground with my back to the van. As I did so, I flicked my phone backwards, hoping it would go far enough under the van so as not to be seen. The fact that you ended up with it suggests that I succeeded.' He gave me a grin. 'Anyway, a split second later, the driver came round the corner of the van. He picked me up and roughly bundled me back inside. That's when I acquired this cut.' He indicated the nick over his eye.

Sue had been sitting with her mouth half open, a look of deep shock on her face. 'Sam, that's terrible. What happened when the others got back?'

Sam laughed ironically. 'Actually, not much. I don't think the driver wanted the other two to find out that he'd allowed me to get out of the van. He just got back in the front and we drove off.'

'What about the guy who'd taken your phone?' I said.

Sam grinned. 'Oh, yes, that was another thing. He didn't realize the phone was missing at that point, but I'll get to that in a minute.'

The next notable event was Sam's transfer to the other van just outside the town of Stone. It sounded as if the two parties had been in constant contact with each other, because the transfer appeared to be judged almost to the second. Sam told us that he assumed he had reached their destination due to the fact that they had turned down what seemed to be a bumpy track. However, no sooner had they stopped than Sam had been roughly bundled out of one van and into another.

He said, 'That's when the guy who'd taken my phone realized he'd no longer got it. He went ballistic and demanded I tell him where it was. I told him that I didn't know what he was talking about, but I guess that I wasn't too successful at concealing my triumph. He threw me down on my face and went through all my pockets. He searched in one or two other places which I wasn't so thrilled about but he then realized that I hadn't got it."

Once they had got going again, it was approximately fifty minutes before they ended up at their final location. Because of their speed, frequent bends and occasional stops, Sam had realized that they were now driving along 'A' and 'B' roads. Apart from that, he had no idea of his new location, not that he could have informed anyone if he had.

'How was it at the house?' Sue asked.

'The place itself was fine. Unfortunately, there were no other properties visible from my window. Even so, I thought it wouldn't do any harm to have some method of signalling someone if the opportunity presented itself. I started to investigate the room. After the first hour, I think I knew everything there was to know. To my delight, one of the items I did find at the bottom of the wardrobe was a decent rubber torch. That was great, but I didn't really think there was much chance of me managing to get anyone's attention. I guess that's why they put me in the room they did.

'Anyway, I thought it was worth a try. Apart from anything else, it gave me something to do. I began experimenting with the torch. After sundown, and when I had the light off in the room, I could see the beam of that torch right over on the edge of the wood. It was faint, but still noticeable.'

'Wasn't that a bit risky?' I asked. 'If one of them had seen the light, you might have been in deep trouble.'

'To be honest, Bruv, I didn't much care. I figured that the worst they could do was take the torch off me, and I'd already found a nice little hiding place for that. If they'd come and accused me of trying to send signals, I'd have just denied it.'

Sue smiled as she said, 'And where was your hiding place?'

Sam grinned back at her. 'Another of my little discoveries was a roll of masking tape on a shelf high up in the same wardrobe.

'I noticed that there was a three-inch wooden panel that came down below the bottom drawer in the chest of drawers. It looked just deep enough to hide the torch. When I'd finished signalling, I used the masking tape to tape the torch behind the wooden panel. No one would have found it unless they'd known where to look. In any case, as it happened, it was all unnecessary. No one saw or suspected anything.'

I smiled inwardly. That was typical of Sam. It was like his communicating in code and hiding things in ornaments with secret compartments. He was always thinking of ways to conceal things.

'How did you feel when you saw the signal from the wood?' I asked.

'I can't tell you how shocked I was when I saw the light. I had to look two or three times before I allowed myself to believe it.'

'You must have felt pretty good, though?'

'Oh, I can't tell you. I felt like dancing round the room.'

We had a bit of a laugh, but then a look of disgust came over Sue's face as she asked, 'When did they take your leg?'

'Right at the start. They seemed to be highly amused by it. One of them asked me if I'd mislaid my parrot. Every time he came up to use the toilet, he'd shout, "Pretty Polly, pretty Polly," and burst out laughing. I got a bit sick of it, but he thought it was hilarious.'

"I don't know how you coped on your own,' Sue said. 'Not knowing what they would do to you.'

Once again, Sam stared across the restaurant. 'Most of the time it wasn't too bad,' he said. 'But I must admit, it got more difficult towards the end. Believe it or not, it was harder when I knew that Rob and the police were outside. I don't know why. Perhaps the knowledge that my rescue was close, I felt I had more to lose. Whatever the reason, I certainly felt a bit more twitchy.'

Sam suddenly changed the subject. 'Anyway, I know all about that. What about you? How did you find out what had happened to me? And how did you discover where I was being held?'

So, for the next half an hour, Sue and I filled him in with all those details. This obviously started with my unanswered messages. When I arrived at the point when I realized for the first time that John Smith was involved, Sam's expression changed from one of deep interest to one of horror.

'You mean that man was involved in my kidnapping?'

'So it would seem,' I said.

Sam did not say a word, but the expression on his face spoke volumes. The initial impression was of deep anger. However, after a moment, another emotion began to make its presence felt. There was an unmistakable sign of fear that appeared in his eyes. That, at least, I could help him with.

'Sam, you have no need to worry about Smith anymore.'

His eyes swivelled to look at me, but he still did not speak.

I was pleased to see that the fear had been replaced with hope.

I gave a faint smile. 'It's probably about time we told you some of the other things that have been going on,' I said.

'Have they caught him?' he asked.

I said, slowly, 'Sam, he's never going to be able to hurt anyone again.'

He looked confused.

'He's dead,' I said.

Sam appeared to be having difficulty processing this information. Eventually, he said simply, 'What happened?'

So, I resumed my account of our engagement with Smith. I showed him the text messages I had received and made sure he knew how stressed I had been over his situation. As Sam scrolled through the messages, I suddenly remembered that I had received one that I would rather Sam did not see. I was just going to take the phone from him when he came across it.

All of a sudden, he froze, staring at my phone. I knew he had seen the message from Smith about his friends bringing a bit of symmetry to his legs.

There was a pause for a few moments as no one spoke. Then, Sam said quietly, 'I hope it wasn't a pleasant death.'

As it has been Smith who was responsible for Sam's disability, I understood why he felt the way he did, but having witnessed Smith's demise, I knew I would not have wished that on anyone.

After another fairly lengthy pause, I said, 'Let me tell you what happened.'

I told him about our final trip to Mount Saint Helens. I described the spectacular view, the distant rumble and almost imperceptible tremor of the ground, then the volcano blowing her top, and the rest of the team running for the vehicles and tearing away from the scene. I described Kevin's and my sprint for the Land Rover and our subsequent encounter with Smith.

Sam listened with fascination as I recounted the events. When I got to the point where Smith had been engulfed by the volcanic cloud, his overriding emotion appeared to be one of relief. However, after a moment's thought, something else suddenly occurred to him.

'If you were that close to Smith, how come you managed to survive?'

I explained Steve's belief that we had been saved by the contours of the ground at that point. Then I filled him in with our frantic drive down the track away from the killer cloud. As I moved on to the journey back home and my attempt to find out what had happened to Sam, Sue stopped me.

'He's missed out a bit,' she said.

Sam raised an eyebrow.

'Have a look at the back of his neck.'

I shot Sue a glance. I would have preferred it if Sam had not discovered about my close shave.

After giving me a quick glance, Sam pushed himself to his feet and moved around behind my chair. As I had half expected, he went and sat back down without saying a word. He was never one to make a big deal about things, but one glance at his face told me that he appreciated how close I had come to losing my life. He actually looked quite shaken.

'It's not too bad,' I told him. 'It was quite sore for a couple of days, but it's getting better every day.'

There was silence for a few seconds as once again, Sam gazed across the café.

Eventually, he said, 'Next time Kevin comes asking you if you want to go with him on some kind of expedition, can I suggest you say "No"?'

I laughed, but he was obviously deadly serious.

This was made crystal clear as he added, 'You do realize we could both be dead now?'

'Oh, come on Sam, that's a bit melodramatic.'

He became quite feisty. 'Nonsense! The bullet that shattered my leg was only a foot away from having the same effect on my head. And it very much looks as if you had an even closer shave.'

'That may be true, but the person responsible in both cases is now dead. He's not going to show up in any future trips.'

'So, you think he was responsible for the eruption as well?'

'No, but if he hadn't attacked Kevin and me, we'd have been able to get clear before the volcanic cloud got to us.'

'That's irrelevant. If that cloud had been slightly to one side, you'd probably not have made it anyway.'

He was probably right. In any case, I was not going to continue the argument.

'Well, let's forget it. The main thing is that we're both alive and well. Shall I continue with my story?'

Sam stared at me for some time before dropping his eyes to his empty plate. 'OK,' he said, 'let's hear the rest of it.'

So, I told him about contacting Andy Phillips and explaining the situation to him. I mentioned Sam's message in which he had spoken of the white van and I said something about keeping notes of the goings on at his flat.

'They told me you provided them with the details about the van,' Sam said.

I grinned at him. 'It's a good job I know you so well, Sam. I remembered your penchant for secret compartments and suspected you'd hidden your notes where people would be unlikely to find them. It took me a while to figure it out, but when I caught sight of the house, I was sure I'd found your hiding place.'

Sam was beaming. 'Well done, Bruv. It never crossed my mind that someone else might have to find those notes.' Then he became more serious. 'It's a good job you sussed it out,' he said. 'If you hadn't found the registration of that van, it might have taken them weeks to find me.' He suddenly thought of something else. 'Incidentally, perhaps it's a good job I did hide that book.'

'Why's that?' I asked.

'You know I told you that they suggested I shove some clothes in a bag? Well, while I was up in the bedroom, I could hear the other bloke opening and closing drawers and cupboards. When I'd finished filling my bag and we were back downstairs, I asked him if he had found it. He looked blank and asked me what I was going on about. I said, "Whatever it was you were looking for in my cupboards."

'That annoyed him, but he didn't say anything. I assumed they knew that I'd seen them outside and wanted to make sure I hadn't left any record. If they'd found the book, I don't think things would have gone very well for me.'

Knowing what a delightful bunch of people we were dealing with, I suspected he might be right. Anyway, after Sam's little interjection, I went on with my account.

I explained how the news had come through to us from the police in dribs and drabs. The hope when we had some positive news, and then the frustration as, once more, the trail appeared to go cold.

Sam was particularly interested when I reached the point at which the police had identified the property where he was being held. He had a broad grin on his face when I told him that they had got me out of bed to come and signal to him.

'I knew learning Morse code would come in handy one day,' he said, laughing.

I went on to tell him about my various night-time jaunts to the house. He was not particularly surprised when I told him about the man and his dog following us into the wood. After retreating from the window, he had heard the growling of the dog and guessed it must have picked up our scent. Sometime later, Sam had returned to the window to find out what was going on. He had watched the two crossing the area of scrubland between the property and the wood and had continued to watch until he had seen the two on their way back. Realizing that there was very little chance of us trying to contact him again that night, Sam had decided to go to bed.

Over the next few minutes, I gave Sam the remaining details about that morning's events. He was fascinated over how many people had been involved in his rescue. It was not like him to get particularly emotional about anything, but the fact that so many resources had been mobilized to affect his release appeared to really touch him. I was fairly sure that, in the future, other revelations would come out about the morning's events but, for now, that was the end of our discussion.

We were just contemplating what to do with the rest of the day when my phone rang. It was James Beckford and he asked to speak to Sam. So, I passed my mobile to Sam and waited.

After a fairly short and one-sided conversation, Sam ended the call.

'He wants me to go into the police station and tell him all about my captivity,' he said.

So that is what happened. He gave them all the details he could remember about his abduction and imprisonment. They also wanted any information he could supply about the people who came to his flat, including detailed descriptions.

The following day, the three of us, having travelled back down to Maidenhead, were having a late lunch together when I received a text from Andy Phillips. It read as follows:

Hi Rob, I could do with meeting up with you fairly soon. Would it be possible to meet you at the Fox and Hounds at 7:30 this evening?

It was, so I sent a text agreeing to the rendezvous.

After lunch, Sue excused herself to go back to Slough to speak to her parents. Although she had been in regular contact with them since our return from the States, she had not yet explained to them about her new-found faith. She wanted to share it with them and tell them the effect it had had on her life. Thinking this might prompt a fairly lengthy conversation, I arranged to give her a ring in the morning.

As she left, she gave me the kind of look which I interpreted as, 'What about you? Are you going to say anything to Sam?'

This caused a slight dilemma for me. I genuinely wanted to tell Sam about becoming a Christian, but I had a pretty good idea how he would react. As it turned out, when I did broach the subject with him ten minutes later, I discovered I was absolutely right.

'Oh, for goodness's sake,' he said. 'Not you as well.'

As I started to explain, he interrupted me.

'Listen, Bruv, I don't want to know. If you want to deceive yourself about the existence of some benevolent sky fairy, that's up to you, but don't try to include me in it.'

'Have you stopped to consider how illogical that reaction is?' I asked.

His head swivelled round. 'What do you mean?' he snapped.

'Well, you've hardly looked into the subject at all. The only time you had any contact with the issue of the Bible or creation science, you were starting to waver.'

'Nonsense!'

'I'm sorry Sam but, when we were in the Congo, you admitted that you were beginning to consider their position. You said that their arguments were logical and scientifically sound.'

'I don't remember saying that.'

'Well, whether you remember it or not, you did. But now you seem to be dismissing it from a position of almost total ignorance.

You said that you'd look into the subject when you got home. Can I ask, did you do that?'

His silence was all the response I needed.

I continued, 'So, why do you think you're qualified to decide on the authenticity of the Bible? When it comes to most major decisions in our lives, we usually find out something about the subject before we decide what to do. Why do you think we should abandon that principal when it comes to Christianity?'

For a few seconds, there was a hesitation as Sam considered how to respond. When he did, he said, 'I don't see why I should require an extensive knowledge of the Bible in order to reject it. I know enough about science to understand that there's no requirement for any kind of god to create this universe.'

'Is that so, Sam? But when we were in the Congo, you said that their explanation of the evidence made scientific sense. You remember all that information about creatures like the bombardier beetle and the green woodpecker? You had absolutely nothing to say to refute their position.'

There was another uncomfortable silence, so I went on: 'Sam, if I could find some arguments which would challenge your position, would you be prepared to discuss it?'

There was another hesitation, so I added rather provocatively, 'Or are you going to insist on sticking to an irrational rejection of the Christian faith, irrespective of any challenges there might be to that position?'

Sam always hated any suggestion that he was being irrational in any way. I could see the flash of annoyance in his eyes, but his lack of a retort strongly suggested he had no immediate answer.

Eventually, he said, 'There are enough brilliant scientists who have completely rejected Christianity to convince me that I don't need to rediscover those arguments for myself. I choose to reject the claims of Christianity based on their work.'

'And what about the brilliant scientists who accept the Bible?' I asked.

He shrugged. 'Who knows? Perhaps they've experienced some kind of tragedy in their lives which cause them to want to hang on to a comforting myth.'

'So, you're willing to gamble your eternal destiny on the say-so of others—others who also haven't really looked into the subject.'

'Well, firstly, I'm not sure my eternal destiny comes into it,' he said. 'As far as I'm concerned, when I die, I'll be dead. That's it. No more Sam Granger.'

'Yeah, as far as you're concerned. And what if you're wrong? What if these people you put your faith in have spent no more time in honest investigation than you have? You think that's rational, do you?'

I could see his rising annoyance as he said, 'Just drop it! I'm not interested!'

I shrugged. 'OK, have it your own way. But I still think it's completely illogical to reject something you know nothing about.'

Sam did not respond and, unfortunately, that was the end of the discussion.

At 7:15 pm that evening, I set off to meet Andy Phillips at our usual meeting place.

I immediately saw him sitting at the same table where we had sat nine days earlier. Waving to him, I went straight to the bar. When I joined Andy at his table, I was holding a glass of Coke with ice. Noticing this, he looked up at me and raised an eyebrow. 'Are you feeling OK?' he asked with a grin.

I laughed. 'Actually, there's been a significant change in my life,' I said. 'I'm sure I've never been over the limit when I've been driving, but now, if I'm in the car, I don't drink at all.'

'Well, being a policeman, I should congratulate you on that, but what caused the change?'

This seemed like an ideal opportunity to tell Andy about my new-found faith. However, rightly or wrongly, I was impatient to know why he needed to see me.

'I'll explain about that in a while but, first, I need to hear what you've got to say. You're the one who set up this little rendezvous, so I assume you've got some new information.'

He nodded. 'I do. Our colleagues in Derbyshire obtained a warrant to search the home of Dr Charles Thompson. His computer contained files which included information about you and Sam, as well as the personal details of a number of other individuals. When I asked for a list of names, most of those names seemed vaguely familiar to me, so I decided to check back through our records.'

He paused; I waited.

‘They were the details of all the British members of your expedition to the Congo.’

This was frustrating. ‘Wasn’t Thompson’s place searched as part of the original investigation?’ I asked.

‘Yes, it was. Unfortunately, somehow, this was missed and they didn’t find enough evidence to prosecute on that occasion. I suspect it’ll be different this time. We believe he’s almost certain to have been the person who supplied Sam’s address to the kidnappers. We still have some work to do, but I’m confident that we’ll soon be able to prove that.’

This was good news, but he had another bombshell. ‘What’s even more significant is something we’ve learned about the friend of the Barkers who suggested they rent out their property to the couple from Gloucester.’

I raised an eyebrow.

‘It turns out that Charles Thompson is an acquaintance of Mr Barker. We don’t think he himself had any idea how the property would be used, but it seems that Thompson knew the property would be empty for the relevant period. Anyway, I’ll certainly be pushing for us to revisit that previous case in the light of this new information.’

‘Good,’ I said with feeling.

However, Andy still was not finished. ‘There’s something else. I received a new communication from the Washington Police. They found another phone that John Smith appeared to have been using for his various illegal ventures.’

The phone had been studied and nearly all the contacts

identified. This had led to the arrest of two other men who the police suspected were involved in the kidnap and imprisonment of Jim Redfern. Their investigations into these crimes were still ongoing, but it certainly sounded promising.

On the following morning, I had a question on my mind to which I was very keen to receive an answer. I was just about to give Sue a ring when my phone rang. The timing was highly inconvenient, but I was delighted to see Kevin's name displayed. I answered the call.

'Hi Kevin, how are you?'

'Great, thanks,' he said. 'I hear they found Sam. How is he?'

'He's had a rough time over the last few weeks, but he's a tough cooky. I'm sure he'll be fine.'

'Great. And how's your neck? Believe me, Rob, I thank God every day for you and the fact that you managed to get me away from that ridge. I can't believe how close we were to losing our lives.'

'Oh, I'm fine, thanks,' I said. 'The neck's healing well. Yeah, it does seem like a bit of a miracle that we got out of there.'

When it came to enquiring about people's health, there were a couple of folks I was very keen to find out about. 'How's Jim?' I asked.

Kevin sounded concerned. 'He's in a bad way, Rob. Really, it's a miracle he's still alive. But, because the venom was in his system untreated for so long, there have been a number of complications. There's been a significant amount of soft tissue necrosis surrounding the bite sites, and I'm afraid the doctors are concerned that there may also be some lasting kidney and neurological damage.'

There was silence as I pondered the gloomy news. Then I asked, 'What about Cecil? How is he?'

'The news there is far better. He did need a skin graft, but this was to a much smaller area than they had first feared. Steve says that he's in good spirits and asking for updates on everyone else. He'll be delighted to hear about Sam.'

'That's great news,' I said.

'Anyway,' Kevin went on, 'apart from checking on how you and Sam are, I wanted to give you an update on that anti-creation group in Westminster.'

I have to admit, the drama over Sam and his rescue had rather put them out of my mind. All the same, I was very keen to know what Kevin had learned. However, when he told me his news, I just burst out laughing.

It turned out that the two members of that group flying out to the States had absolutely nothing to do with our Mount Saint Helens' trip at all. Apparently, they had just gone on vacation.

'Sorry about the misunderstanding,' Kevin said. 'My friend's become more and more involved in the group. The good news is that he believes he's now been completely accepted by all the other members. The group had started to get rather agitated as a result of our trip, and that agitation caused my friend to jump to an incorrect, but completely understandable conclusion. He doesn't much like coincidences, and those two heading for the States prompted him to act before he was in possession of all the facts. He asked me to apologize for any additional stress this has caused.'

Kevin's news reminded me of something. 'By the way,' I said, 'I had an email from Jack late last night. We're planning to keep in touch.'

'That's great.'

I felt a little guilty as I owned up to Kevin about the suspicions I had had concerning Jack and Briony working for Smith. As it had turned out, their home being in Florida and their two speakers coming from England had indeed been a complete coincidence. This had come as a great relief to me. In spite of Jack's initial reluctance to engage in conversation, I had subsequently become surprisingly drawn towards him. It was quite possible that we would be contacting each other fairly regularly in the future.

Kevin was pleased about this, but he had some further news of his own. He went on to tell me that there was an official high up in the Home Office who was also part of the anti-creation group at Westminster. It seemed that he was a great friend of Jennifer Davies—the woman at the Ministry for Education. Kevin's friend had learned that it was this man who had been responsible for terminating the police investigation following our Congo expedition. When Andy Phillips had tried to identify the woman, we now knew to be Jennifer Davies, he had been told to drop that part of his investigation.

I found that interesting. As far as I knew, there was nothing at all to connect her to Charles Thompson or John Smith, but obviously someone had been very keen to prevent Andy from looking too closely into the activities of this lady. I wondered why that might be.

As at the end of my last adventure with Kevin, there seemed to be a number of unresolved issues. However, there was at least one situation that was no longer of any concern: that of John Smith himself. I was still horrified about the manner of his demise, but I was undeniably relieved that he was no longer any kind of threat to Kevin or anyone else who decided to join him on future trips.

The call from Kevin had been very welcome and, with the exception of the news about Jim, it had been pretty positive. However, as soon as our conversation was over, I made the call to Sue that I had been about to make when Kevin had called.

As I waited for Sue to answer, I drummed my fingers on the coffee table. There was no reply. When her answerphone announcement finished, I said, 'Hi Sue, I could do with having a quick chat. Can you give me a ring when you pick this up?'

As I hung up, there was a knock at the front door.

I swung the door open and, there, with a big grin all over her face, was Sue. 'Hi Rob, I saw it was you, but I didn't really see the need to answer.'

I grinned and stood back so she could come in.

'How are things?' she asked as she entered the lounge.

'Pretty good, thanks. I'm hoping they'll be even better in a minute.'

Sue sat down at one end of the settee and looked up at me. 'What do you mean?' she asked, slightly puzzled.

I felt a little nervous as I said, 'Well, we've spent quite a bit of time together over the last few weeks. It must have been obvious that I've really enjoyed sharing that time with you.' I paused and swallowed hard. 'Sue, I'd very much like to get to know you better. Can we discuss this over an Italian this evening?'

She bowed her head, and it felt as if my heart was attempting to punch a hole in my ribcage as I waited for her answer.

The End

ENDNOTES

1 www.youtube.com/watch?v=zYH8o_4blcQ

2 Ham, Ken, *Is There Really a God?* (DVD), www.answersingenesis.org.

3 Spetner, Lee, *Not by Chance*, (New York: Judaica Press, 1998), p. 138.

4 Batten, Dr Don, *Biology: Limits to Variation,* (audio cassette), www.answersingenesis.org

5 Mount Saint Helens Historical presentation. Some historical information from www.mountsthelens.com/history-1.html.

6 Details on the Mount St. Helens eruption on May 18, 1980. Austin, Dr Steve, *Mt. St. Helens* (DVD), Institute for Creation Research.

7 Details of the route to Mount Saint Helens: www.aaroads.com>guides

8 History of geological thinking. Mortenson, Dr Terry, *Noah's Flood; Washing Away Millions of Years* (DVD), www.answersin genesis.org.

9 Details on Hutton and Lyell. Mortenson, Dr Terry, *Millions of Years: Where Did the Idea Come From?* (DVD), www.answers ingenesis.org.

10 Finely laminated strata. Austin, Dr Steve, *Mt. St. Helens* (DVD), Institute for Creation Research.

11 Ager, Derek, *The Nature of the Stratigraphical Record,* (London: Macmillan, 1981), pp. 46–47. Reported by: Mortenson, Dr Terry, *Noah's Flood: Washing Away Millions of Years.*

12 Flat strata layers in the Grand Canyon. Mortenson, Dr Terry, *Noah's Flood; Washing Away Millions of Years* (DVD), www.answersin genesis.org.

13 Bent layers in the Grand Canyon. Snelling, Dr Andrew, *Grand Canyon* (DVD), www.answersingenesis.org.

14 Details on rapidly formed canyons. Austin, Dr Steve, *Mt. St. Helens* (DVD), Institute for Creation Research.

15 Ibid.

16 Gould quote on the extreme rarity of transitional fossils. Gould, Dr Stephen Jay, 'Evolution's erratic pace', *Natural History,* Vol. 86:5, (May 1977), p. 14.

17 Quote on the rapid formation of fossils. Currie, Philip J. & Koppelhus, Eva B., (Mineola, NY: Dover Publications, 1996), p. 11. Reported by Mortenson, Dr Terry, *Noah's Flood; Washing Away Millions of Years* (DVD). www.answersingenesis.org.

18 Quote on the rapid formation of rock. *Eastern Daily Press* (Norfolk, UK), 5

Oct 1994, p. 7. Reported by Mortenson, Dr Terry, *Noah's Flood; Washing Away Millions of Years* (DVD). www.answersingenesis.org.

19 Fossils of modern-day creatures in dinosaur layers. Werner, Dr Carl, *Living Fossils Evolution: The Grand Experiment* (DVD), www.TheGrandExperiment.com.

20 Details on Spirit Lake. Austin, Dr Steve, *Mt. St. Helens* (DVD), Institute for Creation Research.

21 Details on coal, and logs in Spirit Lake. Austin, Dr Steve, *Mt. St. Helens* (DVD), Institute for Creation Research.

22 Information on radiometric dating. Snelling, Dr Andrew, *Radiocarbon and Radiometric Dating* (DVD). www.answersingenesis.org.

23 Some of the information on forestry regrowth came from the website, www.weyerhaeuser.com/company/values/citizenship/mount-st-helens/

24 Information on radiohalos. Snelling, Dr Andrew, *Radiohalos* (DVD). www.answersingenesis.org.

LIST OF IMAGES

address for the article https://creation.com/the-earth-how-old-does-it-look, p. 166.

Image 12: A fossilized fish in the process of eating its lunch. Public domain, p. 167.

Image 13: Vertical logs floating in Spirit Lake. Public domain., p. 185

Image 14: A drained swamp. Photo by Steven A. Austin PhD. Used with permission, p. 215.

Image 15: A tree stump running vertically through many rock layers. Photo by A. Snelling PhD. Used with permission, p. 225.

ADDITIONAL NOTES

It will be obvious from the endnotes that many of the details in this book about the famous eruption of Mount Saint Helens on May 18, 1980, as well as the conditions it left behind, were gleaned from Steve Austin's brilliant DVD on the subject.

- Chapter 4—The eruptions in 1980 and resulting geologic evidence.
- Chapter 5—Finely laminated rock strata.
- Chapter 6—Canyons.
- Chapter 8—Spirit Lake and logs.
- Chapter 9—Coal

I would highly recommend that anyone reading this book, who is interested to know more about these events, should watch that DVD. It is extremely informative.

I would also recommend that readers of this book take a look at the following websites.

- www.mountsthelens.com
- www.mshslc.org
- www.weyerhaeuser.com

There are so many fascinating facts to learn about Mount Saint Helens which do not feature in this book.

FURTHER VIEWING

Many of the details in *Set in Stone* were taken from the DVDs listed below. I would recommend anyone reading this book to also view these DVDs for more detailed coverage of these subjects.

- Dr Steve Austin, *Mount St. Helens,* (Compel Media, 2012). This DVD gives details on the eruptions of Mount Saint Helens in the 1980s and the conditions created as a result. It was the inspiration and primary source of information for this book. There are many other fascinating details presented by Steve Austin on this DVD which do not appear within this book.
- Dr Terry Mortenson, *Noah's Flood; Washing Away Millions of Years*, (Answers in Genesis, 2006). This DVD provided details on the history of geological thinking, as well as additional information on the formation of fossils and rock strata. It also includes information on radiometric dating techniques and the biblical record of the Flood.
- Dr Terry Mortenson, *Millions of Years: Where Did the Idea Come From*, (Answers in Genesis, 2005). This DVD shows how geological thinking changed from the eighteenth century up to the early part of the twenty-first century. It also explains how people within the Church began to compromise when it came to the biblical text as a result of these unbiblical ideas.
- Dr Andrew Snelling, *Grand Canyon*, (Answers in Genesis, 2009). This DVD provides many fascinating facts about the Grand Canyon including information on folded rock strata. Many of these details are used to question how long it took to form these geological features.
- Dr Andrew Snelling, *Radiocarbon and Radiometric Dating*, (Answers in Genesis, 2009). This gives information on

radiometric dating for the layman. It is a tremendous DVD to watch if you are new to the subject of radiometric dating techniques and how they are supposed to work.

- Dr Andrew Snelling, *Radiohalos*, (Answers in Genesis, 2012). If you want to dig deeper and understand why radiohalos pose such a problem for the conventional view of millions of years, this is the DVD for you. It does take some thinking about, but it is well worth the effort.

Finally, I have done my best to source all the quotes in this book accurately. As a blind person, to a large degree I have had to rely on others to help me with this task. I have also relied on other material for descriptions of certain aspects of the book. Please forgive me if I have inadvertently overlooked anything.